Interactive Business Communities

Interactive Business Communities

Accelerating Corporate Innovation Through Boundary Networks

MITSURU KODAMA
Nihon University, Japan

Routledge
Taylor & Francis Group

LONDON AND NEW YORK

First published 2011 by Gower Publishing

2 Park Square, Milton Park, Abingdon, Oxon OX14 4RN
711 Third Avenue, New York, NY 10017, USA

Routledge is an imprint of the Taylor & Francis Group, an informa business

First issued in paperback 2016

Gower Applied Business Research
Our programme provides leaders, practitioners, scholars and researchers with thought provoking, cutting-edge books that combine conceptual insights, interdisciplinary rigour and practical relevance in key areas of business and management.

British Library Cataloguing in Publication Data
Kodama, Mitsuru, 1957-
Interactive business communities : accelerating corporate
innovation through boundary networks.
  1. Strategic alliances (Business) 2. Business networks.
  3. Knowledge management. 4. Reengineering (Management)
  5. High technology industries--Management. 6. Strategic
  alliances (Business)--Case studies. 7. Business networks--
  Case studies. 8. Knowledge management--Case studies.
  9. Reengineering (Management)--Case studies. 10. High
  technology industries--Management--Case studies.
  I. Title
  658.4'038-dc22

Library of Congress Cataloging-in-Publication Data
Kodama, Mitsuru, 1957-
Interactive business communities : accelerating corporate innovation
through boundary networks / by Mitsuru Kodama.
    p. cm.
  Includes bibliographical references and index.
  ISBN 978-0-566-08928-2 (hbk) -- ISBN 978-0-566-08929-9 (ebook)
    1. Business networks. 2. Strategic alliances
  (Business) 3. Technological innovations. 4. Knowledge management. 5.
  Organizational change. I. Title.
  HD69.S8K62 2011
  658'.046--dc23

                                                                    2011022440

ISBN 13: 978-0-566-08928-2 (hbk)
ISBN 13: 978-1-138-26330-7 (pbk)

Contents

List of Figures   *vii*

Acknowledgements   *ix*

Preface: The Era of Convergence and Collaboration   *xi*

PART 1   **BACKGROUND AND THEORETICAL FRAMEWORK**   **1**

Chapter 1   Convergence and Collaboration   3

Chapter 2   Boundary Vision and Interactive Business Communities   27

PART 2   **IN-DEPTH CASE STUDIES**   **63**

Chapter 3   Co-creation and Co-evolution Models through Platform
                       Business Innovations – ICT Industry Cases   65

Chapter 4   Hybrid Innovation in the Semiconductor Industry   91

Chapter 5   Chunghwa Telecom's Hybrid Innovation   113

Chapter 6   HTC's Strategy Transformation – Strategies for Building a
                       Company Brand   133

Chapter 7   Technology Integration through Boundary Vision   149

PART 3   **DISCUSSION AND CONCLUSION**   **167**

Chapter 8   IBC and Boundary Networks Lead the Way to Innovation   169

Chapter 9   Conclusions – Creating Knowledge Integration Firms   195

References   *203*

Index   *209*

List of Figures

1.1	Convergence and collaboration	4
1.2	Types of interactive business communities	6
1.3	Converged services with mobile phones	8
1.4	Building interactive business communities through corporate networks in different industries	10
1.5	iPhone/iPad business models	11
1.6	Business structures for electronic publishing	11
1.7	Formulating businesses with the smart grid concept	14
1.8	Photovoltaic business value chain expansion	16
1.9	Increases in automotive electronics	16
1.10	Formulating automotive semiconductor businesses	18
1.11	Affiliations among companies focusing on automotive batteries	20
1.12	Innovation systems	24
2.1	Existing various boundaries	29
2.2	Knowledge integration firms	31
2.3	Evolving corporate innovation	33
2.4	The seven boundary vision capabilities	34
2.5	External knowledge integrative capability	37
2.6	Strategic integrative capability	38
2.7	Intentional and incidental emergent strategies	38
2.8	Forming innovative organizations with organizational integrative capability	41
2.9	Leadership integrative capability	45
2.10	What about the 'system'?	47
2.11	Systems thinking – top-down approach	49
2.12	System LSI 'top-down design'	49
2.13	Systems thinking – bottom-up approach	50
2.14	Systems thinking – top-down and bottom-up approach	52
2.15	Top-down and bottom-up mobile phone module design	53
2.16	Architectural innovation	56
2.17	Digital appliance platform (UniPhier)	58
2.18	Building business ecosystems with platform strategies	60
3.1	Co-creation and co-evolution among knowledge innovators	68
3.2	Types of platform business models	69
3.3	Synergies through co-creation and co-evolution	76
3.4	Types of business models and collaboration networks	79
3.5	Google's platform business – collaborations and synergies through IBCs and boundary networks	83
3.6	Collaborations and synergies through IBCs and boundary networks – NTT DOCOMO's platform business	84
3.7	Co-creation and co-evolution through IBC and boundary networks	88

4.1	Semiconductor sector business model	92
4.2	Qualcomm's IFM (Virtual IDM) business model	95
4.3	TSMC's hybrid innovation through knowledge integration	100
4.4	Changes in TSMC vertical boundaries – value chain integration	101
4.5	New integrated model in TSMC	103
4.6	The new hybrid innovation-based firm in the semiconductor industry	107
4.7	Hybrid innovation (the Fujitsu case)	111
5.1	Marketing and sales system IBC	121
5.2	Product/service development and Joint-development IBCs	123
5.3	Creating vertical value chains with boundary networks	129
5.4	Chunghwa Telecom's corporate capability for boundary vision	131
5.5	Chunghwa Telecom's business design capability for boundary vision	131
6.1	HTC's value chain	141
6.2	HTC's alliance strategies	145
7.1	Boundary networks at J-Phone and Sharp	152
7.2	Hit products created through 'urgent projects'	157
7.3	Corporate capabilities for Sharp's boundary vision	162
7.4	Business design capabilities for Sharp's boundary vision	164
8.1	Forms of IBCs in boundaries for three levels	174
8.2	IBC and boundary networks	176
8.3	Three features of dynamically changing IBCs	183
8.4	Elements of IBC management	184
8.5	IBC and boundary network patterns (pattern one and two)	187
8.6	IBC and boundary network patterns (pattern three and four)	188
8.7	IBC and boundary network patterns (pattern five and six)	188
8.8	Innovation through leadership integrative capability	191
9.1	Convergence accelerates hybrid innovation!	197

Acknowledgements

I would like to express my sincerest gratitude to all the people who provided support in the writing of this book.

I crossed over from the science and engineering fields to the social science fields (business studies) through the chance intersection of the two triggers of theoretical and applied inspiration. The theoretical inspiration is due to the intellectual stimulation I found in *The Theory of the Knowledge Creating Company* by Dr Ikujiro Nonaka, Professor Emeritus at Hitotsubashi University. As a new area of interest for me, this was highly influential in motivating me towards business studies and research. I would like to take this opportunity to express my gratitude to Professor Nonaka for this inspiration.

The second trigger, the applied inspiration, goes back to the time I joined NTT. When I joined the company, I really hoped I would be assigned to the NTT Laboratories, but the personnel supervisors informed me that I was more suited to business than to research. One often hears that new employees in Japanese corporations are not assigned to their desired divisions; nevertheless, this assignment would turn out to have a big influence on my worldview. The close interaction between people in the business department greatly changed the framework of my own thinking and behavior (a big change from the microscopic worldview I had practiced in fundamental research in science and engineering as a graduate student, to the more realistic worldview of business), and gave me the opportunity to experience action and understanding of things through the practical lens of business and management.

Through this I was able to experience a wide range of interactions for many new processes that were applied in daily business activities. I would like to offer my sincerest thanks to my bosses and seniors at NTT (including NTT DOCOMO) for the wide-ranging practical instruction that they provided. The combination of these two practical and theoretical inspirations triggered me to move away from the world of business people into the world of academia, and even today, these two elements continue to inspire me in my business studies research.

I am also deeply grateful for the interviews and materials provided by business people working in the case study corporations presented in this book. These company people create new knowledge by encouraging dynamic and practical processes on a daily basis through IBCs and boundary networks, the central theme of this work.

I am currently working on new theories about my observations and discoveries of new business phenomena that emerge from corporate workplaces (both at the macro and micro level). Business success and failure in corporations and organizations does not follow general laws such as those found in the natural sciences, although there are uniformities in the logic of these. However, the business phenomena of strategic activities are extremely complicated and diverse, and dynamically change in response to circumstances. This means that developing a strategy based on a previously successful concept does not necessarily guarantee repeated success. This is because no matter how refined strategic planning is in its rationality and analysis, realistic businesses formulate and execute strategies that depend on dynamic contexts that include customers and fellow business people, by asking 'who', 'why', 'when', 'with whom', and 'how', and are based on important practical process elements at the micro level.

This means that business people must have a dynamic and comprehensive strategic view, while at the same time engaging in thinking and action that focuses on minute practically applied processes and details to specifically formulate and execute strategies. In other words, 'God is in the details'. I believe that research into these practical human processes is of great importance, and the concept of 'boundaries' described in this book does not only refer to the interactive micro processes between human beings, but also provides a framework through which strategic formulation and knowledge integration processes can be analyzed and understood. Further research into the theoretical and applied aspects of this field can be expected.

Finally, I would like to take this opportunity to express my sincerest gratitude to Mr Martin West, Commissioning Editor and Ms Donna Shanks, Assistant Commissioning Editor, Gower Publishing, without whose deep level of support, assistance, and consent to publish, this book would not have been possible. I also would like to express my gratitude for a grant-in-aid for scientific research from JSPS and Nihon University's College of Commerce.

Preface: The Era of Convergence and Collaboration

Technological innovations including the rapid expansion of Information and Communications Technology (ICT) and development of environmentally friendlier systems are forcing changes across various fields in society, economies, corporations, and industries in general. While ICT continues to evolve as a platform enabling people all over the world to network and interact with one another to announce, share, create, store, spread and connect with a diverse range of information and knowledge, environmentally friendlier systems are becoming critical technological infrastructure needed for sustainable economic and social systems.

The emerging new business models using ICT platforms represented by groundbreaking products such as Apple's iPhone and iPad, and new technological infrastructure for sustainable economies based on the smart grid concept and electric vehicle systems and so forth are set to transcend diverse technologies and industries and dramatically alter the conventional strategic model that focuses on competition between companies.

This recent phenomenon of fusing together different technologies including ICT to develop new technologies and products, requires business models based on new rules that span different industries; the phenomenon known as 'convergence'. And it is bringing even more complexity to the traditional competitive business model. Convergence is rapidly accelerating strategic alliances, joint development and ventures, strategic outsourcing, M&A (Mergers and Acquisitions) etc. in companies and their customers, and triggering dramatic changes to existing corporate boundaries. This means the collaborative strategies linking differing businesses are moving beyond the simpler competitive business modes and becoming increasingly important as core drivers to business strategies. In other words, modern innovative businesses have an urgent need to move beyond strategies that focus on corporate competitiveness to incorporate collaborative strategies with a range of industries (and companies) including clients.

Also in recent years, individual companies have been faced with the challenge of global business expansion that includes developing countries, which brings a pressing need for leadership that can formulate and actualize these collaborative strategies with global partners. As well as those issues, the knowledge economy of the twenty-first century brings with it great changes to individual lifestyles and employment values while simultaneously changing perceptions about the way collectives such as corporations and non-profit entities (communities etc.) should exist or think.

Especially in business organizations, the adoption of knowledge management techniques for storage and use of the knowledge of individuals and organizations, which has accompanied the rapid expansion of ICT, is transforming corporations at the global level. However, it is important to note that no matter how much ICT adoption transforms business, the most fundamental elements of corporate strategy at the grass roots level are individual values, individually accumulated knowledge and innovations in core competencies. Further, to implement sustainable businesses and ICT businesses that traverse different industries as mentioned, companies need strategies to develop external sources of knowledge and core competencies that the company does not possess with participation from clients. Importantly, innovative companies in the twenty-first century require leadership that brings continued business innovation through collaborative strategies that focus on communication and coordination with others.

Therefore, company leaders must face up to the task of creating organizational platforms that promote collaborative strategies, actively work to formulate interactive business communities (IBCs) within the company and with partners outside the company, including clients, and improve the company's core competencies while at the same time absorbing the core competencies of leading partners and working to converge and integrate the company's own core competencies. The strategic activity of corporate leaders who work toward the formation of IBCs is a factor that will result in continued creation of new value for clients. 'IBC' means an unofficial or official organization that promotes strategic activities through interactive collaboration between members of the business community with various specialized knowledge and interactive collaboration strategies across multiple business communities.

These condensed collaboration strategies will be encouraged through the formulation of IBCs across diverse organizations within and outside companies. The formulation of an IBC within a company is a key factor in improving the company's organizational capability, while formulating inter-company IBCs that include clients can trigger mutual synergies of core competencies. In this book, integrating the diverse core knowledge within and outside companies is referred to as 'hybrid innovation' (systems integrating closed innovation and open innovation that can be thought of as equivalent to 'half open innovation').[1]

Moreover, the central concept behind collaborative strategies linking different business types is the promotion of 'co-creation' and 'co-evolution' through the formulation of IBCs. Co-creation means working with partners and clients to establish new businesses, economies and societies, while co-evolution means working with partners and clients not only for the evolution of the IBC itself, but also to develop those social and economic communities.

For companies, the most important issue in implementing collaborative strategies is how to create interactive business communities with client participation inside and outside the company to bring about co-creation and co-evolution. For these reasons, community leaders must have the leadership potential to form the IBC within the company, and provide leadership that aspires to global partnerships and client collaborations that transcend the conventional short-sighted competitive strategies within industries and inter-industry competitive strategy views.

This book discusses the mechanisms for realizing new business innovation through the formulation of interactive business communities from the point of view of strategies, organizations, technologies, operations, and leadership. The book also focuses on the process behind the formulation of IBCs and on company leaders' management and

---

1   IBC formation is basically a 'ba' (Nonaka et al. 2008). David Teece cites the following in the Foreword of 'Managing Flow' (Nonaka et al. 2008) (xiv) – 'Nonaka's frameworks recognize the importance of shared context or place (what Nonaka calls "ba")'. 'Ba' need not to be limited to a single organization – it can embrace suppliers, customers, governments, and competitors. Perhaps it's a half-open model of innovation. No doubt future writings will bring clarification.

leadership style through in-depth case studies of high-tech corporations in the United States, Taiwan and Japan. The book describes the ways these business leaders overcame various existing boundaries (technological, organizational, corporate and industrial) to encourage formulation of interactive business communities through new 'boundary vision' strategic thinking and bring about business model innovation through these new convergences.

The Book is Structured as Follows

Part 1 (Chapters 1 and 2) discusses theory. Chapter 1 describes the background and significance of this book, the importance of convergence and collaboration in recent years and refers to a number of business cases. The chapter also describes the major managerial elements that promote the 'hybrid innovation' resulting from the knowledge integration process within companies and externally prompted by collaborative strategies brought about by IBC formulation. In discussing convergence and collaboration, Chapter 2 describes the formulation of IBCs as organizational architecture within and outside companies with participation from clients and partners, and how new corporate boundaries that transcend industries, companies, organizations and technologies are defined to promote strategy transformation in business enterprises. It then describes the 'boundary vision' concept that is fundamental to IBC formulation, and seven capabilities that support boundary vision.

Part 2 presents case studies (Chapters 3–7). Chapter 3 describes cases of American and Japanese business innovation in the ICT field. This chapter clarifies the mechanisms involved in bringing about the product and service innovation processes that lie at the heart of the information revolution in the ICT industry. There are three main types of 'knowledge innovators' involved in the growth of ICT and digital businesses – 'platform innovators,' 'application innovators' and 'content innovators'. As case studies of 'knowledge innovators', this chapter deals with Apple's business innovations through strategy transformation that enabled the company to expand from its PC business into the multimedia business with iPod, iPhone and iPad; with Google's business strategy through an open platform model; and looks at the business innovations undertaken by NTT DOCOMO in the mobile phone businesses. These cases illustrate how IBC formation became the base for these innovation strategies, and even now continues to foster 'co-creation and co-evolution' as a business ecosystem.

Chapter 4 describes business model innovations in the semiconductor industry through collaborative strategies between companies with client participation. This chapter looks at the examples of the world's largest 'fabless' company, Qualcomm and eSilicon in the United States, the world's largest 'foundry' company, TSMC in Taiwan, and 'New IDM' company, Fujitsu in Japan. The chapter then describes how these companies have formed IBCs with clients and partner companies all over the world and realized new value chain vertical integration that transcends corporate boundaries to produce business model innovation through co-creation and co-evolution.

Through the case of Chunghwa Telecom in Taiwan, a major communications carrier, Chapter 5 describes how the IBC formed within and outside the company has become the well-spring for dynamic organizational capability at the core of its corporate competitive superiority. The chapter presents the important network platform that emerges as a result of new knowledge created when knowledge embedded in groups or personal knowledge is integrated through IBC 'boundary networks' traversing the company's internal and external organizational boundaries.

Chapter 6 presents an example of corporate strategy transformation through the formation of an IBC. In a departure from its role as a PDA mobile device specialized subcontract manufacturer, Taiwanese high-tech company HTC formed an IBC with its partner corporation to develop a range of world-first mobile terminals including PDA phones and smartphones to build the most competitive business process in today's smartphone market.

Chapter 7 presents an example of product development through the formation of an IBC within a company. This chapter illustrates product innovation though the process of converging technologies undertaken by Sharp. The chapter shows how the IBC enabled the diverse knowledge within the company to combine to trigger new product innovation with both creative product development and efficiency.

Part 3 (Chapters 8 and 9) covers discussion and conclusion. Through various case studies, Chapter 8 presents the leadership and management styles of corporate leaders who have realized hybrid innovation through IBCs and the boundary networks created between IBCs.

Chapter 9 discusses managerial implications and conclusions reached through the application research in this book.

Mitsuru Kodama, November 2011

PART 1

Background and Theoretical Framework

CHAPTER 1

Convergence and Collaboration

1.1 New Business Models Transcending Different Technologies and Industries

The most excellent core technologies in cutting-edge ICT, energy, automotive, semiconductor, biotechnology, medical, and material science fields are scattered across companies and organizations all around the globe. Innovation in these superior core technologies is the source of new products and services. Until recently, one of the strategic goals for high-tech corporations has been to develop and evolve products through independently sustained technological innovation. However, recent years have seen a growing demand for not only higher-functionality and higher-performance products, but also demands for investment in low-cost products, wider-ranging product lineups and shorter product development cycles. Conversely, increasingly diversified customer needs and value shifts have caused 'disruptive innovation' (Christensen 1997) that creates unexpected user needs born out of new product values.

Viewed in the context of the global market, international corporations are under pressure to come up with new global marketing and creative product strategies as demand expands in developing countries and matures in domestic markets. Thus, there is an increasing necessity for high-tech companies of the world to develop new products and services based on new technologies created through convergence of differing technologies in order to distinguish themselves from other companies in the area of new product development. The reason for this is that there are already a lot of cases of new and unconventional product and service development that merge technologies from differing fields. There is greater and greater need for business strategies that respond to convergence, as convergence is creating business structure, products and service developments that combine and integrate differing services and technologies across a range of industries.

ICT evolution has shortened business processes and supply chains in all sorts of industries, has sped up decision-making and streamlined management, and has given rise to new e-business models that merge and connect different industries (Kodama 2008). The biggest impact on the ICT industry is coming from companies like Google and Yahoo with their search and advertising businesses, multimedia distribution businesses with Apple's market-leading iPod, iPhone and iPad mobile devices, NTT DOCOMO's i-mode mobile phone business model, and Sony, Nintendo and Microsoft game businesses. These businesses do not only concern themselves with the technological aspect of product innovation in ICT development, but are the result of service innovations through new marketing strategies that create new markets. These product and service innovations promote 'co-evolution' across the whole ICT industry to create a dynamic 'business

ecosystem'. The fundamental source of the Internet businesses with i-mode/iPod/iPhone/
iPad, and game businesses such as PlayStation/DS/Wii/Xbox is this dynamically creative
business ecosystem forged through this co-evolution (Kodama 2009a).

Higher technological performance, diversity and rapid evolution of ICT is bringing
even more complexity to the business models that corporations should adopt. In this
dramatically shifting modern corporate environment of rapid technological innovation,
shorter product life cycles, mature markets in developed countries, expanding markets in
developing countries, and the search for new business models in the evolving ICT field,
companies have to strive to create new business models and develop new technologies.
Companies need to pursue innovations that can provide customers with new value
through the drivers of converging technologies and cross-industry ICT business creation.
For these reasons, not only is the merging and integration of different specialist knowledge
within companies important, but especially important is the integration of knowledge
between corporations.

To bring about new products, services and business models through convergence that
creates ICT businesses across industries and merges technologies, what sorts of strategies
and organizational actions should a company undertake? What is the role of leadership
and management in all of this? These are some of the many issues confronting many
global corporations. Although there is diversity in the details of industrial and corporate
strategies, in recent years, 'collaboration' is a key corporate concept for adapting to the
'convergence' world view (or for creating convergence individually) (see Figure 1.1).

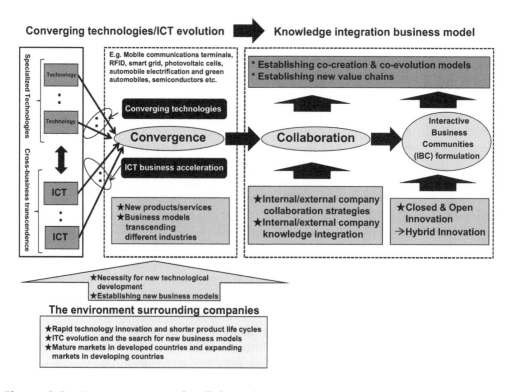

Figure 1.1   Convergence and collaboration

In promoting these 'collaborative strategies', not only is it necessary to integrate the specialized knowledge among the different organizations within a company, it is of the greatest importance to create globalized networks with prominent international partners to integrate the specialist knowledge scattered around the world with the company's own internal knowledge. The driver for collaborative strategies that accelerate knowledge integration within and outside companies is the formation of 'interactive business communities' (IBCs hereafter). An IBC is an 'organizational platform' that evolves core corporate knowledge within a company, actively searches for the best knowledge around the world, and integrates it with the company's core knowledge. As described in Section 1.4, the concept of knowledge integration through the formation of an IBC involves the concept of simultaneously combining 'closed innovation' and 'open innovation' (hybrid innovation) (see Figure 1.1).

1.2 Collaborative Strategies through IBC Formation

As mentioned, patterns of corporate behavior and organization are changing as ICT evolves, technologies merge and business environments are transformed. This means that strategic business transformations through company-external strategic alliances, joint development and venturing, strategic outsourcing, M&A, virtual corporations, that include resources outside companies such as knowledge and personnel, not just the resources confined to business units in the conventional corporate organization, are becoming more and more essential. In the area of marketing as well, marketing strategies based on new concepts such as customer participatory marketing, supply of customized goods and services for specific customers, personalization, and customer dealings (meeting of hearts and minds, building confidence and trust etc.) that form new relationships with companies are also important.

The main issue in promoting business innovation with this kind of strategic view is not how to engage in strategic business and operations only with the company's internal resources (knowledge, personnel etc.) but how to formulate IBCs of various collectives through collaborations (including virtual collaborations using ICT networks) with resources external to the company, including customers, and create innovative businesses.

Generally, this means a collective formed from range of elements both inside and outside the company working towards achieving the corporate organizations' business goals. Organic collaboration is important to integrate knowledge between various organizations within a company (different business units and specialist organizations). IBCs are also human networks that consolidate diverse knowledge within and outside a company including customers' knowledge. Companies that continue to create new knowledge (new products, services and business models) are engaging in strategic business and operations through organic linking of a range of IBCs both internally and externally.

Collaborations between different business units and specialist fields within a company promote total optimization of company business processes and supply chains by combining the entire company's creativities and efficiencies (Kodama 2007a). The collaboration with external partners in different industries that accompanies convergence raises the potential to achieve new business innovation and solve new problems (Kodama 2007b). In other words, accessing and absorbing diverse knowledge inside and outside a company can be a trigger towards innovation (new knowledge creation). For example, project-based organizations that span across a company's internal and external resources can enhance a company's organizational capability to spur the new knowledge and creative work needed to form new products, services and business models (Kodama 2007c).

Figure 1.2 illustrates three general categories depicting corporate business communities that consider the external environment (external partners, customers etc.). Type One is a closed IBC within a corporate organization. This IBC is formed between all business units and specialist departments, and functions to share a variety of information, knowledge and decision-making (between the upper and lower levels of the organization; top, middle and lower layers; and between branch stores and offices etc.) in the daily running of the company as well as strategic business. Projects and CFTs (cross-functional teams) in a company are also a type of IBC organizational system.

The Type Two IBC is a collective of affiliates and outsourced companies, and functions to share a variety of information, knowledge and business creativity in routine outsourcing affairs and across strategic alliances. The Type Three IBC is a strategically-based direct channel and new marketing community between companies and customers from large corporate to general users (e.g. various systems for carrying out projects with special monitoring, consultation via private channels, customer-participatory development projects for new products and services that reflect various special customer needs and deal with complaints).

In the long-term, sustained corporate innovation and continued creation of new business depends on how the IBC is formed. Therefore, in analyzing future corporate strategic activity, rather than only considering one's own company's organizational

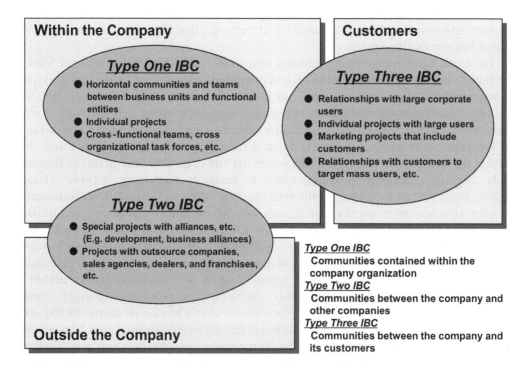

Figure 1.2   Types of interactive business communities

architecture, it is important that strategic and organizational philosophies continue to be discussed with the IBC of internal and external collectives that includes customers, considered as an analytical unit for organization.

The following section introduces recent business cases (relating to PDAs, RFID solutions, the smart grid, solar cells business, automotive computerization and development and environmental vehicles) involving collaborative strategies through the formation of IBCs. Business innovation in these fields has created convergence at the technological and industrial level including ICT, and this has resulted not only in the formation of IBCs based around collaborative strategies for product and service innovation through knowledge integration within a company, but at the same time resulted in promotion of collaborative strategies through IBC formation with external partners.

Integration of new core internal and external organizational knowledge is accelerated within these IBCs and between different IBCs. Formed within and outside companies and including customers, organization networks that emerge from the formation of IBCs do not only encourage the knowledge integration process and expand existing value chains, they also promote 'co-creation' and 'co-evolution' among all stakeholders including one's own company, other companies and customers (see Figure 1.1).

1.2.1 NEW ICT BUSINESS CENTERED ON PDAs

With their global top-level service and technology, the Japanese mobile telephone services are producing new services and products through the merging of different technologies across the boundaries between different business areas, industries and organizations. These developments are creating value chains with new strategic frameworks.[1] As representative Japanese carriers NTT DOCOMO, KDDI and SoftBank move toward realizing the new products and services of the future, these companies are actively developing strategic affiliations across a variety of industries including manufacturers of mobile phone, computer and communications equipment, semiconductor vendors, content providers, international communications carriers, financial institutions and automobile manufacturers.

The business strategies of NTT DOCOMO and other mobile communications carriers lie in the realization of product and service convergence (see Figure 1.3). Providing consumers with seamless usage environments through convergence that includes mobile, fixed, broadcasting and home networks, these companies are able to give users more comfortable and user-friendly services using their mobile telephones with information appliances, automobiles, broadcasting equipment and mobile terminals, and also with medical, social welfare and educational services. These converged methods of linking services and lifestyle tools with mobile phones are the strategic goals of mobile phone carriers.

'Convergence strategies' like this prompt the creation of new value chains through the expansion of business from existing corporate domains into new areas. Especially, the formation of IBCs among different types of businesses enables access to a range of different knowledge, and promotes dialogue between business people along the knowledge boundaries. The creative abrasion and productive friction between business

---

1   Using mobile phones and smart phones, the digital content 'mobile content market' and the 'mobile commerce market' for goods, services and transactions are expected to grow dramatically in future.

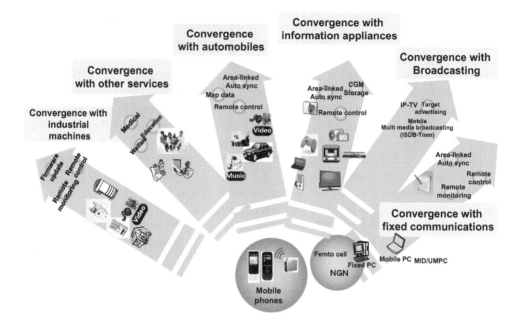

Figure 1.3   Converged services with mobile phones

people at the knowledge boundaries inspires new knowledge, and increases the creativity necessary to realize new business models (Kodama 2007b). Focusing on the mobile phone business in Japan in recent years, the new business models observed include electronic money businesses and credit card businesses, as well as the merging of broadcast and communications (the development of the One seg mobile phone and multimedia broadcasts through mobile phones etc. merging digital terrestrial broadcast and Internet businesses with mobile phones), and businesses merging mobile phones and automobiles (Telematics), which are the result of new value chains brought about by collaborative strategies between different companies.

For example, looking at the Telematics business, the first issues confronting car manufacturers are how to deal with safety and environmental concerns. Facing the tough environmental regulations and sharp increases in crude oil prices of recent years, automobile makers are pressured to develop 'clean' cars with greater fuel efficiency. As demand for hybrid car development expands into the future, Japanese car makers, e.g. will have to strengthen relationships with their current automotive parts manufacturers (Denso, Aisin etc.) and at the same time, forge collaborations with electronic manufacturers (Hitachi, Mitsubishi, Toshiba, Panasonic, NEC, Fujitsu, Sharp etc.). There is also an urgent need for the development of semiconductor chips (microcomputers and system LSI, described in the section on automotive computerization) that are able to deal with informatization and safety/environmental needs; this is bringing stronger collaborations between influential semiconductor vendors and car makers around the globe (Japanese semiconductor makers, Motorola in the US, Freescale Semiconductors etc.). To make cars even lighter in future, car makers are also forging strategic alliances with a range of steel and materials companies (companies such as GE and DuPont that develop plastic, aluminium and other materials).

The second issue facing car manufacturers is the need to respond to automotive informatization demands. Just as if the modern automobile were like a stand-alone computer or mobile phone, it cannot be designed with only phone and email functions, but must be designed with multimedia communications functions that meet customers' needs (for reading articles, listening to music, watching video etc.): functions for accessing the whole range of content, and in-vehicle e-commerce functions. For these reasons, car manufacturers are promoting joint development in communications equipment with various software and IT vendors, building links with Apple to expand on-board music delivery with iPod, and forming joint businesses through strategic alliances with mobile phone carriers such as Toyota's alliance with KDDI, and Nissan's alliance with NTT DOCOMO.

Automobile manufacturers have also linked up with a range of prominent content providers, and have embarked on automobile-based wireless Telematics services (on-board bi-directional information transfer). 'Toyota G-BOOK', 'Nissan Carwings', and 'Honda Premium Club' are some of the brand names. Various content providers and automobile manufacturers are also looking at ways to create new content businesses. As well, collaboration between automakers and Microsoft is accelerating the computerization of car navigation equipment to support Telematics services with the Windows Automobile car navigator OS, as well as raising theperformance of conventional navigation functions.

The new challenge for automakers is to meet the demand for a more comfortable on-board experience with greater levels of safety, while tackling environmental problems. This is why automotive companies are forming IBCs with a range of external business partners, and as these IBCs are networked with automotive makers at their core, the knowledge available in each of the IBCs is merged and integrated to create new knowledge (new products, services and business models). These collaborative strategies can result in the creation of new value chains.

Figure 1.3 illustrates the current state of business networks formed through the creation of IBCs between the different and varied industries of mobile communications carriers, financial and credit card institutions, broadcast, retail and advertising businesses, and automobile industries in Japan. Working towards realizing new value-added mobile Internet services, Japanese Mobile phone carriers are using these network relationships to promote collaborations with leading Internet businesses such as Yahoo and Google. SoftBank also maintains a strong relationship with Apple for its successful iPhone and iPad exclusive sales in Japan.

In this way, mobile phone carriers are promoting coordination and collaborations through the creation of relationships between companies, formed with strategic alliances and capital investment, and expanding their own corporate boundaries and value chains. Figure 1.4 describes the business networks structured from groups of different companies with NTT DOCOMO, au (KDDI) and SoftBank at the hubs, and the central role these companies play in information and knowledge storage and circulation needed for the realization of new business models. The knowledge integration process brought about by the formation of IBCs between different businesses is an important element in the creation of the new value chains needed to form new business models.

In the PDA world of smart phones and next-generation PCs, the Apple iPhone and iPad business model has created a data distribution platform of the type required for digital content circulation for accounting, payments and verification etc. similar to i-mode in Japan. Behind the explosive popularity of iPhone and iPad is the promotion

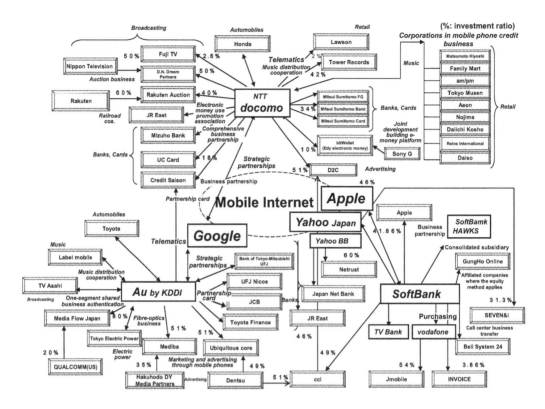

Figure 1.4   Building interactive business communities through corporate networks in different industries

of participation with service providers and software developers (including consumers) linking Apple's accounting platform across a range of music, broadcast, video, book, game, corporate information, education, medical, and other industries. The network effect based on this type of positive feedback helps to create a business ecosystem through co-evolution between the various industries involved.

A big difference between Apple's App Store and i-mode is the maximum possible lowering of hurdles to participation from content and application businesses, and the dramatically better user interfaces in the PDAs. The excellent iPhone and iPad platforms also offer the user new experience and value, and spur users themselves to find new creative uses for the devices (see Figure 1.5).

Electronic book services with iPad and Kindle etc. mean that content different from that of traditional paper books can be created and with it potential for new businesses for the computerization and circulation of existing book content; something that cannot be done only in the framework of existing markets. These developments have the potential to fundamentally transform conventional publishing and book distribution/retailing businesses. (see Figure 1.6).

Notably in the US, iPad (including iPhone) and Amazon's book reader Kindle are positioned to become global de facto standards. With a Kindle in America, buying regular books has become unnecessary since the electronic environment is in place. As a portable study or text book library, not only do these devices facilitate private, business,

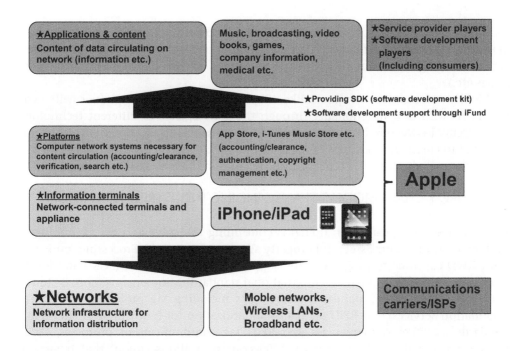

Figure 1.5   iPhone/iPad business models

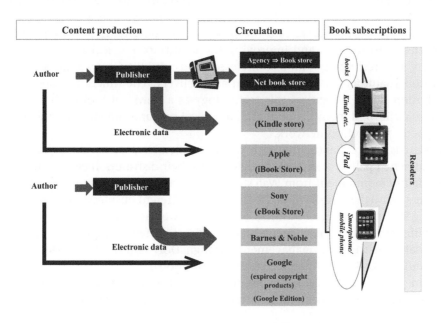

Figure 1.6   Business structures for electronic publishing

educational and leisure uses, but they also have the potential to trigger dramatic change in educational and other markets. This means that there is potential for new synergies to appear, merging book content with various content services (video, music, advertising, games etc.).

Mobile information terminals like iPhone/iPad and mobile phones will evolve into PDAs with new functionality through the convergence of different technologies. Convergence between ICT technology, diverse content and applications will bring greater potential to create new business models. In this way, convergence will create new value chains that will dramatically transform the business models of existing industries.

1.2.2 SUPPLY CHAIN MODELS TRANSCENDING INDUSTRIES WITH RFID

Radio Frequency Identification (RFID) is continuing to evolve as a key technology for tracking more and more assets and property all around the world. Processing innovations using RFID continue to progress in the supply chain management (SCM) and logistics processing fields. EPC Global,[2] an international standardization organization, is studying the potential for global standard technologies including tag protocols, EPC IS (EPC Information Services) and RFID tag data standardization for use with SCM. To establish standards for wireless frequencies and RFID tag communications protocols, ISO air interfaces under the ITU (International Telecommunications Union) that traverse the barriers between industries and business have been examined.

For SCM, RFID makes it possible to increase product and asset visibility, and can be used in the medical area, e.g. to track high-cost medical equipment, implements and pharmaceuticals, and accelerate the processes of identifying locations, managing drug dispensing to patients and improving the quality of medical services in general. For retailers, this technology can also increase goods visibility in warehouses and retail outlets through automated stock shipment and delivery. The American Food and Drug Administration (FDA) recognizes this technology as a powerful tool in preventing the influx of unauthorized medical goods and biological preparations through the American medical goods distribution network.

Wal-Mart is also collaborating with major retailers and demanding that suppliers use RFID-attached pallets and cases for delivery to their distribution centers and outlets. This mandatory requirement from Wal-Mart has had a big impact on manufacturers and distributors around the world. For this reason, many different businesses and industries are considering RFID for a range of business activities. As well as this, uses for this technology are spreading into various areas, such as the FDA's counterfeit drug prevention programs, and materials and weapons management through DoD (United States Department of Defense) and NATO (North Atlantic Treaty Organization).

Even in Japan, practical and experimental applications are appearing in various areas such as sales and marketing (department stores, mass retailers), convenience stores

---

2   EPC Global is an international organization concerned with RFID codes (Electronic Product Code (EPC)) issuance, systems examination and service support. This organization was originally the MIT Auto ID Center in the US, but transitioned to its current state in Autumn 2003 with member participation from EAN international, UCC in the US, Wal-Mart, P&G, Gillette and other corporate users and suppliers. Also, academic research is being carried out through the Auto ID lab with participation from member universities including the University of Adelaide in Australia, and Keio University in Japan (currently seven universities including MIT). EPC Global membership is not limited to corporate and associate retailers, but also includes a range of memberships in the appliance, airline, medical and logistics fields.

(automated payments), game centers (private information management), transportation (cargo etc.), perishable foods (traceability), distribution (source tagging – attaching tags at the point of production), printing, events and forums, disabled person support and solution businesses.

When considering the introduction of RFID in an open business environment, the issue to consider is whether introduction should be 'closed use' or 'open use'. 'Closed use' means use within a company or factory setting, whereas 'open use' refers to the transfer of property rights accompanying distribution, similar to commercial transactions between different companies. Up to now RFID has mostly been introduced as closed use systems in factories and offices, enabling companies to use their own specifications for the tags and the data recorded in them.

However, with the momentum that began with Wal-Mart's 2005 requirement for suppliers to attach RFID tags to supplied goods, there is now an urgent need for the establishment of standardized technology and regulations so that the RFID tags can be used and shared among businesses as an internationally standardized tool for commercial transactions. Thus, a standardized system that includes RFID tag frequencies and systemic components is indispensable. This brings with it the pressing need for collaborative strategies among companies from a range of different industries and business areas.

1.2.3 THE SMART GRID BUSINESS MODEL – TRANSCENDING INDUSTRIES

Facing up to the radical solutions required for modern environmental problems, high-tech companies from all over the world are pouring efforts into the construction of the 'smart grid' (the next-generation electric power distribution network) by converging power system technologies with ICT. There has been a lot of attention focusing on photovoltaic and wind-turbine power generation to reduce CO_2 emissions, but since the reliability of these systems is dependent on the weather, they can also cause instability in power supply systems. The smart grid, however, can overcome these problems through the fusion of electric power and ICT technologies. As the next-generation energy supply system, the smart grid will also be able to deal with reverse power flow from household power supplies and control complex power supply systems (see Figure 1.7). To develop and construct the smart grid, cutting-edge ICT control and battery technologies will have to be assembled in conjunction with electrical system technologies such as power conditioners to optimize distribution between the supply and demand sides.

In Japan, measures to create new value chains through collaborative strategies crossing over organizational boundaries between businesses and industries are being undertaken through applied research into smart-grid centered energy infrastructure, by joint ventures established between such organizations as the Tokyo Electric Power Company, Nippon Oil Corporation, Mitsubishi, NTT group, Tokyo Gas and the Tokyo Institute of Technology (see Figure 1.7). These companies are bringing together a range of leading technologies including photovoltaic and fuel cell technologies, and will be conducting experiments for proof of concept both inside and outside Japan over the next five years. Market expansion in this field is expected internationally in countries such as the USA, China and India, and the companies involved are considering steps towards commercialization of their research achievements.

These companies have dispatched researchers and engineers to the Tokyo Institute of Technology on a special joint industry-university mission, forming a body of about

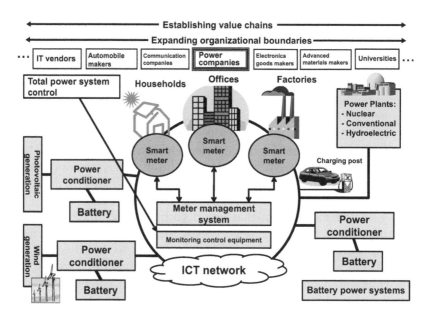

Figure 1.7　Formulating businesses with the smart grid concept

50 people including the academic researchers involved, and dubbed 'Team Japan'. Tokyo Electric Power Company, NTT group and Nippon Oil Corporation are developing electricity and heating usage methods that maximize effectiveness with office and household solar power generation combined with batteries through the ICT-controlled smart grid. Mitsubishi has been developing systems to use electricity generated with solar and wind to charge electric vehicles, while Tokyo Gas is involved in developing infrastructure to supply electricity with new types of fuel cells. The Tokyo Institute of Technology has also enlisted many world-class researchers in the renewable energy field to focus on solar power generation. To achieve the next-generation energy infrastructure, collaboration strategies between different companies that merge and integrate all of these technological elements will be pivotal to the success or failure of smart grid businesses.

1.2.4 SOLAR CELL BUSINESSES TRANSFORMING EXISTING VALUE CHAINS

For a sustainable society, the important challenges to be tackled are the creation of low-power electronic equipment, and the generation of the level of power required for propulsion using solar cells and secondary batteries. From the perspective of new business models for solar cell makers, new energy management is needed that uses ICT for control and maintenance of energy in households, buildings, towns and cities, both nationally and globally.

To promote the use of solar cell modules around the world, grid parity[3] must be achieved. This is a big issue for solar cell makers as they work to bring costs down to achieve grid parity and continue to strengthen the industry and turn a profit. One

---

3　Grid parity refers to the situation where the energy generation cost of new forms of energy such wind and solar is comparable or equal to the cost of electricity generation with existing systems or the boundary point cost.

example is the Japanese solar cell manufacturer Sharp – a company that has accumulated much technology and know-how in solar cell and module development and manufacture over many years. Sharp has defined its business process of supplying solar cell modules destined for integration into systems as its own corporate boundaries.

However, solar cell manufacturers of the future will have to build power generation stations and thus become involved in the broader electricity generation business, working towards total optimization of power generation costs. This means that Sharp will dramatically expand its value chain, and change its company status as it opens out into wider-reaching power enterprises. As these power generation costs come down, the solar energy world is expected to expand. When that happens, the electricity created with sunlight must be smoothly transferred to the peripheral power distribution grid. One of the increasingly important research issues for solar cell makers such as Sharp is how to develop system technologies to alleviate and stabilize power generation fluctuations due to cloudy skies or short and long generation cycles.

As a company with an eco-positive vision, Sharp is making efforts towards 'energy creation', 'energy conservation', 'energy storage' and 'energy delivery'. 'Energy creation' means solar cells, while 'energy conservation' means LCD panels (e.g. the world renowned LCD television brand 'AQUOS') LED lighting systems and other energy conserving products. 'Energy storage' means battery systems, while 'energy delivery' means home energy management systems. Sharp is aiming towards new business models founded on these solution businesses.

Figure 1.8 illustrates the expansions in Sharp's existing value chains. These expansions to existing value chains will be triggered as solar cell manufacturers transcend technologies and industries in response to smart grid convergence. Another big issue for solar cell makers is the challenge of global expansion, gaining public recognition around the globe for solar cells, and creating a 'megasolar' business. This is because unless large gigawatt-scale power stations are built, these businesses will not grow very much. Therefore in creating the megasolar business, not only national and government support is required, but to establish a truly global business, solar cell makers must form collaborative strategies with commercial businesses, power companies and communications carriers etc. just like the smart grid strategies mentioned earlier.

Working toward this kind of future megasolar business, electronics companies the world over will have to merge and integrate core knowledge scattered across physics, chemistry, electronics, mechatronics, semiconductors and ICT etc. using collaborative strategies to produce the necessary electronic and solar cell innovations.

1.2.5 AUTOMOBILE COMPUTERIZATION AND DEVELOPMENT BRINGING NEW TECHNOLOGICAL INTEGRATION

In recent years, automobile computerization has become a key driver of the electronics industry. A luxury automobile has around 70–80 microcontrollers and car navigation and car audio systems and so forth are using system LSIs, with implementation of these technologies predicted to become even more common (see Figure 1.9). Eventually semiconductor electronics will propel vehicles as we leave behind internal combustion vehicles and move toward the electric vehicle world of tomorrow, although even in the internal combustion automobiles of today as electronics are used more and more often to replace mechanical systems, continued growth in this area of automotive electronics

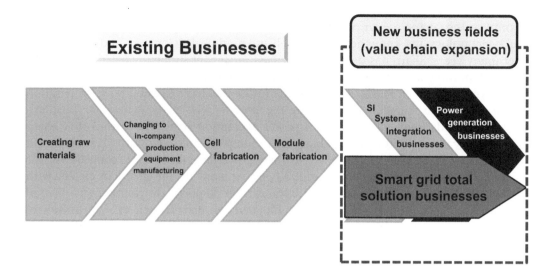

Figure 1.8   Photovoltaic business value chain expansion

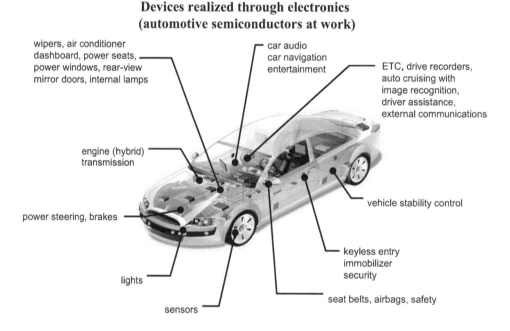

Figure 1.9   Increases in automotive electronics

is still expected.[4] Electronic control in computerized vehicles makes it possible for even greater functionality, reliability and performance. Vehicle computerization can also contribute to achieving safety, environmental and comfort targets.

For the long-term supply process from proposal activity in the R&D stage through to maintenance with this kind of automotive computerization, layered collaboration frameworks between car manufacturers, ECU (electronic control unit) makers (sometimes called first tier. There are also second tier, third tier etc.) and semiconductor suppliers are already standard business practice (see Figure 1.10). However, with the even greater level of automotive computerization and EV developments of recent years, automakers are forming more and more direct collaborative strategies that include a wide range of electronic manufacturers and semiconductor suppliers[5] to replace the layered alliances between ECU makers and semiconductor suppliers.

For example, Nissan's technical center acts as the central hub for Nissan's global development system. Indispensable to Nissan's R&D activities, the center deals mainly with product planning, design, prototypes and experimentation. One of the features of the center is that it integrates automotive technological development with product development to achieve Nissan's corporate vision to enrich people's lives. As a fundamental driver enabling Nissan to succeed in the extremely competitive world of automobile development, the center is always equipped and ready to master the latest technology. In March 1999, Nissan had to rethink its engineering strategies and formed its wider ranging global strategic alliances with Renault. This helped the company strengthen its financial structure, and establish and steadily pursue the 'Nissan Revival Plan (NRP)' to achieve profitable growth.

Nissan now routinely engages in these global collaborations to achieve the dramatic cost and delivery cycle reductions demanded in today's business environment. Symbolizing the strategic collaborations at Nissan's base, in 2007 the company built a new technical center nearby called the Nissan Advanced Technology Center (NATC), an innovatively designed building that houses a collection of cutting-edge technological

---

4   Operations manually performed in the past such as opening a window by rotating a handle are now performed by power windows, and power steering to reduce the heaviness of steering wheel operation at low speeds is also increasingly popular. Electronics and semiconductors etc. are implemented in these areas. Microcomputers for purposes such as engine control are employed in areas that are not normally seen, to optimize ignition, reduce fuel consumption and NO_x emissions, and clean up exhaust gasses. Microcomputers are even used in the airbag technology designed to reduce injury in the event of a collision.

Microcomputers are also used to raise the front suspension and lower the rear suspensions during sudden braking to maintain vehicle stability. Anti-locking brakes (ABS) are becoming standard equipment. Also controlled by microprocessors, this type of brake system is designed to avoid loss of driver control due to wheels locking during sudden braking in wet or rainy conditions by automatically softening the brakes as they are applied to prevent skidding. Moreover, in-vehicle entertainment systems – stereo, radio, navigator etc. – use the latest LSI systems (SoC – 'system on chip') consisting of 32 bit microprocessors and multicore devices.

The latest cars use microcomputer functions for rear-vehicle monitoring, automatic headlight tracking, laser readers to prevent collision, and the 'around view monitor' system that creates an overhead view of the car for easier parallel parking etc.

5   Semiconductor makers are also restructuring with the convergence that comes with the computerization and informatization of vehicles. In Japan, NEC Electronics and Renesas Technology merged to strengthen their total solution businesses all the way from microcomputers through to high-functionality system LSI semiconductors for mobile phones, smartphones, digital appliances and automobiles. In the past, the semiconductor business has been partitioned into 'design, development and manufacture' sections; however, nowadays in Japan, to meet diverse customers' needs and cost reduction requirements as well as to respond to the technical innovations accompanying convergence, semiconductor businesses use a vertical integration business model called Integrated Design Manufacturing (IDM) to improve efficiency through partially separated manufacturing functions. Foundry companies specializing in manufacture are also holding onto their own strengths while moving into the upstream value chain areas of design and development.

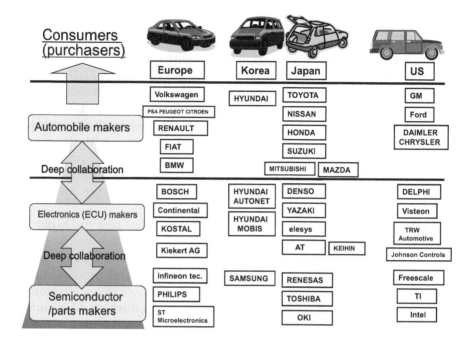

Figure 1.10 Formulating automotive semiconductor businesses

development capabilities to provide society with safe and environmentally friendly cars and enable more efficient research and advanced development for the cars of the future.[6]

The center develops leading safety and vehicle technologies enabling prompt application of ideas conceived in the research and development department to actual products such as environmental electric power trains and ITS (intelligent transport systems). This is not only a place for researchers, but also fulfils a strategic goal for creative innovation through collaboration with parts manufacturers and suppliers.

Vehicles are described as 'total integration of technology'. Collaboration between suppliers and automakers is especially important since roughly 80 per cent of components in vehicles are provided by suppliers compared to 20 per cent or so that are made by the automaker itself. Other important research issues include human interfaces, various usage environments, safety and reliability and so forth, as well as the need for ever-shorter vehicle development cycles that have a direct effect on business performance. Integration of this sort – automotive design and planning, component coordination and so forth – is a feature of the competitive vibrancy of Japanese manufacturing corporations.

However, as globalization steams ahead, companies must continue to form collaborative strategies with best partners around the world. One important technological theme is the assembly and mounting of high performance software and hardware sections as automotive computerization increasingly incorporates software parts such as semiconductors and sensors. As these mounting processes become more complicated, knowledge integration of various specialist technologies also becomes more important,

---

6   A published photo of the NATC: http://www.geocities.jp/morinosato4jp/c22_natc/natc_main/natc_main_info60. htm.

which means developmental frameworks involving collaborations with a more diverse range of partners than the older-style supplier networks are on the rise.

NATC aims to speed up development and commercialization of advanced technology and create new value for the automobile society of the future. To achieve these goals, this newly conceived office environment or 'Workplace'[7] is a forum for encouraging collaboration with researchers inside and outside the company to develop world-class technologies, and because it is necessary to achieve collaboration through even closer partnerships between suppliers and advanced technology development, Nissan is embarking on new projects with various suppliers based on mid to long-term plans.

To develop new technologies, improve product potential and deal with production and investment issues more efficiently, Nissan invites suppliers to begin participating earlier in the product development stages of a project, and forms close relationships with suppliers. These new kinds of mid to long-term partnerships improve efficiency and are an important element of the Nissan company (Nissan calls this the 'project partnership system').

Collaborative strategies with partnerships formed at the early stages through this policy can increase the potential to (1) encourage suppliers to use specific advanced technologies, (2) ensure adequate time for technical advancement to the level required for application to motor vehicles, and (3) allow for even further technological advancement through collaboration between Nissan and its suppliers and others.

1.2.6 DEVELOPING ENVIRONMENTAL VEHICLES THROUGH NEW BUSINESS COMMUNITIES

In the battery business, collaborations and industrial competition that transcends organizational boundaries are also fast evolving (see Figure 1.11). The main competitive market is in high-capacity lithium-ion batteries. Since lithium-ion battery technology is important for environmental vehicles and the smart grid mentioned earlier, there is interest and participation from all kinds of businesses involved in the automotive, electronics, materials, energy, and residential fields. Although Japanese companies have held superiority in the battery technology field for quite a while, there is a global tug of war emerging as Korean and other players quickly move into the area.

Toyota, maker of the leading environmental vehicle the Prius, has been using the conventional nickel-hydride batteries, but has decided to use the lithium-ion batteries in new models to be released from 2011. Batteries are constructed at Toyota, but production is also planned to begin at Panasonic EV Energy, a battery company set up as a joint capital investment with Panasonic. Slated for inclusion in the Prius brand minivan to be released in early 2011, this will be the first time lithium-ion batteries will be used in a mass-produced hybrid vehicle. Lithium-ion battery models are also planned for subsequent hybrid vehicles following on from the Prius.

Nissan are also scheduled to release a lithium-ion EV in December 2010, the 'Leaf'. The batteries for these vehicles will be manufactured by Automotive Energy Supply Corporation, a joint investment with the NEC group, and the company is gearing up

---

7   As a new concept office, the building features a uniquely stepped design overlooking the lower level, a 200–person capacity collaboration room, a prototype workshop for quickly turning ideas into reality, a communications space for promoting mutually enhanced ideas through exchange and gathering of new information, and an auditorium for fostering technological exchange activities.

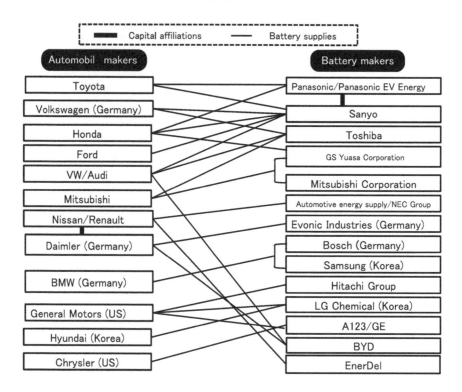

Figure 1.11 Affiliations among companies focusing on automotive batteries

to manufacture 500,000 units in America, Japan and Europe by 2012. The company is planning to bring down costs through external sales to other major automakers in addition to its French Renault ally.

First applied by Sony in 1991, demand for lithium-ion battery technology in mobile phone and notebook computer applications has exploded, because the batteries are generally capable of 1.5 times the output of the nickel-hydride batteries with about double the storage capacity, and they have good potential to power electric vehicles. Costing several thousand dollars per vehicle, however, they are more expensive than nickel-hydride batteries and push up production costs. There are also issues regarding safety and output improvements, and as yet no decisions have been made regarding the most balanced specifications and design. Corporations are pouring resources into R&D and facility construction for development and manufacture, because to develop a battery that became an industry standard would result in great profit. GS Yuasa Corporation, Toshiba and Sony are moving toward factory construction with large capital investment. Also, Hitachi has merged Shin-Kobe Electric Machinery Co. and Hitachi Maxell to form Hitachi Vehicle Energy, and plan to supply lithium-ion batteries to General Motors in the United States from 2011.

The cell market for the completed lithium-ion battery product is worth about 10 billion US dollars. Sanyo and other Japanese players hold roughly 60 per cent of this market, but there is a rapidly increasing presence of Korean and Chinese participants. LG Chemical of Korea has been selected to supply Shanghai Automotive in China and Volvo in Sweden and is negotiating contracts with four companies including Ford Motors in the US. The company is supplying these modern automotive groups and others and is hurrying to construct a mass production line with these major contracts as a driving force.

In 2009, BYD (Guangdong China) formed an alliance with Volkswagen in Germany in the electric vehicle field. They also formed one with Daimler in March 2009 to jointly develop electric vehicles. International manufacturing technology is coming up to the standards of Japanese makers. Having the same cost reduction strategies as Japanese players, and looking at their supply contract closure and development and capital expenditure, they have the power to quickly catch up with Japanese manufacturers' market share depending on the speed of their decision-making.

GE also has invested in and continued to support the American venture enterprise 'A123Systems', established in 2001, who are supplying batteries to GM and Chrysler. Another US venture company manufacturing lithium-ion batteries, EnerDel, has contracted to supply batteries for Think Global's 'City' and Fisker Automotive's luxury plug-in electric vehicles, and began collaborating with Nissan in research for better conductive materials to produce improved vehicle batteries in 2009.

From developments like these it can be seen that car makers are actively pursuing collaborative strategies with electronics manufacturers and emerging venture companies because they don't have the developmental and manufacturing know-how for battery technology. On the other hand, since batteries have a wide range of applications, battery makers are forming relationships between corporations to supplement their technology and know-how through the formation of mutual IBCs with leading automakers to absorb the knowledge required to apply battery technology to automobiles (technical specification and reliability issues etc.).

Collaborative strategies through alliances for development of parts other than lithium batteries, such as motors, are also becoming more and more important for the development of environmental vehicles. Competition between major electronics manufacturers for the development and manufacture of fundamental environmental vehicle parts is bringing down costs, improving performance and promoting wider diffusion through global markets. Motors for Hybrid and electric vehicles are equivalent to the engine and transmission in a gasoline-powered vehicle. Although Toyota and Honda are manufacturing within their companies, the market for environmental vehicles is also expanding in developing countries and causing more demand for low-cost mass production technologies than ever before. The major electronic manufacturers are leading the way in cost and performance competitiveness with basic parts formally supplied through in-company production or affiliate corporations.

Toshiba, a manufacturer of high-performance industrial motors for elevators, the Shinkansen (Japan's high-speed trains) and others, is taking its advanced technology and developing it for automotive applications. The company has been highly praised by Ford for its superior new systems for efficient conversion of electricity into propulsion. Beginning in 2011, Toshiba will construct a factory in Houston, Texas in the United States, at a cost of around 40 million USD, and start production of 120,000 units in the spring of 2012. Positioning itself in a growth area of the automotive business, Toshiba is developing other customers as well as Ford, and is planning to raise future production capacity to 300,000 units per year. Toshiba will also supply Honda with new-type lithium-ion batteries for their electric two-wheelers, and is continuing supply negotiations with Volkswagen as well.

In the world of environmental vehicles, the US major automakers are lagging behind the Japanese players. Ford has plans to construct a factory in Michigan as its strategic base for hybrid and small car manufacture with a 10 million dollar investment, reducing the financial burden and speeding up commercialization with externally supplied motors.

As mentioned earlier, collaborative strategies between major auto and electric manufacturers are becoming more and more common in the automotive battery area. As well as Toshiba's partnerships, Hitachi is planning to supply GM with motors, and Meidensha of Japan are to supply Mitsubishi for their electric vehicles. Since major Japanese electrical companies have the worlds leading technological ability to manufacture basic parts, there is more and more movement to form strategic alliances centered on these Japanese manufacturers.

1.3 Organizational Capability Innovation through Collaborative Strategies

Convergence across developmental technologies and industries involved in PDA and RFID solutions, the smart grid and solar cell businesses, automotive computerization and development, semiconductors and environmental vehicles promotes innovation through the new business networks created by IBCs (Type Two IBCs, see Figure 1.2) formed through collaborative strategies with external businesses.

It is also important to form IBCs for collaboration between the different organizational structures within a company (Type One IBC, see Figure 1.2), as well as the external collaborative strategies formed with other companies through convergence. This is because the organizational capability of a company is determined by dynamic sharing and integration across organizational boundaries of diverse knowledge possessed by people, groups and organizations, through the IBCs inside and outside the company. Integration and merging of different knowledge through collaborative strategies is not only important outside the company, but also inside the company to trigger innovation for products, services, and ICT business development and growth through convergence of technologies and industries.

Diverse knowledge possessed by human beings is the well-spring of organizational capability. This tacit knowledge is 'embedded' (Brown and Duguid 1991) in individuals as skills, core competencies, and know-how. The process of knowledge integration must involve the accumulation and integration across organizational boundaries of knowledge possessed by the people in the various organizations within the company. However, obstructions to knowledge integration may arise from conflict or friction between knowledge-possessing business people working at organizational boundaries, which can hinder collaborative strategies (Leonard-Barton 1995). This is because business people with different backgrounds and experience conduct themselves according to their own unique mental models and path dependencies (Rosenberg 1982, Hargadon and Sutton 1997), and may express uneasiness or opposition when confronted with new or foreign knowledge. Therefore, companies or organizations that have these types of mental model may be unable to avoid competency traps (Levitt and March 1988, Martines and Kambil, 1999) and core rigidities (Leonard-Barton 1992, 1995) and lose opportunities for innovation (Christensen 1997).

On the other hand, innovation is enabled through the source created when business people recognize and understand new and foreign knowledge across their organizational boundaries. Constructive and creative interaction and dialogue between business people across these pragmatic organizational boundaries trigger new knowledge that promotes collaborative strategies within a company and induces innovation (Leonard-Barton 1995).

The 'dynamic view of strategy' that includes vibrant IBCs and networks between IBCs is the architecture that achieves knowledge integration across multiple organizational boundaries, and is necessary to acquire the organizational capability needed to maintain the corporate competitive-edge.

1.4 The Collaborative Strategy through Knowledge Integration Model

This section discusses patterns of the process of knowledge integration through collaborative strategies, and the relevance of IBC formation. Until recently in the era of mass production, innovation has been fully controlled by individual companies through traditional hierarchical organization with closed, independent systems. However, in the age of convergence with its ever-changing and diversifying business environment, the old closed innovation system is causing problems for many companies as they strive to achieve new innovative success (e.g. Sawhney and Prandelli 2000; Chesbrough 2003). In the past, innovation has been managed as closed and independent systems operating according to the company's internal hierarchical framework. In this way, the company had full control of the innovation process, and retained most of the intellectual properties associated with it. In this corporate system, companies seriously considered internal knowledge integration and IBC formation (Type One IBC, see Figure 1.2) (see Figure 1.12, pattern A). Even now, these closed corporate innovation systems are adopted in industry and enterprise mainly because they are perceived as having business advantages through the creation of vertically integrated value chains.

However, to succeed in the R&D and production capacity competitiveness of today's world of dramatically changing high-tech enterprises, many companies are actively working to form all kinds of alliances with other companies and universities to embrace these business environment changes (or create a new business environment themselves). There are specific causes behind the convergence phenomenon, as described below.

Firstly, more than ever in today's world of rapidly diversifying technical innovation and higher performance standards, R&D is faced with continually increasing challenges that must be overcome. Secondly, the cost of R&D and production facilities is going up and up, which means that a company operating independently would have to bear a significantly greater financial burden. These are current issues in areas such as semiconductor development, biotechnology and medical goods where there is demand for cutting-edge technology. The third cause is the emergence of changing business processes accompanying the development of ICT, and new business models crossing between companies and industries, such as the iPhone and iPad phenomena. Fourthly is the need for radical re-thinking of developmental methods and improved efficiencies to recover developmental costs in a world where product life cycles are getting shorter and shorter. The fifth reason is the rising demand for solutions such as RFID, the smart grid and solar cells, and the demand for customization and packaging (grouping of different

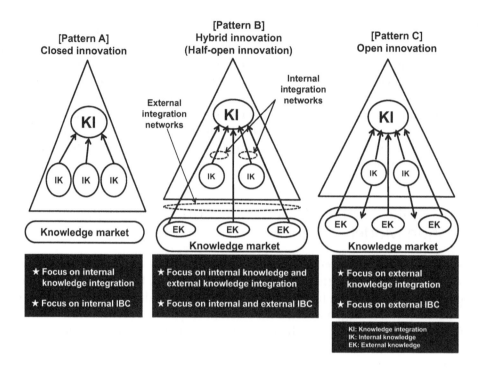

Figure 1.12 Innovation systems

products). The sixth cause is the rising need for strengthened global management that can support regional corporate governance in responding to the rapid market growth in developing countries.

These are the reasons why companies must avail themselves of the high-quality and diverse knowledge that is born through the convergence and consolidation of knowledge existing in different technological fields and industries. In a world where business resources are changing though the convergence phenomenon, companies cannot rely solely on their own resources (core knowledge such as technology, know how, skills etc.), and must make efforts to form strategies to make the best use of the resources available through partnerships with prominent corporations and universities all over the world.

In these innovation systems, knowledge integration of internal and external knowledge through internal and external IBCs formed through collaborative strategies inside and outside companies, and those networks (internal integration networks and external integration networks) themselves are both of critical importance (see Figure 1.12, pattern B). This kind of innovation system is referred to as 'hybrid innovation' in this book. Also called 'half-open innovation', hybrid innovation simultaneously incorporates elements of both open and closed innovation systems.

In these systems, knowledge integration that transcends corporate (industry) boundaries is needed for corporations to recognize the importance of external partners' skills and creativity and understand that the traditional models of closed and autonomous production and intellectual property innovation systems are inadequate. For a company to remain competitive in the knowledge economy, this kind of distributed innovation management requires a new type of governance approach through administration that integrates the multitude of useful knowledge dispersed inside and outside the company and among its customers, through the open systems of IBCs and networks created between IBCs. The author has significant theoretic and practical propositions regarding the structure of business systems for knowledge integration models in hybrid innovation systems.

Obviously companies must maintain and develop their own core competencies (e.g. Hamel and Prahalad 1994) that are difficult for another company to replicate, but they must also embrace open innovation in response to changing business circumstances (see Figure 1.12, pattern C). While open innovation means that a company makes use of another company's ideas and technology, it can also mean that the company shares its own ideas with another company so that the other company can use those ideas to increase the value of innovation.

To encourage efficient innovation, companies can open their own business model and strengthen it by embracing even more ideas and technologies from outside the company. Companies should release more of their know-how (patents, licenses and technological know-how etc.) and simultaneously construct business models based on new ways of thinking that promote synergies with other companies' business models (mutual business model strengthening between the companies involved) (Chesbrough 2003, 2006). In these types of corporate open innovation systems, the 'horizontal specialization' business structures used mainly by the digital industries and semiconductor manufacturers, there are advantages to the adaptation of business models that create bigger returns through 'selection and convergence' of a company's resources.

This book emphasizes that the ground source for innovation is the new knowledge gained through the formation of IBCs and associated networks that merge and integrate the boundaries between technologies, organizations, companies and industries. The 'dynamic strategy view' consisting of diverse IBCs and IBC networks (called 'boundary networks' in this book) existing inside and outside companies and including external partners and customers, brings with it the new organizational capabilities needed for innovative creativity. Through in-depth case studies, Part 2 of this book illustrates the mechanisms that bring about new innovation with the formation of organizational architecture realized through diverse IBCs and their networks, enabling corporations to dynamically integrate knowledge and create new innovations.

Chapter 1 Conclusions

1. There is greater and greater need for business strategies that can cope with convergence, as products and service developments and business models that merge and integrate differing technologies and services and use ICTs across a range of industries.
2. The rapid pace of technological innovation, even shorter product lifecycles, mature markets in developed countries, rapidly growing markets in developing countries, and the search for new business models with ICT developments means that business environments are changing dramatically, and corporations must find new structures for their business models and technological developments.
3. The central strategic theme in adapting to (or creating within) the changing 'convergence' environment is strategic collaboration within and external to companies.

4. In promoting these collaborative strategies, not only is it necessary to integrate knowledge in specialized fields in the different sections within a company, it is of greatest importance to create globalized networks with prominent international partners to integrate the specialist knowledge scattered around the world with the internal knowledge of a company.
5. 'Interactive business communities' (IBCs) that accelerate integration of knowledge from different sources are the engine that propels 'collaborative strategies' within and outside of companies to create 'hybrid innovation'.
6. IBCs are also an 'organizational platform' to bring about new value chains and 'co-creation' and 'co-evolution' in business models.
7. 'Hybrid innovation' (half-open innovation) is an important element promoted through knowledge integration inside and outside a company through collaborative strategies operating through internal and external IBCs, and among networks of IBCs.

2 *Boundary Vision and Interactive Business Communities*

2.1 Hybrid Innovation and Boundary Vision

In the knowledge economy, the diverse knowledge held by human beings is the source of valuable products, services and business models that create fresh competitiveness. Referring to several cases, Chapter 1 discussed a range of new products, services, and business models born through boundary transcendent convergence spanning diverse technologies and industries, and giving rise to value chains of new strategic models. Therefore as corporations move to create new businesses, companies must gain new understanding of the managerial processes that bring about new knowledge through dynamic sharing and integration of the knowledge in people, groups and organizations across organizational boundaries. The most important element as companies work to acquire the organizational capability required to maintain a competitive edge is the formation of IBCs – organizational architecture (organizational design concepts) that realizes dynamic knowledge integration across multiple organizational boundaries.

To establish the capability of creating diverse IBCs, practitioners must have the ability to gain new insights from varied and complicated boundaries, called 'boundary vision'. Boundary vision presents new propositions, such as 'knowledge integrative capability' – the ability to integrate new and unfamiliar knowledge from different sources; 'boundary architecture' – corporate design that realizes new business models defining new corporate boundaries through the integration of different boundaries; and 'boundary innovation' – innovation processes transcending the boundaries between industries and corporations. Hybrid innovation is one of the modes of boundary innovation. Boundary architects' new perspective on the dynamic process and leadership to utilize boundary vision to develop a grand design to create new boundary architecture, and to develop a new business model, is a critical management element in the current age of convergence.

How should corporations use this 'dynamic view of strategy' to bring about innovation in the rapidly changing market environments of the convergence era? As business people, managers and so forth (practitioners) face up to real issues in the daily running of businesses, they are asking:

How can we acquire new knowledge, base a strategy on it, and execute that strategy?

What do we managers have to do to share and integrate knowledge within our own company and across the boundaries with other companies?

What type of leadership do we need to practice to find and pursue new businesses?

How much should we commit to high-risk business?

... and so on.

These are the sorts of issues facing managers and business people who have to bring about new innovation by merging unfamiliar knowledge through strategic thinking and action that focuses on diverse boundaries. In the high-tech business fields, as illustrated by the case studies mentioned in Chapter 1, innovations are more and more often brought about through the high-class core technologies dispersed around the world. This means that management that can integrate from a multitude of perspectives the excellent knowledge dispersed inside and outside the company and in customers through an open system, is becoming more and more necessary in the age of convergence and the wealth of valuable knowledge that it brings. In other words, at the same time as developing and accumulating core competitive competencies within a company, critical in the knowledge economy is the concept of hybrid innovation – the concept of generating new products, services, and business models through knowledge integration and adoption of core competencies from outside the company (see Figure 1.12 in Chapter 1).

What kind of management does a corporation need to gain a competitive edge through hybrid innovation? One answer is a message for corporate leaders saying: 'Let's create IBCs inside and outside the company by making the best use of boundary vision.'

As already mentioned, there is a strong tendency for knowledge and creativity, in other words innovation, to occur at the boundaries between different specialist fields. Companies are segmented into specialist departments, business units and so forth; and further, there are a great many divides between corporations, industries, and business sectors. There are also innumerable visible and invisible and macroscopic and microscopic boundaries existing between these partitions. For new knowledge creation and innovation in convergence business fields, stiff competition and changing circumstances, many companies have to transcend different industries and corporations at the global level. This is why corporations need to execute strategies to integrate the diverse knowledge across the multitude of boundaries between various sections of the company, between the company and other companies, and between the company and customers.

Certainly, knowledge is the primary source of a company's competitiveness. As well as the sectionalized organizational boundaries between practitioners in companies, there are also knowledge boundaries at the micro level due to the different values, specializations and backgrounds that practitioners have (see Figure 2.1). This means that the unique mental models and path-dependent knowledge that practitioners use for innovation can also be an obstruction to it (Kogut and Zander 1992, Nonaka and Takeuchi 1995, Leonard-Barton 1995, Brown and Duguid 2001, Spender 1990, Carlile 2002).

Many practitioners are aware of these 'invisible walls' between and within corporations, their specialist departments and customers. Furthermore, there are much greater stresses and complexities in dealing with external partners and customers in the context of new business, than in internal company relations. So, how should knowledge and organizational boundaries be overcome, and how should diverse knowledge from different practitioners be managed to bring about new knowledge?

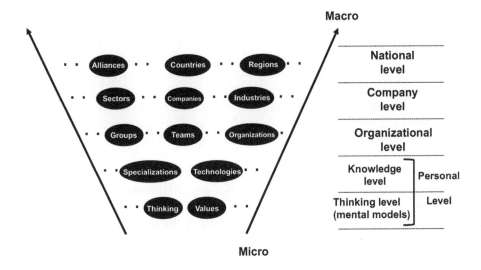

Figure 2.1   Existing various boundaries

The author's field work up to the present identifies 'boundary vision' – networking concepts and behavior patterns that bridge between diverse boundaries inside and outside corporations, which business people use to share knowledge and create new knowledge. Boundary vision is an awareness of these diverse boundaries, and a view that new business and corporate strategies can be designed through convergence along these boundaries. More specifically, boundary vision is a view and a way of thinking that should be acquired at all levels of management not only for optimizing vertical and horizontal boundaries around corporations to adjust to circumstantial (market) changes, but is also a conceptual system for adapting company boundaries to create new environments (markets) and bring about a hybrid innovation.

The first characteristic of boundary vision is that it acts as a trigger for dynamic optimization of a company's main business value chains by changing the vertical boundaries both in and out of the company. The second characteristic of boundary vision is that it searches not only a company's core business domain but also different business domains to spur new business,[1] dramatically changes the company's horizontal boundaries and finds relationships between completely different types of knowledge and the company's knowledge. Boundary vision is therefore an enabler that creates new knowledge through the merging and integration of different types of knowledge. Examples of this can be seen with Apple's expansion through strategy transformation of its PC business to its music distribution and mobile phone businesses, and in Japan, with 7-Eleven and NTT DOCOMO's move into financial service businesses. These are big changes to horizontal boundaries through these companies' boundary visions.

As described in Figure 1.12 in Chapter 1, traditionally, innovation in a mature industry was carried out through research in closed and independent systems within a company's hierarchy, and the company had complete control and retained most of

---

1   Boundary vision embraces the concept of peripheral vision. Refer to Day and Schoemaker (2005) for more information about peripheral vision.

the intellectual property rights. The governance mechanism for this type of closed innovation gave rise to the company's unique core competencies and was the source of its competitiveness. However, increased business efficiencies for entire companies began to appear through changing the vertical boundaries that define value chains with outsourcing to access resources (knowledge) that companies did not have.[2] During soft times, it was advantageous to create vertically integrated value chains within a company and with affiliate companies through close technological resources interdependencies and coordination between business units within a company.[3] The conventional automobile industry is a good example of this.

On the other hand, when markets are fluctuating rapidly, and in the technological environment that comes with convergence, the organizational capability for dynamic processes that can assemble resources flexibly in response to change by taking positive steps to find knowledge outside the company while at the same time strengthening and maintaining the company's core competencies through selection and consolidation, has become increasingly important.[4] This is the 'hybrid innovation' process that creates new products, services, and business models by improving and developing the company's own core competencies, dynamically adopting other companies' core competencies and merging company-wide and inter-company knowledge.

Corporations need this dynamic process to integrate widely dispersed knowledge and if necessary, restructure in response to changing circumstances. This means companies must always be ready to redraw the vertical and horizontal boundaries from which their business models are formed to adapt to shifting business environments or to create convergence – new and intentional business transformations (in this case 'horizontal boundaries' refers to a company's main business alliances, or drivers defining strategic domains of business related to their main business and new business).

In realizing new business models, it is important to dynamically integrate internal knowledge through internal integration networks that link the company's internal

---

2   For more about transaction cost theory and corporate boundaries, refer to Teece (1982).

3   Although path dependent close integration within a company is a strength, if a big problem happens in tight interdependencies in changing circumstances it can create a weakness (e.g. Siggelkow 2001; Hargadon and Sutton 1997; Henderson and Clark, 1990). Further, there is a danger that the strengths of propriety technologies or value chains can turn into weaknesses due to market fluctuations or the emergence of disruptive technologies (e.g. Levitt and March 1988; Martines and Kambil 1999; Leonard-Barton 1992, 1995).

4   Dynamic capability (Teece et al. 1997) refers to attempts to build dynamic theories based on existing resource bases theory, and dynamically integrate and restructure competencies within and outside companies to adapt to changing circumstances. 'Capability' refers to the business processes of merging and restructuring resources within and external to corporations to maintain a competitive edge. 'Dynamic capability' means the process of improving existing routine capabilities for adjusting and exploiting existing corporate resources in response to changing circumstances (e.g. Zollo and Winter 2002; Winter 2003). Improving existing routines and operations contributes to incremental innovation of existing business. In periods of low business uncertainty and relative stability, or in soft market conditions, companies apply dynamic capability to decide upon strategies and execute them in a planned analytical way. So-called 'learning before doing' Pisano (1994) – establishing and executing detailed strategic plans – is an important element of this dynamic capability in market structures where the various players can be easily identified in value chains with clear corporate boundaries.

More recently, the idea of dynamic capability was modified and reinterpreted by many researchers, notably Eisenhardt and Martine (2000), who sorted out the tautological problems relating to the interpretation of capability, and clearly illustrated the relationship of dynamic capability to competitiveness. They described dynamic capability as 'the corporate strategic and organizational processes and routines of using resources (integrating, relocating, acquiring or liquidating) in and out of the company to adapt to, or create changes in markets', and inductively derived the concept of corporate dynamic capability as necessary in both soft and fast-paced market conditions. Especially in highly uncertain fast-paced market conditions where industrial corporate boundaries are blurred, rather than adhere to the 'learn before doing' rule, the simpler 'learn by doing' rule is of greater importance (Eisenhardt and Sull 2001).

boundaries (people, organizations, different specialist technologies etc.) and external knowledge through external integration networks that link the company's external boundaries (between corporations, between the company and its customers, across different industries etc.). New knowledge is created by transcending this array of boundaries with the knowledge integration process working through internal and external integration networks. In this book, companies that achieve hybrid innovation through this kind of process are called 'knowledge integration firms' (see Figure 2.2).[5]

Not only focusing on growth in their main business areas, knowledge integration firms use 'boundary vision' to create new business opportunities through clever combinations of diverse knowledge acquired with prudence and ambition from strategic alliances, strategic outsourcing, joint development and venture, M&A etc., whether it comes from within the company, from groups of companies, from the same or different business fields, or from customers.

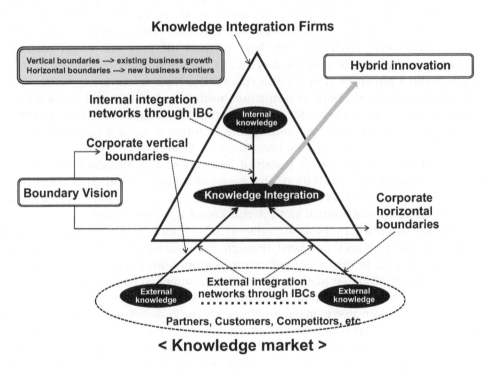

Figure 2.2   Knowledge integration firms

Source: based on Kodama (2009b)

---

5   For the most recent discussion about knowledge integration firms refer to Kodama (2009a, b).

Examples of this can be found in the digital home appliance field (Slim TVs, DVD recorders, digital cameras etc.) with leading Asian companies (such as Panasonic, Sharp, Canon, Sony and Toshiba in Japan, and Samsung and LG Electronics in Korea) – these companies are constantly rethinking and restructuring their vertical boundaries (R&D, component and device development, manufacturing, marketing, distribution, services etc.) to create business models. Although Panasonic, Sharp, Canon, and Samsung black box their proprietary R&D, component, device development and production technologies through vertical integration, these companies also promote flexibility through outsourcing and overseas manufacturing with 'established production techniques' (technology that can be copied) and procurement of 'proven technology' from other companies. At the same time, these companies engage in restructuring of vertical boundaries through joint developments and service and marketing alliances formed through M&A and strategic alliances with other companies in the same business area.

Fabless companies concentrating their resources on R&D and product planning, such as Apple, Qualcomm and Nintendo, define their vertical boundaries clearly with 'selection and consolidation', to provide the end user with a final product created through collaborative strategies with best partners all over the world (designers, manufacturers, distributors, and retailers etc.). Communications carriers such as NTT DOCOMO and Chunghwa Telecom also concentrate their resources on R&D, product planning, and communications infrastructure businesses, to create and develop mobile telephone business value chains through collaborative strategies with their global best partners (mobile phone and communications equipment makers, software vendors, semiconductor makers, content providers, corporate businesses etc.).

Hybrid innovation consists of sustained innovations that transform core business and radical breakthrough innovations that create new business, although the processes that realize these two types of innovation require the formation of internal and external integration networks (for internal and external knowledge integration).

To realize sustained innovation, value chain optimization is required to adapt to changing circumstances (markets) through the creation of internal and external integration networks. In the case of radical innovation, however, new value chains need to be created to establish new markets (business environments) for the innovation. This is why the boundaries where different knowledge intersects must be identified, and external integration networks created to merge and integrate the knowledge. The vibrant structure of internal and external integration networks based on boundary vision dynamically transforms corporate vertical and horizontal boundaries (see Figure 2.2). And IBCs are the foundations for these network structures.[6] IBCs, dynamic networks linking practitioners, and networks between different IBCs (called boundary networks hereafter) promote hybrid innovation by connecting the multi-tiered knowledge spread across these networks, and raise innovation potential within industries and across different industries.

---

6   Here, from the micro perspective, 'network' refers to human networks of people or knowledge, or from the macro perspective refers to networks between groups, organizations and companies. These can be networks spanning the various layers of management inside and outside companies and including customers, and between different organizations. There has been much research to date about the relationship between innovation and networks spanning corporations (e.g. Powell and Brantley 1992; Powell, Koput and Smith-Doerr 1996; Rosenkopf and Tushman 1998); however, most of the analysis here focuses on the macro level within corporations or between corporations. By contrast, this book considers network dynamism from the micro perspective focusing on practitioners in corporations.

2.2 Advancing Corporate Innovation through Boundary Vision

As previously stated, boundary vision is a conceptual framework that enables optimized design of corporate vertical and horizontal boundaries to bring about hybrid innovation. To get the most out of boundary vision, there are seven important capabilities (discussed later) that must be nurtured. Boundary vision is not just specific short-term strategies to achieve corporate objectives, but also encompasses its practitioners being able to draw up long-term grand designs. Moreover, boundary vision is a structural capability conjoined with the creativity to decide what type of IBCs need to be formed to realize strategies.

By rethinking existing vertical and horizontal boundaries, boundary vision redefines and reinvigorates corporate boundaries (the design of corporate boundaries, called 'boundary architecture' hereafter) for strategy transformation. 'Strategy transformation' means changing value chains by redefining horizontal and vertical boundaries to bring about new products, services, and business models (in Figure 2.3 this is represented by expanding horizontal boundaries (Past Present) and expanding vertical and horizontal boundaries (Present Future).

As companies work towards realizing the goals of strategy transformation, they use IBC external integration networks to absorb and integrate knowledge arising from synergies among partners, customers, and competitors in the knowledge market with their own knowledge. Corporations use the dynamic structure of IBC internal and external knowledge integration networks to integrate knowledge inside and outside a company and enable the realization of product, service, and business model targets.

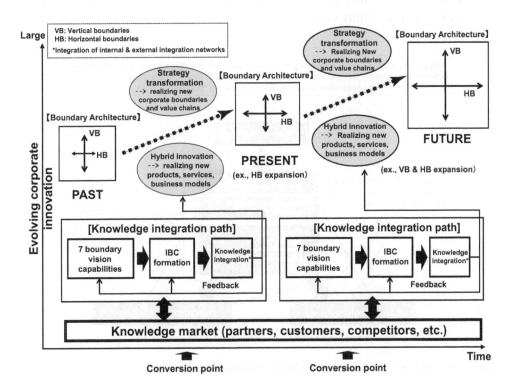

Figure 2.3   Evolving corporate innovation

Usually, the path illustrated in Figure 2.3 (boundary vision IBC formation knowledge integration – referred to as a 'knowledge integration path' hereafter) is not just unidirectional and linear, but is actually a trial and error feedback process for hypothetical testing to achieve hybrid innovation for these new target products, services and business models. In past, present and future time axes, corporations always accomplish strategy transformation for new products, services, and business models by constantly redefining their boundary architecture through on-going knowledge integration paths (see Figure 2.3).

2.3 The Seven Boundary Vision Capabilities

There are seven capabilities required for business leaders and managers to increase the quality of their boundary vision to promote hybrid innovation. They are: i) external knowledge integrative capability; ii) strategic integrative capability; iii) organizational integrative capability; iv) leadership integrative capability; v) systems thinking; vi) architecture thinking; and vii) platform thinking. Capabilities i) to iv) are managerial elements related to a company's 'corporate capability', whereas capabilities v) to vii) are 'business design capabilities' that enable the establishment of specific business strategies. 'Corporate capability' means the strategic and organizational capabilities needed for sustained hybrid innovation. 'Business design capabilities' refers to imaginative design and conceptual capabilities needed to develop plans for new products, services, and business models, and the boundary architecture (corporate boundaries) design abilities needed to bring about hybrid innovation (see Figure 2.4). The following sections describe each of these seven capabilities individually.

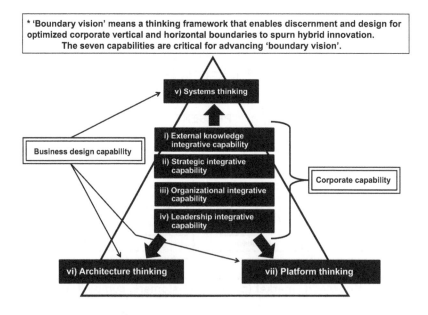

Figure 2.4   The seven boundary vision capabilities

2.3.1 EXTERNAL KNOWLEDGE INTEGRATIVE CAPABILITY

As one of the 'corporate capabilities', 'external knowledge integrative capability' is the ability to recognize unfamiliar knowledge with seemingly little relevance (or no relevance at all) and then find a relationship to one's own knowledge, and merge and integrate it with one's own knowledge. Much of the existing research in this area to date asserts that the interaction and merging of different types of knowledge can be a source of new innovation (Kodama 2007a). Therefore, the first important step for managers and leaders depends on whether they can grasp external knowledge integrative capability and practice it to identify relationships of unfamiliar knowledge to existing knowledge, and then find new meaning.

In cases where experience and knowledge are lacking (e.g. when young people enter a company), thinking frameworks (mental models) limit practitioners to routine or specific tasks in the workplace. Later on, however, as people (staff) gain more knowledge and experience, and learn on-the-job in different departments and specialist fields, they begin to recognize and understand different thinking frameworks and different knowledge relationships. The author calls these concepts 'shared thought worlds' and 'harmonized knowledge' (Kodama 2007c). Conversely, the more practitioners with specialized knowledge (e.g. research and engineering specialists) refine and deepen their fields of expertise, the greater the risk that they may become unable to break away from thinking frameworks based on their particular knowledge.

On the other hand, innovative and modest 'reflective practitioners'[7] have a strong tendency to grasp things from a perspective that transcends specializations, work abilities, organizations, corporations and industries. These people understand different mental models and thinking frameworks, and do not shirk away from absorbing and learning from unfamiliar knowledge. These 'innovative practitioners' have a fundamental 'human capability' of creating new knowledge themselves. Innovative practitioners create multi-tiered IBCs – organizational platforms necessary for generating value through the creation, utilization and sharing of knowledge. So, how do innovative practitioners create IBCs to form new business concepts?

As Bernard Simon[8] once pointed out, there are limitations to human knowledge capabilities. This is why in the world of management, organizations are segmented into layers, and work abilities partitioned. Obviously, corporate activities consist of a number of business processes (basic research, applied research, marketing, product development, manufacture, sales, distribution, after service etc.) and there are a diverse range of business contexts. No human being is fundamentally capable of performing all tasks from new product or service R&D to sales and support (and even if such people did exist, they would be very few in number).

---

7   Innovative and modest reflective practitioners are referred to in this book as 'innovative practitioners.'

8   Simon describes the rationality or knowledge limits of limited human cognitive and information processing capabilities as 'bounded rationality'. In other words, there is a limit to how much information the human being can process, therefore a human being cannot be completely rational. So, in asking the question of why human beings form organizations, Simon argues that it is possible to make rational and objective judgments within the context of a limited domain, and that the organization is a social instrument used to reduce the complexities of the world to a domain that can be grasped by limited human understanding. In this way, the formation of organizations with layered structures allows complicated decision-making to be dispersed throughout the number of subsystems (so-called modularization). He asserts that this enables high-level decision-making that would be impossible for individual people to achieve. For details refer to Simon (1996, 1997).

Boundary networks of IBCs or multi-tiered IBCs are indispensable for the conceptualization and actualization of excellence in new products, services and business models because these networks transcend organizational boundaries, and a mechanism in which the innovative practitioners in core marketing, R&D and manufacturing departments in new product development create and share their dynamic contexts is needed. These enable innovative practitioners to create and actualize new knowledge (business concepts for new products and services etc.).

Individual innovative practitioners in different departments also have their own unique worldviews and values. At the root of individual people's existence are concepts and modes of behavior that act as fixed paradigms based on past experiences (in different skills and technologies in individual departments such as marketing, R&D or manufacturing). For example, innovative practitioners in marketing never cease to recognize the need to plan products that will provide customers with new value, and find out what kind of product planning will meet latent customer needs – and they do this by dialectical synthesis through the synergies emerging from their own subjective views (about grasping latent demand and assimilating customers) and objective views (about competing products and customer data analysis). However, this does not mean that they have no perspectives regarding technology. They are always paying attention to technological trends inside and outside their own company, always asking whether an uncertain technology can provide customers with certain functions and services, and never lose sight of the effort required to verify concepts for potential usage systems of which customers themselves may or may not be aware.

On the other hand, to develop technology that will satisfy customers, and develop core technology that cannot be imitated by competitors, innovative practitioners involved in research and development or manufacturing never cease to identify new facts using dialectical synthesis of the synergies emerging from their subjective views (ideas about the types of things they would like to develop) and objective views (selection and consolidation based on analysis of technological trends and technological benchmarks from other companies). Similarly, this does not mean that engineers have no viewpoints regarding markets. It's also conceivable that engineers may make feasible proposals to customers that are 'seed-oriented' (as opposed to 'needs-oriented') based on their own independently developed ideas.

By forming multi-tiered IBCs within a company, innovative practitioners create higher order contexts from the new energy released in the collision of paradigms created from various subjective opinions and contexts surrounding markets and technologies. Innovative practitioners understand the diversity of different worldviews and values, and bring about mutual recognition and discipline through creative and dialectical dialogues between different organizations. And they ask how new knowledge is created as individual members share and understand each other's thoughts and feelings, using both self-assertion and humility. It works because it enables individuals to develop a higher dimension of imagination and thought. 'External knowledge integrative capability' is the ability to create and realize new business concepts through abductive reasoning and synthesis of mutually unfamiliar knowledge (see Figure 2.5). The external knowledge integrative capability of innovative practitioners is the driving force behind hybrid innovation.

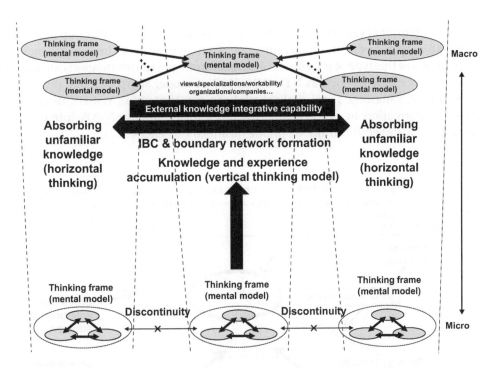

Figure 2.5   External knowledge integrative capability

2.3.2 STRATEGIC INTEGRATIVE CAPABILITY

As another element of 'corporate capability', 'strategic integrative capability' means the ability to create and execute strategies. Academic research has shown that there are different categories of corporate strategy formation processes – intended strategies and emergent strategies (Mintzberg 1978, Mintzberg and Walters 1985). Intended strategies are usually based on strategic planning and decision-making by top management and leadership for sustaining innovation through ongoing improvements to existing business, and are vertical concepts based on existing technological experience and know-how (see Figure 2.6). Upgraded versions of existing products and services through improvements are an example of this.

In contrast, emergent strategies are related to the external knowledge integrative capability mentioned earlier, and are new strategies based on different and new knowledge rather than existing experience and knowledge. Strategies created with horizontal thinking based on unfamiliar knowledge are referred to as either 'intentional emergent strategies', or 'incidental emergent strategies' (see Figure 2.6). Intentional emergent strategies are not the same as the intentional strategies decided upon by top management, but are born in the workplace or from propositions mainly originating in middle management. Intentional emergent strategies are created through processes in which the proposer intentionally finds a relationship between unfamiliar knowledge and existing knowledge (or experience), identifies meaning through forecast, foresight or forethought, and uses brainstorming or imagination to repeat hypothetical testing and create and execute a new strategy.

Mostly, intentional emergent strategies are proposed from the bottom-up and accord with overall corporate direction and mission, rarely appearing to be purely emergent. Some examples of this type of intentional emergent strategies transformation can be found in product developments such as NTT DOCOMO's i-mode, Sharp's mobile phone with built-in camera, Panasonic's anti-shake digital camera, Nintendo's Wii/DS, or corporate strategy transformation in cases of Intel (memory logic), Microsoft (OS Internet), and Apple (PC music distribution/mobile phone business) (see Figure 2.7).

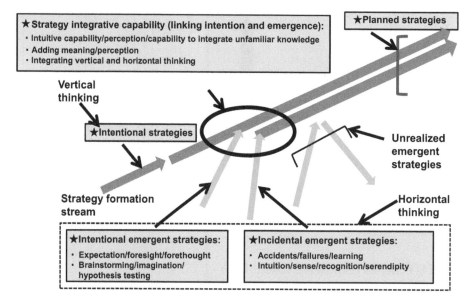

Figure 2.6   Strategic integrative capability

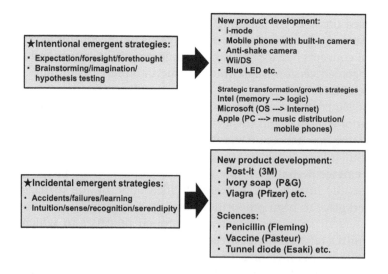

Figure 2.7   Intentional and incidental emergent strategies

Conversely, purely emergent strategies – strategies born of the proposer's sudden imaginative insight, are rare in business, but are observed in the processes of discovery and invention in science and new product development. These are called 'incidental emergent strategies' and give birth to new products and discoveries resulting from scientists' or researchers' intuition, detections, awareness or serendipity based on accidents, failures or continuous study processes. Examples of this type of strategy can be found in new product developments such as 3M's post-it, P&G's Ivory soap, Pfizer's Viagra, or discoveries and inventions such as penicillin (Alexander Fleming), vaccine (Louis Pasteur), and the tunnel diode (Reona Esaki).

Here, the important point is strategic integrative capability to link the intentionality of corporate intentional strategies and the emergence of emergent strategies (intentional emergent strategies and incidental emergent strategies). Specifically, this means incorporating emergent strategies into a company's intentional strategies to create an overall strategy (see Figure 2.6). Strategic integrative capability means merging and integrating vertically conceived intentional strategies based on existing knowledge and experience with horizontally conceived emergent strategies based on unfamiliar knowledge. Integrating vertical concepts with horizontal concepts also ties in with the formulation of the 'external knowledge integration capability' mentioned earlier. Moreover, strategic integrative capability in turn gives rise to deliberate strategies designed to deliver planned results and allow for the appropriate distribution of company resources. In this way, strategic integrative capability fosters the ability to recognize and find meaning needed for merging and integrating existing knowledge with unfamiliar knowledge for hybrid innovation.

Strategic integrative capability is a unified strategy-making capability that aims to make simultaneous use of the conflict between intentionality and emergence. Emergent strategies are based upon the sharing of individuals' introspective thoughts and tacit knowledge and are formed by concept creation through abductive reasoning. Innovative practitioners share a variety of dynamic contexts along boundary networks and through multilayered IBCs to create new knowledge in a flexible and impromptu manner. Once tangible concepts are crystallized into products and services as explicit knowledge, intentional strategies are executed through the whole company's decision-making processes. Essentially, the process of forming strategies by combining emergence with intentionality lies in the creativity and imagination that arises with dialectical dialogue, creative abrasion and productive friction between participants in boundary networks and multilayered IBCs, repeated self-correcting of hypotheses, and finally engaging these hypotheses in a planned and surefooted manner.

The simultaneous use of these two different strategy making processes is an important element of the boundary vision capabilities. In reality, corporations are always advancing individual products and services while conceiving multiple product and service lineups. In other words, as well as upgrading and improving the quality of products and business functions by adding new functionality and so forth, radical innovation (or break-through innovation) of technology or the creation of new markets also exists.

Innovative practitioners in different business and product departments (marketing, development, manufacturing, sales, support etc.) simultaneously develop emergent strategies for new business in tandem with intentional strategies for existing business, across past, present, and future timescales. Strategic integrative capability provides the dynamic strategic formation perspective needed to recognize the coexistence of, and combine, emergent and intentional strategies.

Furthermore, these strategy transforming processes are found in the various spaces and times in organizations and strategies related to individual products and services. As an example, this could mean that at some point in time, top or middle management aims for growth in the present (today) with an intentional strategy for product 'A', and at the same time, uses emergent strategies to search for future (tomorrow) opportunities for innovation for product 'B'.

The case of Panasonic, a company involved in system LSI semiconductor technologies that form the core of their DVD, digital camera, and slim TV products, illustrates strategic integrative capability, in that the company is using intentional strategies to expand their existing product base, while working with emergent strategies to develop new 3D and next-generation TV products. Even from the perspective of organizational systems in the company, the two different strategic forms are managed through simultaneous linkages of the emergent strategies focusing on research, product planning, and development, with the intentional strategies employed in the manufacturing, sales and marketing divisions. Apple and Nintendo also involve themselves in both intentional strategies for existing product base expansion and emergent strategies for new product development.

However, once the company breaks away from the emergent strategy mode to the intentional, and a successful business model is established, top management is prone to lose recollection, and suffer the delusion that they have executed the successful strategy intentionally. As a result, subsequent new product and service development through emergent strategies can become stifled (Christensen and Raynor 2003, Kodama 2007a).

Innovative practitioners on the other hand, always reflect upon these beginnings, even when an intentional strategy brings success. They continue to monitor disruptive technologies and latent needs while re-devising synergies with markets (with customers and so forth). Innovative practitioners engage in emergent strategies to create new concepts by questioning themselves as they aim towards creating absolute product and service value. The case of Apple, with its strategy transformation from PC to iPhone mobile phone and iPad PDA businesses and its music distribution business with iTunes and iPod, is also an example of great success through reinforcement while in the new emergent strategy mode.

Where are the sources needed to engage this kind of strategic integrative capability? They are in IBCs fundamental to the knowledge integration process within and between companies, and the boundary networks that exist across multiple IBCs for consolidating separated elements of human capability. Especially, an important role in all of this comes from 'leadership integrative capability' of leader teams (LT) formed among groups of innovative practitioners in all levels of corporate management, as described in Section 2.3.4.

While innovative practitioners pursue the company vision and their own goals, they self-innovate through intrinsic motivation (a thought or belief about innovation through the individual's daily job routine). This brings about the formation of IBCs and boundary networks in organizations and companies. IBCs and boundary networks foster the improvisation and entrepreneurship needed for the concept creation and abductive reasoning indispensable for emergent strategies, while further embedding strategic discipline as organizational routines and corporate culture to enact and orchestrate visions to ensure competitiveness and profitability for intentional strategies. IBC and boundary network formation sustain robust corporate and strategy character to bring about hybrid innovation even in dynamically changing circumstances.

2.3.3 ORGANIZATIONAL INTEGRATIVE CAPABILITY

The third capability, 'organizational integrative capability', is also one of the 'corporate capabilities'. For the aforementioned external knowledge integrative and strategic integrative capabilities to function, appropriate organizational design is also necessary (see Figure 2.8). As described in Chapter 1, innovation systems in traditional large corporations in the era of mass production usually feature an R&D department in a company-internal research facility, illustrated by Pattern 1. These kinds of R&D departments were usually separate from the rest of the organization (business organizations) and had loose relations with organizations in the operational divisions. R&D achievements were then transferred to those organizations and subsequently converted into products and commercialized. However, there existed the so-called 'Death Valley'[9] between R&D departments and business organizations. This kind of partitioned R&D organizational structure (Pattern A) functioned well enough in times of soft competition and market changes, but in the rapidly changing circumstances and convergence in recent times, the Pattern A organizational system lacks the capability to produce new business innovation in a timely manner.

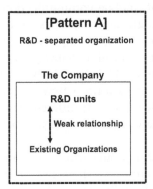

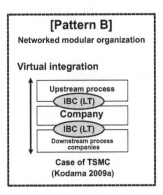

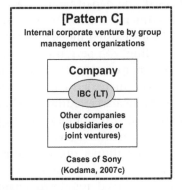

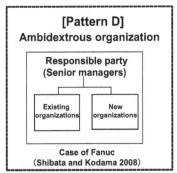

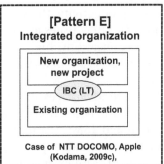

Figure 2.8   Forming innovative organizations with organizational integrative capability

---

9   For details about 'Death Valley' refer to Kodama (2010), Chapter 3.

Countering this, Qualcomm and TSCM formed networked modular organizations (Pattern B) among stakeholders to further business growth in their fabless and foundry semiconductor businesses (Kodama 2009a), as explained in detail in Chapter 4. Sony formed a subsidiary company (Sony Computer Entertainment: SCE) through a joint venture to get its game business (PlayStation) up and running (Pattern C), where the parent company Sony, invested capital in SCE and succeeded with its PlayStation product.

Chapter 3 illustrates new organizations formed as project bases within companies to start up new businesses through collaborative strategies between the new and existing organizations (Pattern E), as undertaken by Apple with its iPod music player development, and NTT DOCOMO's i-mode business.

The well-known Japanese communications equipment company, Fujitsu, saw growth of a company-internal venture organization, by forming a new independent business within the company (NC: Numerical Computing – later became Fanuc) as an 'ambidextrous organization' (Pattern D).[10] Even after Fanuc broke away from Fujitsu, they still made efforts for product technological transformation through the formation of ambidextrous organizations formed between new and existing organizations to deal with new product development using new technology (Shibata and Kodama 2008).

Also, even before NTT DOCOMO was established, the organization existed as a division (mobile communications business division) of NTT's high-performance information and communications department. This department was divided into three business divisions (leased line department, image communications department, mobile communications department), which were overseen and managed by a single director. These three divisions existed independently of each other, and the director had an important role in dealing with personnel issues, decision-making and resource allocation. Subsequently, the mobile communications department branched off to become NTT DOCOMO because of government led communications initiatives, and went on to form a new mobile telephone market. Although the histories of Fanuc and NTT DOCOMO are different, they both existed as ambidextrous organizations within the corporate organizational structure before their separation.

Conventional organizations focus on cost and short-term profits while they aim to innovate incrementally through the operation of their business. These businesses feature a fixed top-down chain of command, and run a disciplined operation that pursues improved productivity through efficient management. On the other hand, new organizations face new issues and challenges in the pursuit of new innovation and growth. In these organizations, high-tech corporations in Japan, Taiwan and America, middle management plays an important role as independent and dispersed leadership to realize innovation.[11]

Although there are advantages and disadvantages to these organizational systems, as shown in Figure 2.8, the best patterns for speedy commercialization can be seen in the cases of Qualcomm and TSMC (Pattern B), Sony (Pattern C), and Fanuc (Pattern D). In these organizations appropriate support and resources (personnel, capital etc.) are assured from top management. Moreover, there is hardly any mutual interference or friction

---

10   Suggested by Professor Tomoatsu Shibata (Kagawa University).

11   In Japanese corporations, the role of middle management is considered to be of central importance (e.g. Nonaka and Takeuchi 1995). In big Japanese corporations, middle management often takes on the role of project leaders and project managers to promote formulation and implementation of strategies for pioneering new businesses, new product development ideas, and specific achievements (Kodama 2007a).

in the loose relationships between new organizations of patterns C and D and existing organizations or parent companies.

Conversely, in the integrated organization case of NTT DOCOMO (Pattern E) successful innovation is born through friction and interference between people and organizations that have different cultures within the same corporation. Similar to NTT DOCOMO, Apple is also an integrated organization (Pattern E), but formed collaborative strategies to share technology and know-how between the existing organization and its new iPod product development project, which served to fortify and develop Apple's existing entrepreneurial spirit in all levels of the company.

However, in the cases of Sony, Fanuc, Apple, and NTT DOCOMO, the defining difference was that the new businesses formed by Sony, Fujitsu, and Apple for gaming devices, industrial machines, and music distribution were completely different from their main businesses. Therefore top management could allow for organizational flexibility (Noria and Gulati 1996, Bourgeois 1981) to effect strategies and distribute resources. In NTT DOCOMO's case, although there was a paradigm shift in its mobile phone business, the company had to involve many stakeholders from within the company because of its strong relationship with the existing business.

Further, the ambidextrous organization (O'Reilly and Tushman 2004) similar to the Fanuc case has also proved successful for new business in American corporations.[12] American corporations practice 'ambidextrous leadership' for the different business objectives of new and existing organizations, and achieve simultaneous short-term and long-term innovation through common vision and shared values. On the other hand, there are many cases among large Japanese corporations like Sony's, where parent companies operate venture subsidiaries. In the past, Japanese corporations have succeeded with synergistic strategies through multilateralization complementing parent companies through the establishment of subsidiaries (creating new business split from the parent company) (e.g. Rose and Ito 2005 and Kodama 2007b).

American corporations are very good at business models using modular organizations, network organizations, and networked modular organizations such as Qualcomm and TSMC; networked modular organizations using ICT virtual integration such as Dell are examples of this (Kodama 2009a).

Although integrated organization within a company to create new business creates a lot of friction, such as in the NTT DOCOMO case, there are advantages to the creation of a new identity through the merging of corporate culture. The biggest issue facing strategic innovation is corporate cultural reform (Markides 1998). To support new strategic innovation in big corporations, strategic innovators create different organizations separate from the main organization.

This can be done by creating a new and separate organization from the main organization (such as the Fanuc case), or by creating a separate company as a subsidiary (such as the Sony case). This organizational pattern is highly effective for new strategic innovation, but it is not without problems. There are issues relating to the long-term merging and harmonization of the new organizational culture with the old. The corporate cultures of Sony and SCE are inevitably different, and Sony faces big issues with how to

---

12   By contrast, other research has indicated that general managers are a source of friction so that interchange between the organizations in the form of a mutual general manager should be limited while interaction at a practical level should be increased (Govindarajan and Trimble 2005).

create strategic synergy among multiple business divisions, or as a corporate conglomerate as a whole. In designing the best organizations for the strategic transformation that comes with changing business and technological circumstances, a critical issue to consider is cohesiveness of technologies and strategies, even though this varies in corporate culture and competitive environments.

Considering common organizational patterns in these innovation cases, there is a need for integrative capability to link the various organizations within the corporation (existing, new, projects etc.) and to link between corporations (external partners and customers). These links between organizations and corporations can be either weak or strong, and vary depending on the level of shared information and knowledge. However, for organizations or corporations to bring about new innovation, organizational integrative capability must be in place to connect organizations and corporations through close collaborative strategies between them, and with customers and external partners. The corner stone of organizational integrative capability is the IBC. Leader teams (LT) of innovative practitioner groups at all levels of management in the corporation formulate IBCs and practise leadership to bring about organizational integrative capability. IBCs in and between companies described in Figure 2.8 are an example of these leader teams.

IBCs are significant not only because they form a community of practice (Wenger 1998) or cohesive business networks to maintain commercial dealings between corporations in the long-term, but also because they form 'small-world structures'(SWS) as cohesive network shortcuts for corporate acquisition of diverse knowledge. These SWSs are also a type of IBC. Also, corporations that aspire to innovation form a number of different SWSs (IBCs) simultaneously, to act as bridges between context and knowledge between different SWSs (IBCs) and create new knowledge for innovation. SWS (IBC) networks (boundary networks) are observed in the process of technological convergence and creating new business models across different industries (Kodama 2007a, 2007c).

2.3.4 LEADERSHIP INTEGRATIVE CAPABILITY

Another of the 'corporate capabilities' is 'leadership integrative capability.' For corporations to create new innovations, it is important to carry out business activity through IBCs that are based on social visions and corporate values. Knowledge that functions as a business resource with competitive value is created through IBCs across multiple boundaries. In an IBC, knowledge and core competencies from inside and outside corporations, including customers and strategic partners, are merged and integrated to produce the corporate capabilities of external knowledge integrative capability, strategic integrative capability, and organizational integrative capability already mentioned.

All leaders in corporations who formulate IBCs to bring about these important corporate capabilities (top level and middle management) must find and share new values for innovation with the leadership of strategic partners within and outside the company, and with customers, as the company works towards achieving its social and corporate visions and missions. The process of sharing, feeling out, and resonating these newly created values with all participants in the IBC through constructive dialogue and discussion in the IBC, is an indispensable part of organizational activity. As such, the philosophy or idea of an 'interactive learning-based community' formed among participants in the IBC is also important (see Figure 2.9).

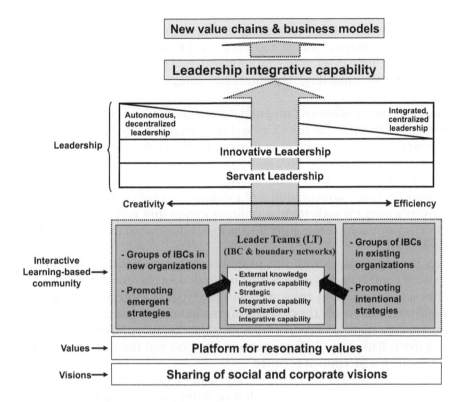

Figure 2.9   Leadership integrative capability

As community leaders resonate values throughout the IBC, they must take on the role of 'servant leadership' by listening to community members, and offering them continued support and motivation, as well as taking on the instructive, coaching and mentoring role of 'innovative leadership' to produce innovative and creative business concepts and processes.

This makes the community members voluntarily participate in decision-making in IBCs and deepen the connections within and between IBCs by creating mutual understanding and virtue. Innovative corporations do not have leadership that relies on old-fashioned fixed hierarchies; rather, new leadership models for successful innovation involve 'innovative leadership' and 'servant leadership' – a new leadership image that aims for growth of individual, group, and organizational communities (see Figure 2.9).

In organizations that promote the emergent strategies mentioned earlier, autonomous and decentralized leadership is needed for IBC community leaders to bring about creative business concepts. On the other hand, in organizations that promote intentional strategies, integrated and centralized leadership is needed for IBC community leaders to effectively improve business processes. Therefore, LTs in the upper levels of corporate management (top and middle management) need leadership integrative capability to strike a good balance between the autonomous, decentralized and the integrated, centralized leadership systems (see Figure 2.9).

LTs are formed from community leaders (the CEO, executives, division managers, department heads, project leaders etc.) at all levels of a corporation (top and middle management, as well as mixtures forming management teams, cross functional teams, task forces etc.) and serve to merge and integrate the knowledge on IBCs in and out of the company, and bring integrative capability (external knowledge integrative capability, strategic integrative capability, organizational integrative capability) to the whole company.

It takes integrative strategy (intentional strategy plus emergent strategy) based on discipline and imagination in the LT to realize 'integrative capability' (Kodama 2007a). In other words, this means integrating the seemingly paradoxical creative/emergent and intentional/planned/deliberate strategic methods.

Through positive discussion and dialogue among community leaders in the LT, they promote thorough understanding of problems and issues, and recognize the value of each other's roles through mutual communication and collaboration. This enables conflicts that arise among community leaders to be transformed into constructive conflict (Kodama 2007a).

Facing the key missions with this process, community leaders need to think about what they can contribute towards creating new value for their own company, or partner companies and customers, by thinking about the types of strategies and tactical actions they should take. Conversely the CEO, having the ultimate decision-making power in the LT, must also take steps to encourage dialogue and discussion inside LTs, to strengthen the interactive collaboration linkages between the CEO and the community leaders, and practice top-down leadership as required.

In this way, the CEO and community leaders can enable coherent leadership integrative capability that embraces both innovative leadership and servant leadership for business creativity and efficiency. Resonance and mutual understanding of values among community leaders in the LT including the CEO is promoted for success in the business of innovation (Kodama 2007a). The integrative synergy of leadership among community leaders forms IBCs and boundary networks, and enables the creation of surefooted value chains and business models for new business through the merging and integration of knowledge across the IBCs.

2.3.5 SYSTEMS THINKING

Due to the convergence of different businesses and technologies, the circumstances surrounding corporations and industries are constantly changing. 'Systems thinking' is an important business design capability for creating new products, services, and business models in the age of convergence. Systems thinking clarifies the structures emerging from the interactive patterns of various factors related to the complex variety of elements that appear in a changing world, and enables the practitioner to gain a complete picture of events and phenomena – in other words, by clarifying the mutual relationships between individual elements and the whole, systems thinking helpss to recognize these structures in the context of total function, and to formulate optimal solutions and measures.

Systems thinking means thinking about a whole body in a unified and inclusive way using the concept of systems, and understanding that in thinking about something that exhibits movement or behavior, there is a group of structural elements linked together to produce that function. This collection of elements acting interdependently as an ordered body is called a 'system.' Systems have borders; it is not possible to understand the functioning or action of the whole by looking at only a single internal structure or function. Systems thinking does not involve thinking about the individual structural elements to recognize a totality; rather, systems thinking means paying attention to the relationships between those elements.

Now, what really is a system? A system is an independent collection of organically linked parts, that has its own boundary; and that boundary separates it from the outside world. In actual fact, almost all of the products, services, and business models that surround us are systems. In the same way, organizations and corporations can be thought of as independent systems, because they consist of multiple business processes organically linked together. In short, our lives are full of systems, and thus it is helpful to view them as such.

One of the factors that characterize systems is relationships. There are relationships inside systems, and there are relationships between systems and the external world. These relationships, between its parts and with the external world have a big influence on the character of the system. For example, in product development and design, there are integral systems formed by complex close interdependent relationships between the parts, and modular systems formed by the interdependence of simple rules – both of which are very different in character. In the former case, changing one part could affect the whole system in an unexpected way, due to the chain of interdependencies. In the latter case, changing one part allows for control of the way the whole system is affected, because the interdependent relationships have rules. This can greatly affect the nature of the whole system, in addition to the nature of the part itself, depending on the relationships that comprise the system.

Systems are assembled from multiple elements according to certain rules to achieve certain objectives. For a system to achieve its objectives, it must have certain functions. For this functionality, several elements are consolidated according to certain rules. This defines the domain of the system. This domain is defined by a boundary, inside of which is called the system, and outside of which is called the environment. There is a relationship between the purpose of the system and its boundary. Larger systems can be divided into partial systems, each working to achieve their own objectives, while the collective, consisting of all the parts, operates effectively and achieve the objectives of the whole. Partial systems are also called subsystems (see Figure 2.10).

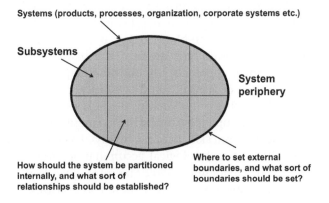

Figure 2.10 What about the 'system'?

Source: based on Shibata and Kodama (2000)

In systems engineering, there are two system design approaches – 'the top-down approach' and 'the bottom-up approach'. The top-down approach is a global way of thinking about things, taking a big picture view of the relevant matters first, clarifying the framework of the whole, and then considering specific details later. Fundamental to systems thinking is the idea that 'the whole consists of various partial elements, and the partial elements exist to form the whole.' In the system concept, it is important to analyze systems in terms of parts clustered together. When an object is thought of as a system, analysis can be carried out, purposes can be clarified, and the system can be improved or developed wholly or partially to optimize it to accomplish its objective. This top-down approach is a core concept in systems thinking.

Using the top-down approach to design a system can be thought of as firstly, defining the objective of the system, and once the boundaries of the system have been clarified, finding the best system functions and then selecting the appropriate elements or subsystems and combining them together. As explained in Chapter 1, in considering the new products, services, and business models that come with the convergence of diverse technologies and industries (developmental businesses such as PDAs, RFID solutions, the smart grid, solar battery businesses, vehicle computerization and development, semiconductors, and environmental vehicles) the top-down approach allows for discernment of different technologies (knowledge) and merging and integration of them as necessary. Here, it is important to begin by drawing up a grand design for a new business as one subsystem in the overarching social and economic system. In the top-down approach, it is important that system thinking ask how to allocate different types of knowledge throughout the whole system, how to define individual subsystems, and then how to achieve the micro designs for these subsystems (see Figure 2.11).

As a specific example, LSI designed for the core of digital products can be considered as designed using a top-down approach (see Figure 2.12). In top-down design, firstly, the specifications of the system are analyzed, and then functions assigned to various subsystems. Then, design solutions can be found through the detailed designing of the subsystems at the bottom. For example, logic synthesis software used to create gate level data from the register transfer level (RTL) description models is a top-down design support tool.[13] Generally, top-down design in system engineering is a design method that works through subsequent layers of detail. In the beginning the entire system is formulated, but at this stage individual details are not considered. The design for individual parts of the system is then refined later on. Finally, refinement continues until implementation. Top-down design is intrinsically linked with black boxing, because in the design stages where internal structures are not considered, they are treated as black boxes.

In contrast to the top-down approach, the bottom-up approach is characterized by the word 'local' – the antonym of 'global' – and obviously, the whole system cannot be understood with localized thinking only. Notably, the Japanese corporate manufacturing concept is said to be this bottom-up type. During the Japanese Edo period, labor-intensive techniques that relied heavily on skill became highly developed, and craftsmanship has since shaped the culture of technological accumulation from the Meiji era to the present. After World War II, Japanese corporations introduced Western manufacturing technologies, repeatedly improved and refined these technologies, and polished high-

---

13   Refer to Kodama (2009a), Chapter 4.

★**Grand design ⇒ Micro design**
What knowledge should be partitioned and how should subsystems be defined?

Top-down knowledge integration

Whole system

Diverse boundaries

Dispersed knowledge

Different fields

Diverse boundaries

Dispersed knowledge

Different fields

Subsystem ············· Subsystem ············· Subsystem

Figure 2.11 Systems thinking – top-down approach

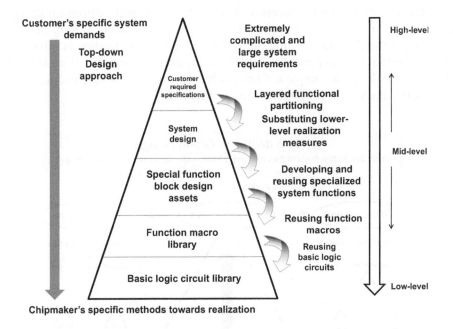

Customer's specific system demands

Top-down
Design
approach

Customer required specifications

System design

Special function block design assets

Function macro library

Basic logic circuit library

Chipmaker's specific methods towards realization

Extremely complicated and large system requirements

Layered functional partitioning
Substituting lower-level realization measures

Developing and reusing specialized system functions

Reusing function macros

Reusing basic logic circuits

High-level

Mid-level

Low-level

Figure 2.12 System LSI 'top-down design'
Source: based on Shiraishi (1999)

quality manufacturing techniques with a bottom-up approach through workplace initiatives arising from interactions between engineers.

Japanese bottom-up concepts such as the KJ method (Affinity Diagram) for problem solving advocated by cultural anthropologist Jiro Kawakita are well known in the QC activities and creative development that spread among Japanese corporations after World War II, and in present-day issues too, pursuing the causes of those problems and eliminating them is also bottom-up approach. Moreover, the KJ method is also a methodology for creative solutions through discussion and brainstorming.

The bottom-up approach is also a way of thinking about purpose when people are not sure what the purpose is, and a way for people involved to share a purpose with each other, clarify differences, and form agreements. Whereas the aforementioned top-down approach can be called a 'hard approach', the bottom-up approach can be called a 'soft approach'. In recent years, the 'Soft System Methodology' (Checkland 1981) systems thinking gaining attention in Europe has been praised as a powerful soft approach for creative problem solving.

Bottom-up design in system engineering begins with designing the details of individual parts that make up the system. Then, larger parts are created by assembling groups of small parts, and finally, the entire system is constructed (see Figure 2.13). In other words, the way the entire system is conceived to realize the macro grand design from component micro designs lies in the notion of the assembly of individual subsystems (knowledge) (see Figure 2.13).

In software development processes, top-down design and bottom-up design both have significant meaning. In top-down design, complete understanding of the entire system is important. Software coding cannot be commenced until there is sufficient detail designed in certain system parts. For this reason, testing of main functions isn't possible until most of the design is complete. Conversely, in bottom-up design, coding and testing can begin once the design for each module is finished.

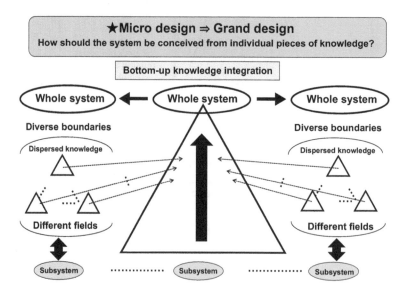

Figure 2.13 Systems thinking – bottom-up approach

However, in bottom-up design, if the relationships between the modules are not clarified, there is a risk posed from design alterations at a later time; it is difficult at the outset to perfectly predict what sorts of problems will occur between the modules. Bottom-up design does, however, offer the advantage of a higher likelihood of reusable code. Even in the system LSI design just mentioned, bottom-up design is still required. The bottom-up method is an approach that first focuses on the subsystems (components), and then after designing in detail, the subsystems are integrated to derive design solutions. Software development in LSI is an example of reusing code from the basic logic circuit library.

Design methods in western technologically advanced manufacturing countries begin with the top-down approach, in which objectives and roles within a development project are first clarified during the planning and proposal stage at the beginning of the product development cycle, the functions needed to achieve those are defined without omission, and clear design rules are laid out by assigning functions to modular units. Then, clear explicit knowledge such as manuals and documentation are used for thorough communication between those involved in the development. Concurrent engineering techniques are used for the various individual subsystem projects, and then finally integrated through modular design[14] methods. These top-down design approaches and methods for architecture conception and realization are especially encouraged in the United States.

On the other hand, the so-called 'integral' design popular among Japanese manufacturing methods leaves ambiguities and redundancies remaining at the planning and proposal stage without defining strict design rules, and the final product is produced with problems and issues arising during development resolved through coordination.[15] Instead of deciding upon top-down design architecture at the outset, there is a strong tendency for Japanese corporations to formulate entire architectures using bottom-up design involving trial and error through organizational coordination and adjustments.

A crucial aspect of 'top-down thinking' and 'bottom-up thinking' is that they complement each other, and are fundamental parts of system thinking that fosters the 'architecture thinking'[16] discussed in the next section. Without becoming transfixed on one thing, it is important to pay attention to the interdependencies and mutual relationships between all system elements, and understand the entire system and the subsystems that comprise it and their workings, as oscillations between grand design and micro design – i.e. macro micro, micro macro. This knowledge integration process

---

14   Depending on the method of manufacturing, in technologically advanced Western countries the connection of each function to the objective of the whole system is always considered – not losing sight of the main purpose in this way increases the possibility that the optimal product will be created to meet that objective.

15   With the increasing complexity and high performance of control functions in automotive computerization of recent years, there is a movement for international standards for certification of safety functions designed around integrated hardware and software. These design concepts will require higher levels of 'systems thinking'. The recent trouble with the Toyota Prius was caused by interference arising between the ABS and regenerative braking systems – the causes of this problem could be traced to a diverse range of technological fields such as hardware, software, and communications networks. Clearly against this backdrop, systems thinking with a top-down approach that spans different technological areas will be more and more important in future.

16   Generally, systems engineering involves a combination of top-down and bottom-up design methods. Overall understanding of a system is important regardless of the methods, therefore in theory top-down design is critical; although in many software projects, existing code is often reused. Reusing existing modules introduces the idea of bottom-up design. Depending on design methods, sometimes systems for partial function are created (design and coding), and then functions are added which meet the required specifications of those systems.

of top-down and bottom-up thinking is the starting point for the new concept creation (see Figure 2.14).

An example of oscillation between grand design and micro design can be found in the mobile phone module designed by Qualcomm in the United States. Qualcomm developed an ultra-compact communications module based on a chipset integrating 3G communications functions and other functions such as GPS. Qualcomm calls this a 'wearable mobile device (WMD)' (see Figure 2.15). Featuring a compact design and low power requirements, Qualcomm is aiming for installation of this product in a range of devices used for health care, medical, automotive, and industrial applications, as well as mobile phones. As the name suggests, Qualcomm expects this device to be installed in a number of wearable items as well. This is also highly likely to contribute to machine-to-machine (M-to-M) technologies where various devices are fitted with communications functions and can share data amongst themselves.

The idea behind this WMD architecture came about through the M-to-M concept that in the ubiquitous era, communications will be carried out not only between people, or between people and machines, but also between machines themselves. From the viewpoint of various economic and social needs, or ideas and concepts about application development, Qualcomm has adopted a total system architecture with the top-down approach based on the modular design concept merging and integrating different knowledge for the various subsystems required to form the whole intended system (systems and business models using WMD), and defining the interfaces between the required subsystems.

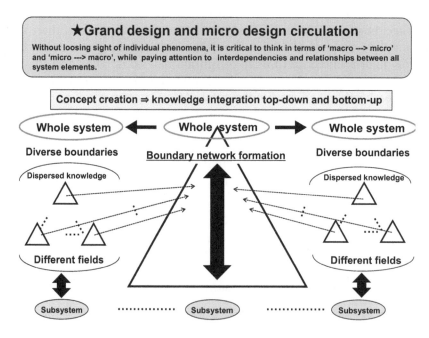

Figure 2.14 Systems thinking – top-down and bottom-up approach

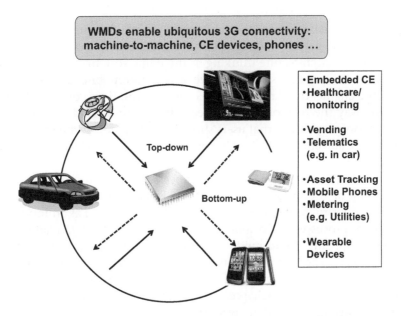

Figure 2.15 Top-down and bottom-up mobile phone module design

Qualcomm is simultaneously taking advantage of its semiconductor hardware and software resources developed over many years through the bottom-up approach and adjusting the interfaces between all the subsystems to integrate the architecture defined by using a top-down approach. In this way, it can be seen that the company is not placing all of the importance in the value of the actual software and hardware-based WMD product, but is focusing on the relationships between the product itself and entire systems (social needs, human behaviors, business processes, business models etc.) through the synergies of the top-down and bottom-up approaches. Qualcomm uses systems thinking to produce new value (achieving the ubiquitous society, e.g.) born in the synergies between systems.

2.3.6 ARCHITECTURE THINKING

'Architecture thinking' is one of the 'business design capabilities'. Architecture thinking is a methodology or technique that actualizes business design products, services, and business models. Architecture thinking and systems thinking discussed earlier can be thought of as the wheels of a car. In architecture thinking, we can think of the services and products, organizations and business models that surround us in our daily lives as systems, and analyze these from the perspectives of the relationships between the parts within a system, and the relationship between this system and the external world. If we put ourselves in the shoes of the designer, all we can do is plan the parts that comprise the system, and how they are connected together.

Our daily lives are surrounded with a wide range of products and services. It seems difficult to find unity or common ground among such rich diversity. However, we can find common frameworks if we review these superficially diverse products and services from a more fundamental perspective. That's the perspective of architecture, and is often expressed in the Japanese language as 'design concept'. A general-purpose thinking can be developed by using the framework of 'architecture' latent in the roots of various products and services, without getting caught up in the usual differences in types of industry, products or services. 'Architecture thinking' is the framework for this type of thinking.

For example, the product system known as an 'automobile' consists of a range of parts such as the engine, the car body, brakes and so forth. If we consider the automobile in terms of the way the relationships between these parts should be designed, and the way the relationships with external users should be designed, we are thinking about the architecture of the automobile. By looking at things from the architecture perspective we can find new aspects.

Architecture is also useful for analyzing processes, since processes are also systems. For example, one of the biggest innovations in logistics in recent years has been the development of door-to-door delivery, which can be understood as an innovation in the architecture of the processes of distribution systems. This involved standardizing the many sub processes comprising the formerly customized distribution routes all the way from shipment to delivery. The essence of the door-to-door delivery innovation can be found in the changes of the architecture of distribution system processes. The semiconductor design processes mentioned in Chapter 4 are also examples of standardizing a business architecture comprising of many sub processes.

Products and services are produced through organizations and business models which can also be thought of in terms of architecture, since they are also systems. For example, a corporation is an organic system that creates value through the organic linking of many parts and functions such as the design, development, manufacture and business departments within it, and these organizations also have boundaries. When thinking about assigning business responsibilities and designing the relationships between different functions within an organization, and where to draw the boundaries between organizations and the external environment, we are thinking about organizational architecture. When thinking about how to form IBCs to represent the relationships between organizations, we must also think about organizational architecture.

Viewed in terms of architecture, mobile phone business models are also different in individual countries. Some mobile phone business models have been realized through collaborations between mobile phone carriers such as NTT DOCOMO, KDDI and SoftBank and mobile phone makers such as Sharp and Panasonic. If we look at mobile phone business models from the perspective of architecture, it is clear that there is a big difference between Japanese and Western versions. Japanese mobile telephone services are provided through closely coordinated organization between communications carriers and mobile terminal makers, and mobile handsets are customized to work with certain carriers. In the West on the other hand, services are standardized and mobile phone terminals can be used with whatever carrier is available. This means that the business model architectures of Japan and the West are different because the boundaries between mobile phone manufacturers and communications carriers are different. This also means that the organizational architecture of IBCs in Japan and the West are not the same either.

The broad scope of the framework of architecture means it is intended as an all-purpose way of thinking to give an overall perspective of an entire system that goes beyond the differences between the individual specific parts. This means that for modern corporations facing the rapidly changing economic circumstances of recent years, architecture is becoming more and more important. Using product development as an example, there are three reasons that can be identified as to why product architecture is important (Shibata and Kodama 2008).

The first reason is that, as objects of design, product systems are becoming larger in scale and more complicated. This is particularly observed in the increases in size and complexity of systems in the area of software. Not only mobile phones and digital home appliances but also vehicles are controlled by built-in complicated software called firmware as results of computerization as mentioned in Chapter 1. These large-scale and complicated systems cannot be developed by individual human beings, so the work of design is allocated to different people and then finally integrated into the complete system, which means that the success or failure of the complicated system development is largely dependent on the way tasks are allocated. In other words, looking at the entire system, efficient ways of allocating work must be decided upon, and product architecture must be planned in advance. The top-down approach in systems thinking mentioned earlier is important here.

The second reason is that technological progress and diffusion is very fast these days and product life cycles have become very much shortened. For example, nearly every household has a digital camera and the market has matured. The first digital camera to appear on the market was Casio's QV 10 in 1995; in a little over 10 years the new digital camera industry has already matured. Modern technological advances and popularization mean that the life cycles of those markets are getting extremely fast. To continue with sustained development in a sharply fluctuating market environment, the idea of designing highly scalable architectures and prolonging product life once developed is important. Planning for single development elemental technologies or products that can be reused in the future happens in the initial stages of architecture conception. In short, the age has come where developmental efficiencies and achievements have become highly dependent on the quality of architecture.

Thirdly, the wave of globalization is also advancing in design and development processes. Whether a company can get the best personnel from around the globe involved in the design and development process now has a big effect on its design and development capability. One effective solution to this is to embark on joint developments with global corporations. Global companies are accustomed to deciding on architecture in advance due to the high mobility of engineers. When embarking on a joint-venture with a global corporation, there are many cases where first negotiations are carried out with an engineer who holds the title of architect. Therefore, for a local corporation to effectively embark on a joint-venture with a global corporation, it must first learn the customary practice of deciding upon product architecture, task allocation, how development should proceed and so forth.

Because of the above reasons architecture is becoming increasingly important in product, service, and business model development. With the current popularity of computer design tools like 3D CAD, it would not be an understatement to say that the most important job of the engineer is to design a superior architecture. As testament to that idea, former Panasonic vice president CTO Susumu Koike, once suggested to his boss when he was still a division director to: 'leave circuit design to the computer. Engineers should specialize in architecture development' (Nikkei Biztech 2004).

Architecture thinking for product development is important for innovation because, there is a potential for highly competitive products to be created through changes in architecture, even though there are no changes at the elemental technological level. Gains produced by this type of major alteration to the relationships between the structural elements comprising a product system have been called 'architectural innovation' by Henderson and Clark (1990).

Architectural innovation can typically be seen in examples of miniaturization and increased performance. For example, Japanese corporations are very good at making thinner and thinner notebook computers by changing the assembly and rearranging the parts in the narrow space inside. Japanese digital cameras also feature advanced high-performance functions produced by both new component development and by manufacturing technique. Further examples of architectural innovation also include Nintendo's DS/Wii and Apple's iPod/iPhone/iPad etc. In other words, big changes to the architecture without much change to the elemental technology can bring about highly competitive product development. Architectural innovation is vastly different to radical innovation, such as the breakthrough development of the transistor which pushed vacuum tubes off the market, or modular innovation, such as core component technological innovation in computers or numerically controlled machine tools (NC) (see Figure 2.16).

Problems hindering architectural innovation are more often organizational problems rather than technological problems. Once a particular product architecture stabilizes, organizational structures and business processes begin to fit themselves in with the architecture. When the connection methods between the parts comprising the product are stabilized, the structure of task allocation within the organization, and the way that information is shared throughout the organization, also begin to respond accordingly to the product architecture. For efficient responses, information and divisions of labor in the organization become more and more fixed and stable, and once an organization reaches this state, it becomes much more difficult to bring about a new innovation through architectural innovation.

		Core Concepts	
		Reinforced	Overturned
Linkage between Core Concepts and Components	Unchanged	Incremental innovation	Modular innovation -Computer -NC
	Changed	Architectural innovation -DS/Wii -iPod/iPhone/iPad	Radical innovation -Transistor -IC

Figure 2.16 Architectural innovation
Source: based on Henderson and Clark (1990)

This problem is particularly noticeable in American corporations. Generally, American corporations have a strong tendency to apply rules and systemize as well as continuing with business specialization and segmentation (this is the top-down approach of systems thinking mentioned earlier). As a result, it is difficult for them to deal with new product architecture created by changing certain product architecture once it has become established in their business structure. Conversely, it's easy to respond to changing product architecture in Japanese corporations thanks to the flexible divisions of labor that exist, for better or worse.

The problem is however, as mentioned in the previous section, that top-down architecture (systems thinking with the top-down approach) has traditionally not been given much attention in Japan. Rather than making clear decisions by using top-down architecture in advance as is done in the West, there is a dependency in Japan on the bottom-up approach, relying on subsequent organizational adjustment capabilities. For this reason, it can be said that there the organizational culture and customs that focus on architecture and the methods and approaches of systems thinking used to conceive excellent architecture are not well cultivated.[17]

As we move into an era of cataclysmic market upheavals, architecture is becoming even more crucial, and the limitations of relying solely on bottom-up coordination capabilities which have served Japanese corporations well in the past, are becoming more and more evident. Japanese corporations need to implement architecture thinking using the top-down approach involved in systems thinking, while continuing to maintain and develop their bottom-up coordination approaches.

2.3.7 PLATFORM THINKING

Platform thinking is one of the important 'business design capabilities'. As a boundary vision capability, platform thinking enables transformation of the existing boundaries of industries, not only in one's own company, but is a perspective that can give rise to new business ecosystem industry structures. Basic definitions of a platform in product development refer to basic technological assemblies common among a number of different products, or modules that act as fundamental central parts of the product. Firstly, let's look at the general idea of a platform in product development.

In the past, product development process activities were advanced to achieve commonality of parts and modules among different device models. Making use of modular design know-how for each part, and designing for functions to be available in all goods in a lineup using common modules has become established basic practice. Platform strategies in product development are design strategies for adopting modules that meet the technical specifications required for each product, based on a fundamental design.

Examples of this can be seen in car bodies, computer motherboards, and core semiconductors (MPU, SoC etc.) used in PDAs. When designing module architecture, it is important to design architecture with modules playing central roles as platforms to make the architecture highly scalable and to lengthen the lifetime of the architecture.

---

17   Methods for excellent architecture realization in the West include DSM (Design Structure Matrix) and AIM (Architecture Improvement Method) mainly proposed by universities and embarked upon as trial and error methods in association with industry. For details about DSM, refer to Eppinger (1991). For details about AIM, refer to Weerd-Nederhpf, Wouters, Teuns and Hissel (2007).

A successfully created platform makes derivative products and complimentary products cheaper and quicker to develop. Therefore in platform thinking, both systems thinking and architecture thinking are needed to decide how to partition the whole system at the outset, and which of those subsystems should be defined as platforms.

Panasonic's digital home appliance product development strategy of recent years is composed of conformity with global technical standards to speed up commercialization and a platform strategy of the company's own unique black box component developments. Panasonic developed their 'UniPhier' system LSI (*Uni*versal *P*latform for *H*igh-quality *I*mage *E*nhancing *R*evolution) integrated platform, that can be used with personal audiovisual devices such as digital cameras, home AV such as DVD recorders and PDP televisions, mobile phones, car AV and so forth (see Figure 2.17). This universally optimized platform breaks down the technological walls that exist between a range of different product fields. Designing system LSI as a platform that can be used in a number of different devices makes it possible to improve the quality of design and the efficiency of development. As shown in Figure 2.17, if common sections can be made into a platform and then featured functions or characteristics developed for individual products later, the level of reliability and development efficiency is much greater than developing the entire product from scratch. It goes without saying that the collaboration strategy embarked upon through the IBC between Panasonic's main R&D department, and design and development supervisors in all product departments played a central role in all of this.

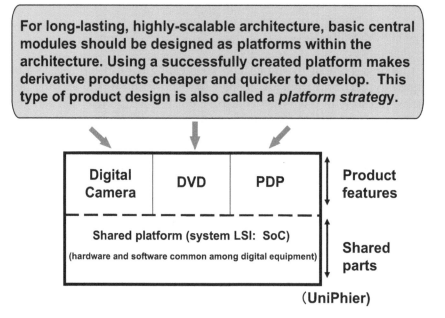

Figure 2.17 Digital appliance platform (UniPhier)
Source: based on Shibata and Kodama (2000)

It is also important to be able to make design judgments about what functions should be included in the system LSI as platforms. If too many functions are produced as platforms, derivative and complementary products may become difficult to distinguish, whereas if there are insufficient functions produced as platforms, design efficiencies won't improve very much. In short, it is not really that easy to judge what degree of platform incorporation will bring about the greatest level of efficiency. Difficult design decisions are needed to design architecture for high-scalability and long product life. The quality of these judgments can have a big impact on a company's product development efficiency.

As another platform concept aside from product development, against the backdrop of IT business advances of recent years, platform strategies are becoming more and more important to business models and corporate strategies. This comes from the idea that customers can be provided with more value by constructing complementary products and services on platforms working as the foundations. Microsoft and Intel have secured positions as platform leaders – Microsoft in software with its Windows operating system, and Intel in hardware with its MPU semiconductors.

Both companies maintain high competitiveness with their products, because positive feedback occurs through the network effect with application and software partner suppliers supplying various applications and software working on Microsoft Windows and Intel MPU. This win-win relationship created between the platform leaders and partner suppliers gives rise to a 'business ecosystem'. Some other good examples of platform strategies in IT businesses are NTT DOCOMO's i-mode and Osaifu-Keitai systems for accounting, transaction and authentication functions, applications and software; the iPhone and iPad application platforms, and Google's android OS for smart phones.

Corporations that aspire to becoming platform leaders need to decide upon a platform architecture that will encourage the independent growth of complementary products for various services and technologies on the platform. In the same way as deciding upon and structuring a platform for product development as previously described, it is crucial for platform leaders to define appropriate boundaries between the company and its partners through systems thinking and architecture thinking, to develop an attractive platform that encourages independent growth for those partners outside the company.

A company that pulls along an entire system consisting of technologies, products and services developed independently by individual partner corporations, with the company's platform at the centre, while inviting and coordinating partner companies (including customers and competitors) is called a 'platform leader corporation.' Microsoft, Google, Intel, Qualcomm, Apple, NTT DOCOMO, Nintendo, TSMC etc. are all platform leader corporations. Platform leader corporations create the platform as an open and modular system to maintain their business leadership, and thus create potential for its long-term progress (Kodama 2009a). Smooth development of this kind of platform strategy can realize business development that isn't really possible with a single company's resources, but has great potential to bring about a business ecosystem through co-creation and co-evolution between corporations, partners, customers and even competitors (see Figure 2.18).

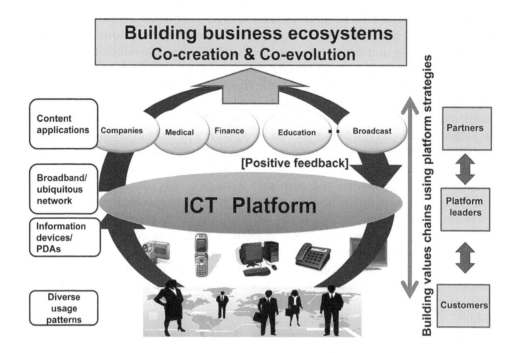

Figure 2.18 Building business ecosystems with platform strategies

2.4 Aspiring for Innovation through Boundary Vision

The preceding sections in this chapter described the seven capabilities needed by corporate leaders and managers to improve the quality of their boundary vision. To practice the leadership that achieves hybrid innovation by conquering and overcoming a range of diverse boundaries, business people must be able to use boundary vision to gain new insight from diverse and complex boundaries. A corporate ethos supporting boundary vision is the corporation's core capability to bring about hybrid innovation and sustained growth. Further, the four integrative capabilities – external knowledge integrative capability, strategic integrative capability, organizational integrative capability, and leadership integrative capability – are related to concrete achievement of business design capability as they mutually complement each other while maintaining congruence.

Business design capability also means a core capability for creating specific product and service strategies or business models. The basic elements of business design capability – systems thinking and architecture thinking – are fundamental capabilities for designing and creating business models optimized for new products and services. Moreover, fundamental to the creation of a business ecosystem with platform thinking are the synergies emerging from systems thinking and architecture thinking.

In the network economy of the future, fusion and consolidation of knowledge between different industries will become even more necessary with the further advancement and diversification of knowledge. High-quality knowledge needed to produce future hybrid innovation will be dispersed throughout the boundary networks linking IBCs across corporations (industries) and between IBCs, and the process of integrating knowledge that overcomes and conquers boundaries in or between corporations will be critical. This is another reason why collaborative strategies with external partners that include customers are going to be more and more important.

Boundary vision proposes new perspectives on the capability to integrate knowledge from different sources, the conceptual ability to realize new business models that merge different boundaries, and further, the imaginative power to bring about hybrid innovation across the boundaries between corporations and industries. Business people need to use boundary vision to create grand designs for new boundary architectures. This process will achieve knowledge integration to create new business models, and become a major component of quality leadership in the twenty-first century.

Companies that encourage hybrid innovation make the most of boundary vision based on the seven capabilities to form the IBCs pivotal to coordination and collaboration with global partners. Particularly, the formation of IBCs across different industries increases the possibility for establishment of a business ecosystem. IBCs existing as new governance models and knowledge networks for the creation, maintenance, and development of business ecosystems are a central framework for knowledge integration firms.

Chapter 2 Conclusions

1. To establish the capability to create diverse IBCs (Interactive Business Communities), practitioners must have the capability to gain new insights from diverse and complicated boundaries, called 'boundary vision'.
2. There are seven capabilities (four corporate capabilities and three business design capabilities) required for practitioners to increase the quality of their boundary vision, and promote hybrid innovation. They are: i) external knowledge integrative capability; ii) strategic integrative capability; iii) organizational integrative capability; iv) leadership integrative capability; v) systems thinking; vi) architecture thinking, and vii) platform thinking.
3. 'Corporate capability' means the strategic and organizational capabilities needed for sustained hybrid innovation. 'Business design capabilities' refers to the boundary architecture (corporate boundaries) design abilities needed to bring about hybrid innovation, and imaginative design and conceptual capabilities needed to develop plans for new products, services, and business models for hybrid innovation.
4. Companies that encourage hybrid innovation make the most of boundary vision based on the seven capabilities to form the IBCs pivotal to coordination and collaboration with global partners.

2 *In-depth Case Studies*

3 Co-creation and Co-evolution Models through Platform Business Innovations – ICT Industry Cases

3.1 Business Model Innovation in ICT Industries

Into the future, companies will have to place increasing importance on generating new business models by establishing innovation process strategies using ICT and digital technologies. The ICT industry is not only affected by product innovations based on ICT technological developments from companies like Google and Yahoo with their search and advertising businesses, multimedia distribution businesses with Apple's market-leading iPod, iPad and iPhone, NTT DOCOMO of Japan's world-first i-mode mobile phone business model, or Sony and Nintendo game businesses. The results of these developments are also service innovations through the creation of new markets with new marketing strategies.

This chapter clarifies the mechanisms involved in bringing about the product and service innovation processes that lie at the heart of the information revolution in the ICT industry. There are three main types of 'knowledge innovators' involved in the growth of ICT and digital businesses – 'platform innovators', 'application innovators' and 'content innovators'. As stakeholders, these knowledge innovators engage in close coordination and collaboration with each other to realize new business models. Knowledge innovators encourage 'co-creation' to bring about new business models, and promote 'co-evolution' throughout the entire ICT and digital industry to nurture the dynamic business ecosystems of business model innovation.

The leading business models of Internet businesses such as i-mode and iPod/iPhone/iPad, or game business models used with PlayStation/DS/Wii and so forth have their roots in a dynamically structured business ecosystem created through this type of co-creation and co-evolution. Just how then, do the actors inside and outside companies go about creating these co-creation and co-evolution business ecosystems? What sort of corporate, organizational and technological strategies are required for co-creation and co-evolution? At the academic level, there is not a lot of accumulated research in answer to these questions. By taking a look at the roles played by knowledge innovators in the world's leading ICT corporations, this chapter considers the relationships needed to foster co-creation and co-evolution, and hence build a business ecosystem.

3.2 Co-creation and Co-evolution Among Knowledge Innovators

As illustrated in Figure 2.3 in Chapter 2, companies in the ICT and digital industries are constantly creating new products, services and business models through the realization of strategy transformations involving new corporate boundaries and value chains in which companies dynamically adjust the boundary architecture elements of their vertical and horizontal boundaries. The basis of these strategy transformations can be found in the seven boundary vision capabilities that serve the knowledge integration process through the formation of IBCs and boundary networks (Figure 2.3 'knowledge integration path').

Mobile telephone carriers that serve large numbers of subscribers and hold substantial mobile communications technologies (e.g. NTT DOCOMO) that have moved into the credit industry, or appliance makers (Sony) that have moved into the game industry (Sony established Sony Computer Entertainment) and financial services (Sony established Sony Bank) are case examples of using knowledge in vertical boundaries (some of the company's business activities) to expand the company's business domain into its horizontal boundaries.

Another example is Apple, who started off in computer development and sales, and later created a new platform for music distribution with its iTunes portal site and the iPod product platform development. Apple expanded its horizontal boundaries into music distribution from its PC business to create a new business domain. To do this, Apple engages in collaborations with content providers from the record industry. Apple also became a player in the mobile telephone business with the introduction of iPhone, and attracts a large number of applications and content providers with its AppStore platform. AppStore provides services in 77 countries worldwide, and since its beginning has accumulated 65,000 applications, and boasts an enormous market now topping more than 1.5 billion downloads. Furthermore with iPad, Apple has also developed an attractive internet business with PDA technology that caters to the e-book market.

Google has developed a business model similar to AppStore with its 'Android Market' by popularizing the company's comparatively open (compared to Apple's) Android OS through collaboration with appliance and mobile telephone makers all over the world. Global mobile telephone makers are able to freely include Android with their new products. Differing from Apple who developed their own hardware and software, Google's strategic objective is not only to increase its advertising revenues by increasing Android's share through net searches from mobile phones, but also to expand its life log business[1] using customer data by creating the Android Market for shopping, viewing history, and location data etc.

Also, SoftBank in Japan, who started out as a computer software distributor, used acquisition and capital investment strategies to transform itself into an Internet and mobile telephone business (portal and content services). As a company that aims to be 'a comprehensive digital information company', SoftBank expanded its horizontal boundaries and business domain to provide content as well as all kinds of communication services including broadcasting.

---

1   A 'life log' is a service that automatically collects personal data, and is optimized for individual lifestyles. Life log services already include behavioral targeting, advertising, recommendations, agents, social graphs, watch-over services, life recorders, contents matching and so forth.

As these companies work towards realizing their goals through strategy transformation, they use IBC and boundary networks to absorb and integrate internal knowledge with knowledge from partners, customers, and competitors to bring about hybrid innovation. To create their own platform, these companies merge their core technologies with core technologies of partners (or partners' platforms), or they use other company platforms to develop unique products and services and provide them to end-users. This is also a pattern of hybrid innovation, which combines internal with external knowledge. In knowledge integration patterns, there are two convergence systems to realize hybrid innovation – closed systems and open systems. These are dependent on individual corporate strategies and the nature of alliances between corporations. Especially, collaborative strategies with partners are indispensable for hybrid innovation.

Collaborative strategies across a company's dynamically structured internal and external knowledge integration IBCs and boundary networks serve to integrate the knowledge needed to bring about hybrid innovation for target new products, services and business models. Boundary vision encourages the dynamic structuring of these internal and external knowledge integration networks and can be an enabler for the dynamic adjustment of a company's vertical and horizontal boundaries, and IBCs and boundary networks are the foundations for these networks structures.

As previously mentioned, knowledge innovators – players who bring about hybrid innovation by dynamically changing the vertical and horizontal boundaries through IBCs – can be described in the context of the ICT industry as 'platform innovators', 'application innovators', and 'content innovators'. These three types of knowledge innovators play an important role in merging different technologies and various business models to develop new business value chains in new emerging industries that span different business sectors, as described in Chapter 1. Knowledge innovators dynamically change corporate boundaries of their companies through the formation of IBCs and boundary networks as well as the structuring of internal and external knowledge integration networks. Through coordination and collaboration with partners, knowledge innovators encourage business model matching and thus enable optimized profit structure generation with individual partners, and as these knowledge innovators collaborate with each other, they encourage co-evolution and co-creation for their objective business models (see Figure 3.1).

Platform innovators mainly serve to develop and provide platforms to act as information distribution infrastructure (ICT systems, handsets, devices etc.) required for realizing new e-businesses and business models. Examples of platform innovators include telecommunications carriers and communications equipment vendors who develop Broadband platforms, and hardware and software vendors for information terminals and game devices such as Apple, Google, Sony and Nintendo. Moreover, companies that provide core technology platforms to develop and manufacture complete or complementary semiconductor and component products (hardware and software) that end up as ICT-related products are also examples of platform innovators. These telecommunications carrier, telecommunications device and component vendor platform innovators mutually co-create and co-evolve to create, encourage and grow new value and supply chains through the synergies between their individual platforms.

On the other hand, 'application innovators' mainly serve to create new business processes and industry value chains to realize new e-businesses and new business models. For instance, these are companies that provide software as a service (SaaS) for cloud computing, application service providers (ASPs), or companies that use platform

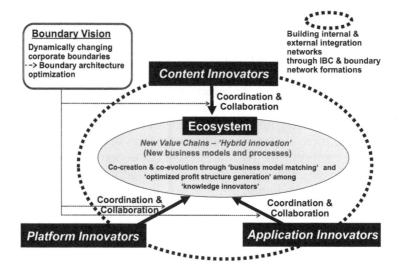

Figure 3.1   Co-creation and co-evolution among knowledge innovators

innovators' software platforms (and hardware in some cases) to create new supply chains or e-businesses and revolutionize business processes. 'Application innovators' also includes players that develop and provide hardware and software components that complement the platform innovators' ICT platform products, or provide additional modules that give new functionality to platforms. The third type of knowledge innovator is the 'content innovator'. These are content holders in various businesses and industries who use new e-business platforms and business processes to provide wide-ranging content services to customers.

All three types of knowledge innovators mutually coordinate and collaborate with each other to establish business formations that feature win-win ecosystem structures. Knowledge innovators create new value chains through hybrid innovation to give birth to a whole host of new businesses (see Figure 3.1).

3.3 Platform Innovation with Diverse Business Models

In the ecosystem business model, the platform provided by platform innovators for technology, products and services is pivotal among the knowledge innovators working with it. Platform innovators provide a wide range of platforms that are not only used by other platform innovators, but also used by application innovators and content innovators to provide a broad range of products and services to end-users. There are several platform businesses that have arisen as a result of the creation of mutual relationships between knowledge innovators.[2] Figure 3.2 illustrates the patterns of these platform business models (just 'business model' hereafter) created by these three types of knowledge innovator, including end-users. The following serves to further clarify these.

---

2   Boudreau and Lakhani (2009) identify three business models – the 'Integrator Platform', the 'Product Platform' and the 'Two-sided (Multisided) Platform'.

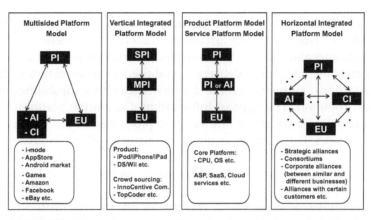

Multisided Platform Model	Vertical Integrated Platform Model	Product Platform Model Service Platform Model	Horizontal Integrated Platform Model
PI ↑ ↕ -AI -CI ↔ EU	SPI ↑ MPI ↑ EU	PI ↑ PI or AI ↑ EU	PI ↕ AI ↔ CI ↕ EU

- i-mode
- AppStore
- Android market
- Games
- Amazon
- Facebook
- eBay etc.
	Product:
	- iPod/iPhone/iPad
	- DS/Wii etc.
	
	Crowd sourcing:
	- InnoCentive Com.
	- TopCoder etc.
		Core Platform:
		- CPU, OS etc.
		
		ASP, SaaS, Cloud services etc.
			- Strategic alliances
			- Consortiums
			- Corporate alliances
			  (between similar and
			  different businesses)
			- Alliances with certain
			  customers etc.

PI: Platform Innovators (MPI: Main Platform Innovators   SPI: Sub Platform Innovators)
AI: Application Innovators
CI: Content Innovators
EU: End Users

Figure 3.2   Types of platform business models

3.3.1 MULTISIDED PLATFORM (TWO-SIDED PLATFORM) MODEL

Firstly, the 'multisided platform (two-sided platform) model' (Eisenmann, Parker and Alstyne 2006) has at least two different types that can be clearly distinguished as individual business development models in which customers, who play an important role in interdependent relationships, simultaneously participate; and businesses that use this platform also provide high-value products and services to those individual customers. As well as saving transaction costs between different customers, this platform also offers product and service diversity, and is characteristic of the Internet shopping mall systems used by eBay, Yahoo, and Amazon etc., that match seeds and needs between customers, or the advertising supported service like Google search engine, or credit card services such as Visa Card. More examples of this business model include newspapers that link advertisers with subscribers, and HMO (Health Maintenance Organization) – one type of American health insurance system that links up patients with treatment organizations.

As well as that, convenience stores like 7-Eleven use the business synergies of the multisided platform model formed from partnerships and partners in businesses different from their convenience store operation to include such things as financial services like ATM machines, distribution services like home delivery, and fee collection services for utility bills. Another example of the multisided platform model is JR in Japan, a rail and transport business who introduced Sony's non-contact 'FeliCa' IC card into their train passes ('Suica Card'), and set up Suica Card readers in train stations and in surrounding convenience stores, restaurants, cafes, bookstores and clothing shops and so forth – thus bringing in a wide range of commercial entities to successfully create a new market. Unlike Internet shopping, the convenience store and the Suica card cases are examples of real-world shopping with the multisided platform model that give birth to network effects between multiple clients.

In more detail, knowledge innovators in this kind of multisided platform model position their businesses as follows: in the world of Broadband and mobile telephone services, platform innovators such as telecommunications carriers and ISPs (Internet service providers) create an information communications network consisting of communications lines and nodes to transmit data, voice and video, and also build systems that enable timely digital content delivery to end-users in combination with the related financial transactions, authentication and content searching capabilities necessary for information distribution. This type of information distribution platform makes use of application innovators and content innovators to provide end-users with a wide range of products and services. For example, content innovators working in Broadband delivery services (for music, broadcast, video, books, games and corporate information etc.) or value-added services (education and medical social welfare and so forth) offer a wide range of diverse applications.

The best examples of success with this model can be seen with NTT DOCOMO's i-mode, Sony and Nintendo's game businesses, the social networking website Facebook, or the online auction site eBay, but there are also web-portals throughout the world that use this multisided platform model to provide a wealth of other e-commerce services. Most platforms in this model, like Google and Amazon, offer open access to participants and external partners (open multisided platform model), although platform innovators offering platforms like i-mode, games (such as Sony and Nintendo) or Apple's AppStore for its iPhone engage in strict and thorough quality-control for the services, applications and content provided on the platform, and function to administer and coordinate external partners. This chapter defines the semi-open multi-sided platform model by contrasting it with the above-mentioned open platform. Apple's AppStore is an example of a semi-open multisided platform model, although initially platform innovator Apple was a strongly vertically integrated organization that controlled application innovators and content innovators (discussed in more detail later).

Application and content innovators use the platforms (technology, products and services etc) provided by platform innovators to provide end-users with products and services as B2B, B2C and even B2B2C. However, there are fixed business rules in the semi-open multisided platform model that exist between application innovators, content innovators and platform innovators. For NTT DOCOMO's i-mode platform strategy of bundling various application services and content, coordination and collaboration based on fixed rules are very important to the company.

In the multisided platform model, collaboration between knowledge innovators is crucial, because knowledge innovators need communication and collaboration and coordination to respond to platform innovators' technological improvements, product and service innovations, and changes to product and service specifications (platform specifications). Also important is the process of platform users collaborating with platform innovators regardless of whether the platform provided is closed or open. Likewise, to invigorate platforms and maximize network effects, platform innovators must engage in the important process of coordination and collaboration with external application innovators and content innovators, who are important complementary players in this type of business process.

The multisided platform is also the core business model of the business ecosystem. The word 'ecosystem' usually refers to biological systems, but business ecosystems are similar to biological systems in that they emerge from the mutual synergies between multiple corporate and organizational groups within, and transactions between participants in a business ecosystem influence other participants due to network effects. In recent years, open platform ecosystem business models like open operating systems or Google's open social model have become more widespread. These enable profits from external partner innovation activities to be shared, and promise profits from network effects at the same time as expanding customer bases. Compared with the 'vertical integrated platform model' discussed later, open platforms have the benefit of lower negotiation and adjustment costs with external partners.

However, in some cases, incorporating partially closed elements as a semi-open platform can serve to coordinate access to the ecosystem (screening external partners, licensing etc.) and adjust the degree of ownership rights to the platform (e.g. the level of external partner investment in the platform), which enables optimal advancement of innovation (quality and quantity), as well as providing quality control for the ecosystem.

3.3.2 SERVICE PLATFORM MODEL

The second type of business model is the 'service platform model'. This includes 'application innovators' who are ASPs or SaaS (Software as a Service),[3] that use the technological platforms (hardware and/or software) of carrier, ISP and product vendor platform innovators to provide the end-user (especially corporate users) with all sorts of applications and software services (business to enterprise (B2E), and B2B systems). Application innovators who develop SaaS and ASP businesses are important business partners for platform innovators, who develop original technology. As well as application innovators, there are cases of corporate users who act as content innovators that use ASP and SaaS to provide services to end-users and consumers (the B2B2C service system – these include e-learning and e-health care services), and there are also cases of platform innovators who simultaneously act as application innovators to provide ASP and SaaS.

On top of that, there are also services called 'PaaS' (Platform as a Service) for developing ASP and SaaS. In the PaaS business model, whole platforms are provided as services. SaaS means services provided for applications via a network, mainly to deal with the cloud computing age, whereas the PaaS business model involves expansion of platforms or entire development environments. 'Cloud computing' is the concept accessing computer resources scattered around the world to provide application services across the Internet.

An example of this is Amazon. As an e-commerce site originally designed for individuals, the company now uses its business systems to provide a platform as a service for server rental, operating systems and middleware that can be freely selected by users, and is now used by many companies around the world including venture businesses. The cases of Amazon, Google, major telecommunications carriers and ISP's that provide cloud computing services to companies are examples of a service platform model, although strictly speaking, the cloud computing services of Amazon and others can be interpreted as one of the services offered in these companies' multisided platform model.

Application innovators use platform innovators' infrastructure (communications networks, handsets, software and ICT tools etc.) to encourage streamlining of their business processes and supply chains to develop their e-businesses. Good examples of these kinds of net business companies can be found in Dell, Wal-Mart, Amazon and

3   This is a service in which the user can optionally select only necessary functions from the software offered by the developer. SaaS is a service concept whereby users can acquire functions they need whenever they want directly from the service provider via the Internet, and they only pay for the functions that they use. High-usability and customization potential combined with multi-tenant technology distinguishes this from the conventional ASP concept.

others. There are also well-known auto and part makers, who as application innovators intentionally use ICT in their business activities across the automotive business supply chain to bring more efficiencies to business processes and shorten product development cycles. In the broader sense, these types of supply chain models are service platform models that span across group companies, client partnerships and between companies.

3.3.3 PRODUCT PLATFORM MODEL

The third type of business model is the 'product platform model'. This model consists of various relationships between platform innovators involving individual interfaces at component and complete product level. In the PC field, Intel's 'Intel Inside' strategy for Microsoft's Windows OS, Qualcomm chipsets for mobile phones, Symbian OS, Google's Android OS, as well as NVIDEA's GPU product platform for a range of tablets, portable media players, notebook PCs and workstations are examples of the product platform model.

Platform innovators who own the core platform technology have contracts to provide this core technology to external partner platform innovators (also called complementary partners). These external partners then use the core platform to develop and manufacture final products or complementary products and provide them to end-users. This means that the ongoing process of coordination and collaboration between platform innovators to keep in step with innovations that greatly change technological standards, or improvements or modifications to core technology, is of the utmost importance.

For example, as part of Intel's platform strategy, the company established fixed rules to encourage complementary players to innovate using Intel's platform while maintaining and developing the entire health of the business ecosystem.[4] Also, as platform innovators, communications equipment vendors engage in close collaboration with communications carriers through partnerships and joint developments for the communications network systems required as platforms for information distribution. In ecosystems that form among the many platform innovators, business models that promote sustained technological innovation not only for a company's platform product, but for sets of complementary or complete products (or services) are examples of this product platform model.

3.3.4 VERTICAL INTEGRATION PLATFORM MODEL

The fourth type of business model is the 'vertical integration platform model'. This business model is used by certain corporations who act as main platform innovators

---

4   Intel promotes coordination and collaboration with external partners to invigorate its platform innovator market with external partners (e.g. the connector market using Intel MPU's or the motherboard and applications markets). Intel also moved into the ASIC business at the base of the chipset business in 1986 to disseminate its flagship MPU products in response to the circumstances of the time. These chipsets reduced the amount of time between commercialization and sales with the new MPU's installed into PCs. Also, by internationalizing with Taiwanese motherboard makers while engaging in some of its own motherboard business, Intel is able to bring large quantities of motherboards installed with its MPUs onto the market. As well as developing motherboards, Intel also contributes interface technology for applications other than processors and chipsets such as PCI, USB, and AGP, where chips in peripherals also use Intel's chipsets integrated with the motherboard, thus establishing Intel's position as a platform leader. However, Intel's complementary vendor external partners (referred to as 'platform innovators' in this book) are shut out of the market, and for Intel to develop and maintain its platform, the company has reinforced 4 levels – (1) work domain within the company, (2) modularization level and interface design, (3) cooperation and competition with complementary businesses, (4) restructuring of internal organizations. See Gawer and Cusmano (2004).

(MPIs) in the development processes all the way from the component level through to completed products (hardware and software). MPIs also delegate business functions to external partners who act as sub platform innovators (SPIs), where the MPI maintains control over SPIs while engaging in close collaboration with them to develop completed products. This kind of vertically integrated business model is called the 'vertical integration platform model'.

Notable examples of this include automotive development systems that function across 'Keiretsu' networks, joint developments between telecommunications carriers and communications equipment makers, and large-scale information development systems for particular clients. The relationships between Japanese mobile telephone carriers (NTT DOCOMO etc.) and mobile telephone makers are described by this business model, where the telecommunications carrier decides upon 100 per cent of the technical specifications for mobile phones and completely controls the mobile telephone manufacturers (Panasonic, Sharp, NEC etc.). Also as a fabless corporation that can be described by the vertical integration platform model, Apple engages in collaborations with best partner developmental makers around the globe for its hybrid innovations for iPod/iPhone/iPad, but maintains strong control over all business processes from development through to manufacture.

Furthermore, Apple's unified iTunes and iPod products do not only vertically integrate hardware and software, but also vertically integrate content. Like Apple, Nintendo is also a fabless company that integrates all business processes from parts through to completed products. In the vertical integration platform model, main control comes from the MPI to maintain commitment and collaboration with SPIs.

In the case of applications for iPhone, Apple initially offered support to development vendors to incorporate the range of applications into the iPhone and controlled this process through vertical integration. Later on, however, Apple opened up their closed application business model by releasing its development tools and APIs to make it easier for external application innovators to participate (at the discretion of Apple). This means that Apple underwent a transformation from the vertical integration platform model to a semi-open multisided platform model with its AppStore business model.

In recent years, businesses using ICT have also begun to casually outsource various businesses to many people over the Internet – a new business model called 'crowdsourcing'.[5] As mentioned in Chapter 1, when a company recruits particular professionals or engineers for closed innovation alone, difficulties can arise with product and service development to match the ever-changing and diverse customer needs of modern times. Therefore, as a closed innovation system that incorporates elements of open innovation, crowdsourcing with its comparatively open human networks has allowed for relatively cheaper procurement methods by enabling the most suitable level of intellectual labor (knowledge and skills) through the processes of 'ordering, recruiting and questioning'.

Crowdsourcing is now practically applied in the fields of R&D, programming, design and music etc., and is a mechanism for aggregating knowledge through public offerings and contest 'among the crowd'. Typical cases include InnoCentive in the R&D field, Threadless, involved in T-shirt sales, and TopCoder, a programming company. These

---

5   Corporations outsource with undefined numbers of people –'the crowd' – to conduct business or solve problems via the Internet. This origin of this word is attributed to Jeff Howe, a contributing editor for *Wired* magazine (US), and first appeared in an article entitled 'The Rise of Crowdsourcing' in the June edition of *Wired* 2006.

business models are examples of the vertical integration platform model used for closed innovation within a company or between companies that has been transformed to an open innovation model. Characteristically, however, platform innovator companies that involve themselves in crowdsourcing businesses maintain total coordination and control via the relationships between developers and customers (outsourcers) in the crowd. In other words from the point of view of customers and developers, the model is open, but the platform innovators have complete control to prevent synergies occurring directly between them. Thus, it can be said that the crowdsourcing business model is an 'open' vertical integration platform model.

3.3.5 HORIZONTAL INTEGRATION PLATFORM MODEL

The fifth type of business model is the 'horizontal integration platform model'. This business model features a platform constructed from strategic alliances, corporate mergers and M&A across different businesses and technologies. Corporations apply this model to expand their horizontal boundaries and reform their boundary architecture for new businesses. In a strategy to expand a company's platform, the vertical integration platform model implies that the company vertically expands its existing business functions upstream or downstream, whereas in the horizontal integration model, companies add new business functions through horizontal strategic alliances with external partners and corporate mergers.

NTT DOCOMO for instance moved into the 'mobile phone credit business' through their strategic alliance with the Sumitomo Mitsui Financial Group, 7-Eleven formed strategic alliances with financial organizations to provide ATM services, while other cases include SoftBank's acquisition of Vodafone's mobile telephone business in Japan. Microsoft's move into the game business, Apple's move into the music distribution business, and Google's expansion from its search and advertising business into operating system and mobile phone businesses are also cases of horizontal business expansion through these companies' 'strategic intent' (Hamel and Prahalad 1998).

Even at the level of services and products, Microsoft's shift into development and sales of its Windows Media Player media distribution product from its operating system and office software, or CATV operators' development of 'triple play services' (telephone, television, and Internet services bundled together) also mean horizontally integrated business models in the broader sense. In platform research, these horizontal platform developments of recent years have been termed 'envelopment strategies' (Eisenmann, Parker and Alstyne 2006), and involve leveraging existing platform functions with user resources to horizontally expand business functions, or bundling complementary products or functions offered by competitors into existing platforms.

The horizontal integration platform model also corresponds to business cases of collaborative strategies through IBCs as mentioned in Chapter 1 (PDAs, RFID solutions, smart grids, solar cell businesses, computerization of automobiles and automobile development and environmental vehicles). Innovation through collaboration with many partners in different fields brings about convergence at the industrial and technological levels including ICT, and the resulting IBCs formed inside and outside companies serve to integrate diverse knowledge and promote platform innovation for products and services. There are plenty of cases of business formations of platform innovators including application innovators and content innovators in a wide range of fields that have achieved this horizontal integration platform model (with particular customers in the same business, or in different businesses or organizations).

Complementary patterns emerge with the horizontal integration platform model when platform innovators collaborate without competing to form new markets, or conversely, platform innovators use M&A and personnel acquisition to absorb new knowledge and engage in new business to compete with other companies. The previously mentioned cases of 7-Eleven and NTT DOCOMO, and alliances through convergence (cases mentioned in Chapter 1) typify this complementary horizontal integration platform model. Notably, these kinds of partnerships, based on strong collaborations with leading partners all over the world, are created in business environments where there are relationships between particular corporations. By contrast, Softbank, Microsoft, Apple etc. challenge existing businesses with a 'competitive' horizontal integration platform model.

These companies decide upon boundary architecture for their vertical and horizontal boundaries to create business models and platforms through the mutual collaborations of platform, application and content innovators, and adjust their horizontal boundaries in response to changing circumstances to create horizontal integration platform models and engage in 'envelopment strategies'.

3.3.6 BUSINESS MODEL MATCHING, OPTIMIZED PROFIT STRUCTURE GENERATION AND THE THREE SYNERGIES

To some degree or other with each of these five business models, the elements of coordination and collaboration are necessary between individual knowledge innovators to bring about win-win business structures. The nature of 'collaboration' implies the creation of business model matching to realize optimized profit structure generation for all involved. Platform innovators, who play an essential role in business models for optimized profit structure generation, have to be mindful of corporate activities purely for their own profit (e.g. overexpansion of the company's business domain through vertical integration of its platform, or giving favour to or ignoring certain application and content innovators). As mentioned, the most important element in maintaining and developing a business ecosystem is the deep collaboration brought about by resonance of values and trust building. Collaborative strategies like this promote co-creation and co-evolution for new business models.

Furthermore, there are three synergies that arise between knowledge innovators during the co-creation and co-evolution processes. The first one of these is 'business synergy'. This refers to knowledge innovators working together for individual business model optimization through mutual creative assessment and alignment through the matching processes. Importantly, knowledge innovators mutually collaborate to bring new and higher value to customers (target users and end-users), and also knowledge innovators must to be able to assess whether costs can be more efficiently reduced by using another company's knowledge instead of their own knowledge. For example, convergence cases mentioned in Chapter 1 are cases of business synergy arising from the mutual integration and optimization of partner companies' business models to create new markets through alliances with different businesses.

The second one of these is 'technology synergy'. This synergy decides whether knowledge innovators can mutually integrate technical knowledge to realize new products and services. An example of this is Google, a company that encouraged the merging of the hardware and software technology of its global appliance and mobile phone manufacturing partners with its Android OS. Google and Sony's collaboration is a case of technology synergy using Android OS to develop next-generation Internet television with Sony's TV development capabilities and rich content (movies, music etc.), combined with Google's software development capability.

The third one of these is 'partnership synergy'. This synergistic element refers to knowledge innovators mutually collaborating to reinforce each other's strengths while supplementing each other's weaknesses to bring about higher levels of synergy and creativity. Long-term partnerships built on collaborative activities establish shared values and trust among all parties involved and contribute to knowledge sharing and integration, while at the same time, partnership synergies can importantly serve to improve the knowledge innovators' reputation. These three synergies are crucial elements of IBC and boundary network formation and the realization of hybrid innovation (see Figure 3.3).

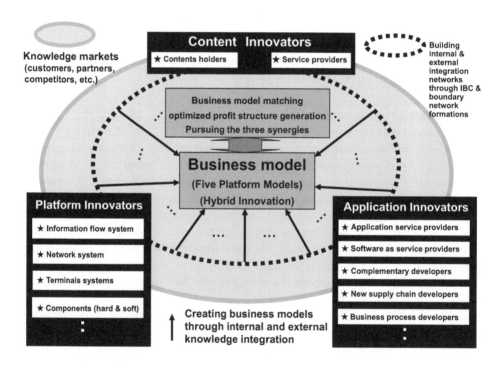

Figure 3.3   Synergies through co-creation and co-evolution

3.4 Collaboration and Business Model Typology

As mentioned earlier, collaboration between knowledge innovators is required with any of these five business models, and thought should be given to the types of collaboration systems that are most suitable for each of them. In the Pisano and Verganti framework (Pisano and Verganti 2008), the essences of the actor's network at the base of collaborations are divided along two axes which illustrate four basic collaboration systems. One axis describes whether the actors participating in the network are in an open or closed system, while the other axis describes whether the network governance structure is hierarchical or flat. Pisano and Verganti describe various cases of four collaboration patterns –'Elite Circles', 'Innovation Malls', 'Innovation Communities', and 'Consortiums' within these two dimensions. While thinking about these four patterns, let's look at the features of these collaboration networks necessary for the processes of construction, maintenance and development of the five business models.

3.4.1 COLLABORATION NETWORKS IN THE VERTICAL INTEGRATION PLATFORM MODEL

In the vertical integration platform model, the network among knowledge innovators is closed, and there is strong leadership from particular knowledge innovators for full control over the professional capabilities of partner knowledge innovators. In this type of network, collaborative relationships are built in hierarchical, integrated and centralized networks between corporations, such as the 'keiretsu' networks in the automotive industry for vehicle development, or the networks across corporations for particular product development projects. Because partner participation is closed, there is limited scope for the network to expand between corporations, and therefore collaboration networks in the vertical integration platform model can be seen as 'elite circles'.

Also, the open type vertical integration platform model represented by 'crowdsourcing' is described by Pisano and Verganti as an 'innovation mall' where platform innovator leadership is hierarchical, integrated and centralized for open collaboration, and proposal evaluation and final decision-making comes from customers.

3.4.2 COLLABORATION NETWORKS IN THE HORIZONTAL INTEGRATION PLATFORM MODEL

The horizontal integration platform model is a business model consisting mainly of different specialist technologies or businesses (or similar businesses) to form professional corporate groups (often called 'consortiums'). Collaboration networks in this business model are closed corporate networks that encourage flat, autonomous and decentralized relationships between specific knowledge innovator corporations that are mutually agreed upon by the participants in these strategic alliances, like the corporate associations accompanying new convergence mentioned in Chapter 1. Compared to the platform innovators above who enact control through collaboration via hierarchical integrated and centralized corporate networks (vertical integration platform model), these autonomous and decentralized collaborations have more potential to bring about creative solutions through the merging of unfamiliar or dissimilar knowledge.

3.4.3 COLLABORATION NETWORKS IN THE MULTISIDED PLATFORM MODEL

The multisided platform model is the ecosystem business model that creates win-win relationships among all stakeholders using a platform to develop unique products and services in which flat governance structures among knowledge innovators mean external players participate in planning. Examples of this type of platform business model included online businesses, credit card companies, Internet shopping malls, i-mode, AppStore, game businesses and so forth, although as mentioned, there are two patterns of player participation in this platform model. The first pattern features set business rules for coordination and transaction relationships to maintain quality control on the platform, meaning that not just anyone can freely participate. NTT DOCOMO's i-mode and the PlayStation/DS/Wii game businesses correspond to this business model. The other pattern is the completely open platform like Google's advertising supported search service where advertisers and hardware and software developers all come together. Other examples include Amazon, Facebook, and eBay. This completely open platform is called an 'open innovation community'.

There are also structures that are neither completely open nor completely closed, that have set business rules for controlling relationships and coordination to maintain platform quality control and optimize (quality and quantity) innovation activities that are called 'semi-open innovation communities' in this book.

Both the open innovation community and semi-open innovation community feature flat governance systems and require an autonomous and decentralized collaboration network for participants. However, the differences between these two types of collaboration network lies in the level to which participants are locked into the community or are free to move in or out of it. In open innovation communities, platform innovators who play the central role of autonomously formulating regulations or organizational culture for the ecosystem have comparatively less influence or control than those in semi-open innovation communities.

3.4.4 COLLABORATION NETWORKS IN THE PRODUCT AND SERVICE PLATFORM MODELS

In the product and service platform models, platform innovators who hold core platform technology link up with platform and application innovators who act as complimentary players to provide end-users with complete and complementary products. In the product platform model, platform innovators with core technology bring together leading external partners (neither as an open system with undefined numbers, or a closed limited system – in other words a 'semi-open' system), and control and coordinate these partners to encourage the partners' innovations, while advancing the platform itself for the company. Also in this model, in the business processes of 'core technology – complimentary technology – assembly – completed products' (there is no assembly stage in the case of services), there is no hierarchy in the relationships between corporations involved – governance is realized by specific platform innovators who control completed products through core technology development and development schedules.

In the service platform model, SaaS and ASP application innovators have to evaluate the software and hardware developed by many platform innovators and combine capabilities to decide what to adopt to provide end-users with a service. Application innovators also need to enable swift feedback with platform innovator corporations for solving problems and issues. In this way, problem resolution and proposal assessment in the service platform model is limited to particular companies; hence hierarchical collaboration is applied.

Therefore, the semi-open collaboration in the overarching hierarchical structure of product platform models and service platform models means that these models are semi-open innovation communities, although there are some examples of the product platform model that use open and flat collaboration. Examples of this business model are typified by open source software organizations such as Linux, Apache, Mozilla Firefox, Wikipedia and so forth. Open source development with Linux and others involves participation in planning from undefined numbers of people in a flat government structure with no hierarchy – the open innovation community mentioned earlier.

3.4.5 TYPES OF COLLABORATION NETWORKS

In the light of the above considerations, each of the business models and their corresponding collaboration networks can be illustrated as shown in Figure 3.4. The point here is to decide on the best type of collaboration to formulate and maintain a specific business model. One axis describes three types of participation; open, semi-open and closed for the actors (or corporations and organizations) in the business model, and also indicates the size of these networks (small, medium and large).

The other axis shows two types of governance structures and organizational characteristics of the actors (or organizations and corporations) involved in forming and maintaining a business model. This same axis also indicates the level of knowledge diversity and unfamiliarity needed for forming and maintaining a particular business model (low or high).

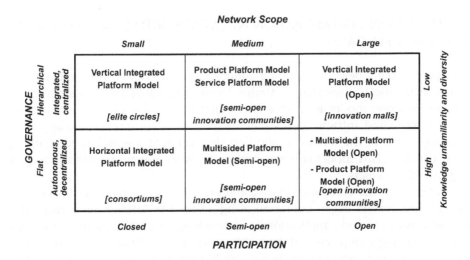

Figure 3.4   Types of business models and collaboration networks

Hierarchical, integrated and centralized collaboration networks are advantageous for actors to polish their common specialized knowledge (or knowledge in similar fields) to overcome issues, and accomplish their strategic targets. On the other hand, flat, autonomous and decentralized collaboration networks are beneficial because they bring about new products and businesses across a wide range of diverse specialist areas and dissimilar knowledge by giving participants a higher degree of creativity and freedom. When viewed in terms of this framework, it can be seen that there are six basic forms of collaboration network for formulating and maintaining each of the business models.

3.5 Combining Various Collaboration Networks and Forming Boundary Networks

As described above, diverse platform models (business models) can be classified as different collaboration networks, but in reality companies can be involved in a range of collaboration network patterns or combinations of different collaboration networks to develop and provide various services and products. A big business issue for companies is that they must optimize their entire value chain by applying the most suitable platform model to all business processes in their value chain elements all the way from R&D, product planning, manufacture, through to sales and support, to create a platform model in which the products and services match the company's target customers. Just like the ICT field, cutting-edge corporations involved in industries where technology and markets are changing rapidly adopt multiple platform models simultaneously, and merge multiple collaboration networks to raise their level of corporate strategy output across the board. This point refers to the cases of Apple, Google and NTT DOCOMO, companies that form IBCs and boundary networks as organizational platforms for combining diverse collaboration networks.

3.5.1 CHANGES IN COLLABORATION NETWORKS WITH BUSINESS MODEL SHIFTS (THE APPLE CASE)

When Apple initially began developing applications for iPhone, the company pursued the same hierarchical, integrated, centralized and closed governance system (a vertical integration platform model as an elite circle) that they had used for the Mac and iPod unified hardware and software developments (including peripherals and applications). Accordingly, some of the iPhone application development was entrusted to important external partners. This model also was part of Apple's competitive strategy to produce distinguishable products.

However, once the company released the product and users got their hands on it, application innovators began communicating across the Internet with each other to figure out ways to include applications and functions that the iPhone did not have – this self-organizing group released over 100 applications within two or three months, something that Apple had not predicted. Apple then responded in March of 2008 by releasing a development toolkit for third parties to develop applications for the iPhone OS platform and offer them to end-users via the iPhone itself.

Apple introduced a profit sharing contract system where profits from for-profit applications are distributed 70 per cent to the developer and 30 per cent Apple. Apple retains control of its platform to screen applications and maintain profit distribution (and participating in the screening mechanism is easier than i-mode's official site – consumers are also able to participate).

In this way it can be seen that although Apple initially engaged in a vertical integration platform model as an elite circle to develop applications, the company gradually loosened its complete control to form a flat, semi-open governance system and moved over to a platform strategy in which many application innovators can independently develop applications. This means the company shifted over to a semi-open multisided platform model from its vertical integration platform model (elite circle), and changed its collaboration mechanisms with application innovators.

3.5.2 MANAGING DIFFERENT BUSINESS MODELS THROUGH COLLABORATION NETWORK INTEGRATION (THE GOOGLE AND NTT DOCOMO CASES)

Google is a corporation that simultaneously applies four business models – the horizontal integration platform model, the product platform model (open and semi-open), the service platform model (semi-open), and the multisided platform model (open and semi-open). With its product platform model (open), Google has created an open source community of third-party 'mashup'[6] software developers, independent software vendors and Google's own software engineers. This community is beneficial for both Google and its partners for realizing product development.

Google also uses the horizontal integration platform model as a consortium to advance its Android OS developed for mobile telephones and smartphones through its establishment of the Open Handset Alliance (OHA) for mobile telephone software development using Android.

OHA promotes the development of Android and plans for the wide-ranging issues for this open source platform such as the operating system itself and the applications that run on it. As a consortium that collaborates in a flat and closed relationship (but open to the participant companies), OHA aims to improve user experience in all areas from communications functions through to the user interface. As the company promotes this business model, Google is able to deepen collaboration and build mutual trust among the OHA member mobile telephone manufacturers. The company also engages in a semi-open product platform model for support and deep collaboration with mobile telephone makers using Android for smartphone development and commercialization.

Google has also established the 'Android Market' for smart phones that have been commercialized by mobile telephone makers – an open multisided platform model that enables users to download whatever applications they like. Anybody can download the application development kit, develop applications and sell them on the Android Market (or give them away free). Google manages the Android Market, while users register their credit card with their Android handsets to buy applications. Looking at this from the point of view of the application providers, 70 per cent of application sales go to the provider while the remaining 30 per cent go to communications and processing fees. The

---

6   A 'Mashup' is a service that combines a number of different technologies or contents from different providers to form a new service. Consisting of combinations of multiple APIs, functions that act as if they were a single web services are also called mashups. Third parties acting on Google's platform use this method to develop a range of Web services. Examples of these are APIs from web services such as Google Maps that are publicly released and incorporated into corporate functions such as customer relationship management (CRM).

communications fees go to the telecommunications carrier, while the processing fees go to the credit card company or some other financial institution – Google doesn't charge anything at all.

The Android Market is an open multisided platform model in which anybody around the world can participate, and unlike i-mode or AppStore, Google does not screen it. Therefore this is self-organizing fertile soil for free release of a multitude of diverse applications, but since Google doesn't control it at all, it could also be a breeding ground for low quality or malicious software. To address this issue, Android Market has a user appraisal and information dissemination system in place.

Google's platform strategy is not only about spreading Android mobile terminals all over the world to increase Google's advertising revenue through the network effects that occur as more and more people use Google's search, Gmail, YouTube and advertising-linked services with the increased dissemination of mobile computing in this open multisided platform model – the company's strategy also promises profits from its cloud computing service – a service platform model.

Therefore, Google provides the Android Market as an anticipatory investment to position itself to turn profits in the future, but Google's platform strategies are wide and varied. Google's hardware platform, said to be the world's biggest computer resource, consists of mammoth data centers each containing tens of thousands of servers spread out across the globe. A range of software platforms are built on this hardware (OS, middleware, applications, content, advertising, personal information … etc). Taking OS platforms, e.g. Google has non-PC operating systems and development platforms for mobile phones and digital appliances – Android – which is a platform operating system to provide Google's services and cuts across the divides between communications carriers, terminal makers and digital appliance makers.

Google's content and advertising platforms are gigantic. The search engine the company developed has converted all data on the Internet into a database and re-sorted it with page rankings. Most Google content is free – because the more the company can find space to display advertising, the more profit it makes. Google's popular YouTube video database, map data, book archive contents etc. have had a huge impact on users. Distributing all of this content for free is central to Google's strategy, since the company increases its advertising sales in proportion to the amount of content it can distribute.

Furthermore, with a different business model to its advertising model, Google stretches its business domain as for-profit cloud computing services, which consist of its GoogleApps[7] application platform providing fee-paying or free applications to corporations and universities, and server appliances for sale to corporations and others.

In this way, Google's four business models include multiple platforms apart from the vertical integration platform model: the horizontal integration platform model, the product platform model (open and semi-open), the service platform model (semi-open), and the multisided platform model (open and semi-open). Across all of these models, Google has a multitude of IBC groups for collaboration with all its different external partners (platform innovators, application innovators and content innovators).

These multiple IBCs exist in the company's horizontal integration platform model between software vendors, semiconductor vendors, mobile telephone makers and

---

7   Google Apps is an abbreviation for Google's application package. This is a set of comprehensive tools used for communication and collaboration. The service is maintained by Google.

communications carriers, whereas in the company's product platform model these linkages exist between mobile telephone makers and appliance makers, while in the multisided platform model participants include software vendors, media companies and advertisers, and in the service platform model, universities and corporate users are included in Google's platforms as consumers.

Google has established boundary networks between all of these IBC networks over which the company shares internal and external knowledge and integrates it to create synergies for the company's strategy as a whole (see Figure 3.5).

NTT DOCOMO and other mobile phone carriers have also constructed multisided platform models (semi-open) with i-mode and so forth, while at the same time engaging in company-branded mobile telephone development, mobile network, financial transaction and authentication platform development with external partners (vertical integration platform model as an elite circle). NTT DOCOMO also has formed a joint development consortium with Renesas, Fujitsu, Sharp, NEC and Panasonic to develop next-generation one-chip LSIs for mobile phone platforms, and an application platform joint development for Linux OS and Symbian OS.

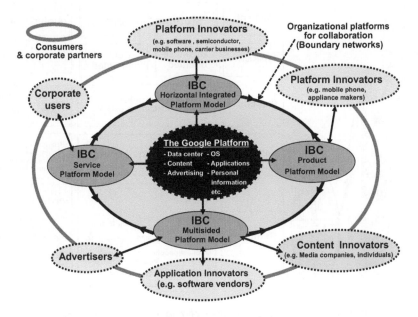

Figure 3.5   Google's platform business – collaborations and synergies through IBCs and boundary networks

These platforms will reduce development costs and shorten development cycles, and relieve mobile phone makers of the burden of having to independently develop basic functions. This environment makes it easier for mobile telephone manufacturers to engage in product strategies that enable them to distribute business resources to focus on developing unique functions and model lineups to come up with distinguishable mobile telephone handsets. NTT DOCOMO uses simultaneous combinations of many different collaborations (networked inside and out oside the company) to deal with these different business models. IBCs for these different collaborations in these individual business models exist internally and externally to NTT DOCOMO, and the company uses combinations of these individual IBCs (boundary networks between IBCs) to share merged knowledge and create boundary networks to deal with these three business models (see Figure 3.6).

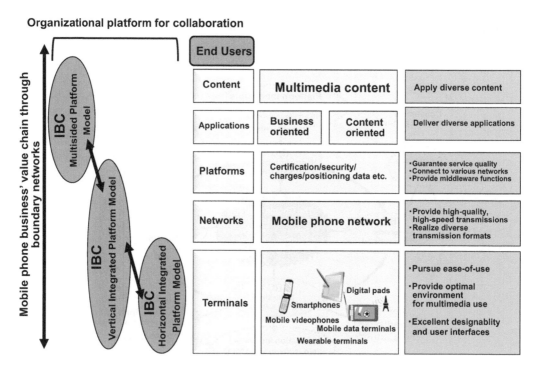

Figure 3.6   Collaborations and synergies through IBCs and boundary networks – NTT DOCOMO's platform business

3.5.3 KNOWLEDGE INTEGRATION THROUGH IBCs AND BOUNDARY NETWORKS

As well as the examples of combining collaboration networks set by Apple, NTT DOCOMO and Google, Chapter 4 discusses innovation firms in the semiconductor industry – the business models of global fabless corporation Qualcomm and foundry company TSMC in Taiwan, – companies that have developed product and service platform models for semiconductor chip and manufacturing systems using a vertical integration platform model called a 'virtual IDM' to integrate all business processes from development and design through to manufacture.

Summing up, the above examples clearly demonstrate that collaboration network patterns exist for individual business models. Corporations have to create win-win business models and ecosystems by forming IBCs and boundary networks most suitable for their strategic objectives based on the nature of their collaborations, although it should be noted that collaboration systems and business models are not set in stone – business models must be dynamically changed, and collaborations promoted through IBCs must respond to changing circumstances and strategic objectives. This is why companies like Apple, Google and NTT DOCOMO use a number of different collaboration patterns and combinations through boundary networks to merge different collaborations at the same time. Forming collaboration networks through IBC and boundary networks formed as suitable organizational platforms enables companies to integrate the diverse knowledge scattered inside and outside the company.

3.6 Coordination and Collaboration Between Knowledge Innovators

When thinking about an ecosystem from the point of view of corporate strategy, what is the best way to create relationships between corporations that will bring about win-win business models through diverse collaboration? To what extent will new business ideas be born through collaboration with other companies? What kind of partners should be selected and what kind of relationships should be built? These are the knowledge integration issues that practitioners face directly on a daily basis, and they raise the question of how IBCs and boundary networks should be formed as organizational platforms for diverse collaboration of the valuable knowledge embedded within and outside of the company.

Practitioners do not get caught up in paradigms of their own ways of thinking and activities; rather, they consciously and voluntarily form organizational platforms by linking up the latent IBCs and boundary networks that exist among partners and customers in existing official organizations, companies and industrial structures, and in the sources of hidden knowledge in the background of different types of business.

The force of the technological revolution going on involving the excellent core technologies scattered around the world in cutting-edge technological fields such as ICT, e-business, contents, electronics and bioengineering cannot be understated. The closed innovation corporations of the mass production era with their hierarchical and independent organizational systems that are completely controlled internally are reaching their use-by date. This really means that in our knowledge-based society, management that openly promotes hybrid innovation through the integration of valuable knowledge across IBCs and boundary networks inside and outside companies is becoming increasingly important to bring about competitiveness.

In the modern knowledge-based society, excellent business models are not created and controlled solely through the power and resources of a single company. Therefore, an important issue to consider is practitioners' understanding of the business model objectives of individual stakeholders. While practitioners need to consider the strategic priorities, core competencies and business models of their own company, they also have to engage in constructive and productive dialogue with all stakeholders for business model matching. Practitioners have to encourage resonance of values and aim for trust building among stakeholders. Resonance of values and trust building are the cornerstones of IBCs and boundary networks.

Within the IBCs and boundary networks, practitioners also have to promote coordination and collaboration among themselves for mutual business model matching for the business model objectives of all stakeholders with important elements of business model matching – the three synergies mentioned earlier – business synergy, technological synergy, and partnership synergy.

For instance, as knowledge innovators establishing a new mobile telephone service, the platform innovators (mobile telephone carriers – communications equipment vendors – mobile handset makers – hardware and software vendors) exchange opinions and engage in dialogue about the carrier's new business model proposal with the application and content innovator stakeholders. While knowledge innovators consider ways to optimize their own business model to match the proposed business model, they also deeply consider, assess and analyze their business model's relationship to their own corporate boundaries. In this way knowledge innovators aim to optimize their boundary architecture – the design of their corporate boundaries. This process means that practitioners in all companies find ways to match up their business model with the new model proposed by the mobile phone carrier and pursue the three synergies.

To build win-win relationships, mutual business model matching and pursuit of the three synergies realizes optimized IBCs, boundary networks and collaboration between the individual companies involved. Nevertheless, IBCs and boundary networks need to be reconfigured among knowledge innovators as knowledge innovators learn from each other and rethink partnerships as situations change. This is an essential part of the 'co-creation process' of raising the level of completion of new business models through mutual learning across IBCs and boundary networks as stakeholders collaborate with each other.

NTT DOCOMO's i-mode, Nintendo's DS/Wii and Sony's PlayStation business models are co-creations resulting from coordination and collaboration through mutual learning among knowledge innovators in different businesses, and Apple's recent iPod/iPhone/iPad products are also the results of co-creation brought about by this type of shared learning among a wide range of knowledge innovators involved in component supply (hardware and software), major record labels for music content, and application and content innovators who produce a diverse range of applications and content for mobile terminals.

Furthermore, as described in detail in Chapter 6, the long partnerships of platform innovators HTC, Qualcomm, Microsoft and Google have given birth to the ecosystem known as the smartphone market through the processes of mutual business model matching and pursuit of the three synergies. Players (NTT DOCOMO with i-mode, Nintendo and Sony with games, Apple with music distribution, and Apple, Google, MS with smart phones, and HTC as a mobile phone maker) who focus on coordination and collaboration realize knowledge integration for new business models through the formation of IBCs and boundary networks optimized for business model matching and pursuit of the three synergies through the process of mutual learning among the many knowledge innovators involved.

New business models co-created by mutual learning are the result of the actual activity of all knowledge innovators in the IBCs and boundary networks. Sustained activities across strong IBCs and boundary networks (strength of networks: the strength of information and knowledge sharing, the level of shared values and trust building, and the existence of formal alliances) leads to creation of new business models and co-evolution of business for the knowledge innovators involved. Knowledge innovators also simultaneously engage in learning through feedback and constant monitoring of business to maintain win-win relationships by optimizing business model matching and pursuit of the three synergies through business model assessment and coordination.

3.7 Knowledge Innovators' Dialectical Thinking and Action

Business model matching and pursuing the three synergies to create a business ecosystem is not an easy task for an individual corporation. In all four business models – the horizontal integration platform model, the product platform model, the service platform model, and the multisided platform model – the key factor for success is the creation of an ecosystem among all stakeholders including end-users.

To build and maintain a new business model as an ecosystem, what kinds of elements does knowledge innovative management need? The results of field research[8] into platform, application and content innovators clearly show that 'dialectical thinking and action' is one way to generate practical knowledge for knowledge innovators.

To develop co-creation and co-evolution, the critical elements here are the leadership integrative capability held by practitioners (see Chapter 2, Figure 2.9), commitment through sustained deep involvement (DiMaggio and Powell 1983), high embeddedness (Granovetter 1973), and resonance of values and trust building (see Figure 3.7).

While working towards social visions and the objective visions and missions of a company, knowledge innovators who create ecosystems need to find and diffuse value with new businesses that include end-users. Knowledge innovators need to engage in dialectical dialogue within IBCs and boundary networks to share and resonate these new values with other knowledge innovators. To do this, knowledge innovators need to practice leadership integrative capability based on dialectical thinking and action, and foster a new leadership style based on the concepts and philosophy of learning from, and teaching stakeholders in an 'interactive learning-based community'.

While platform innovators, who play an especially important role in the ecosystem, promote resonance of values across IBCs and boundary networks, they do not only have to practice innovative leadership as leaders, coaches or mentors to efficiently reform ecosystem business concepts and processes innovatively and creatively, they also have to be good listeners and accommodate external partners (application and content innovators) by offering them continued support by working as 'servant leaders' to raise the level of motivation of all stakeholders.

Leadership through this dialectical thinking and action is not only required of platform innovators but also external partners. External partners must deeply commit themselves to collaboration within the ecosystem, and reinforce the mutual understanding and

---

8   Based on hearings and surveys taken from 37 companies in the United States, Japan, Taiwan, Korea, France, Italy and Israel from 2005 to 2010.

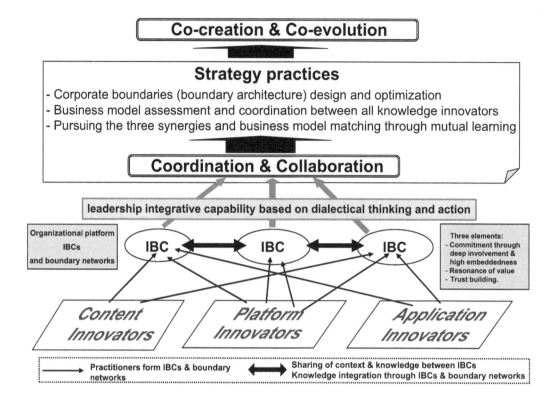

Figure 3.7   Co-creation and co-evolution through IBC and boundary networks

integrity of the alliances within the ecosystem. Leadership in the ecosystem does not depend on the old solidified hierarchical leadership style, but is a new leadership model to achieve innovation that not only aims for growth in a single company, but aims for growth across industries, and ultimately society as a whole. This is the leadership integrative capability needed for successful ecosystems.

Furthermore, the following points also pertain to the managerial character of leadership in leadership integrative capability. Platform innovators have to promote autonomous and decentralized leadership with their external partners to create, maintain and develop an ecosystem to bring about creative business concepts as platform strategies, while at the same time they need a suitable level of integrated and centralized leadership of all end-users and multiple external partners to steer the ecosystem in the right direction.

Therefore, platform innovators have to strike a balance as they simultaneously and dialectically engage in autonomous, decentralized leadership and integrated, centralized leadership applied to the ecosystem. As well as that, stakeholders must also practice leadership based on the philosophies and concepts of 'interactive learning-based communities' to maintain and develop the ecosystem. All of these things enable knowledge innovators to create platform business models based on new value chains, and bring about hybrid innovation through the merging of knowledge across IBCs and boundary networks.

When based on dialectical thinking and action, leadership integrative capability simultaneously promotes commitment through continued deep involvement and high embeddedness, resonance of values and trust building.

The presence of deep interaction among practitioners, the presence of strategic partnerships among organizations that form IBCs and boundary networks, and interactive information and knowledge sharing therein are not the only conditions required for deep collaboration as defined by DiMaggio and Powell, as a high level of involvement in the collaborative process – i.e. the development of strong mutual awareness that practitioners are involved in IBCs and boundary networks – is also essential. The other important element in the formation of IBCs and boundary networks – embeddedness – describes the degree to which collaboration between IBCs is enmeshed in inter-organizational relationships. This element highlights the connection between collaboration and the broader inter-organizational network. Highly embedded collaborations between IBCs were observed as IBC networks centered on platform innovator IBCs began to emerge. This continued commitment through deep involvement and high embeddedness results in well established IBCs and boundary networks as organizational platforms for knowledge sharing and integration.

The second important element in the formation of IBCs and boundary networks is the process of resonating values within them. This is the process whereby all practitioners, in their efforts to fulfill the IBC and boundary network missions and goals, share and resonate values aimed at achieving the target business model. The resonance of values in IBC and boundary networks with partners inside and outside the company gives practitioners the capabilities for dialectical thinking and action that generates the new knowledge upon which the IBC and boundary networks are based.

The third important element in the formation of IBC and boundary networks is trust building. Practitioners need to build a platform for creating relationships of mutual trust while also engaging in ongoing exchange, deep collaboration and involvement, high-embeddedness and high-speed formation at the boundaries of multiple and varied IBCs.

These three elements create tight (with deep involvement, high-embeddedness, shared resonating values and trust building) IBCs and boundary networks among, e.g. ASP application innovators, SaaS platform innovators, hardware and software vendors and particular customer content innovators. Practitioners assess and coordinate the business model and pursue business model matching along with the three synergies to optimize the company's business model among knowledge innovators. The process of mutual coordination and collaboration between knowledge innovators brings about co-creation of a new business model and co-evolution for the knowledge innovators.

The creation of IBCs and boundary networks optimal for co-creation and co-evolution is rooted in the dialectical thinking and action of practitioners. As stakeholders, all knowledge innovators must pursue dialectical synthesis of contrasting elements to realize the true nature of a co-creating and co-evolving ecosystem. Corporations should place strategic importance on creating dialectical relationships between all stakeholders – corporate management that only pursues short-term gain for shareholders is not optimal, because business that only focuses on short-term achievements cannot maintain long-term competitiveness or bring about innovation, which is fundamental to an ecosystem. Strategic management solely from the point of view of corporate finances is not everything. Top management needs to steer its company in a direction towards trust and human values, and understand that an ecosystem is an organic structure consisting of customers, the company (its staff) and its partners.

The business models of Apple, Google, NTT DOCOMO, Nintendo, Sony and others are created through the pursuit of management that dialectically synthesizes contrasting elements (elements that include the company's objective business models, technological issues, and corporate culture) among knowledge innovators to create long-term strategies for win-win businesses among all stakeholders. As knowledge innovators continue their activities through the mutual formation of IBCs and boundary networks, they co-create and co-evolve new business models that span across corporations and customers.

To do this, practitioners must use dialectical thinking and action to build trust and share values, and share deeply their visions and missions with other practitioners across corporations for mutual business success. Encouraging deep dialectical dialogue among practitioners builds resonance of values and trust and increases practitioners' motivation and their commitment through deep involvement and high embeddedness. Resonance of values and trust building also encourages the formation of IBCs and boundary networks to enable deep coordination and collaboration among practitioners. Dialectical thinking and action like this is the wellspring for the creation, maintenance and development of ecosystems and is the driving force behind sustained corporate competitiveness.

Chapter 3 Conclusions

1. There are many business models for platform innovation. The three types of knowledge innovators – platform innovators, application innovators, content innovators – collaborate with each other to encourage the creation, maintenance and development of platform innovation ecosystems.
2. In creating a new business model as an ecosystem, the process of co-creation and co-evolution through coordination and collaboration among knowledge innovators is vital.
3. As knowledge innovators engage in business model matching and the pursuit of the three synergies, they generate a suitable profit structure for the ecosystem.
4. Knowledge innovators create collaboration networks for diverse business models and bring about platform innovation by optimizing these business models through the merging of multiple collaboration systems.
5. As organizational platforms for diverse collaboration networks, IBCs and boundary networks accelerate knowledge sharing and integration. IBC's and boundary networks merging external partners and customers bring about ecosystems through hybrid innovation.
6. Leadership integrative capability founded on the dialectical thinking and action of knowledge innovators gives birth to IBC and boundary networks based on the elements of commitment through deep involvement and high embeddedness, resonance of values, and trust building.

4 *Hybrid Innovation in the Semiconductor Industry*

4.1 Semiconductor Industry Innovations

With the continuing development of horizontal business systems in the semiconductor industry mainly since the 1990s, specialized businesses involved in semiconductor design, manufacturing, and design tools development are appearing one after another. Examples of these 'fabless company' trends can be seen with US companies such as Qualcomm that has a monopoly in mobile telephone semiconductors, NVIDIA with its worldwide share of graphics processing semiconductors, eSilicon that designs the chipset for the iPod, as well as Japanese examples such as MegaChips – companies that specialize in semiconductor design businesses, but don't actually have semiconductor foundry facilities. On the other hand, there are businesses that specialize in ultra-low-cost semiconductor manufacturing such as Taiwan Semiconductor Manufacturing (TSMC) and United Microelectronics Corp. (UMC).[1]

Factors behind these horizontal business developments include the increasing specialization and high performance of semiconductor technologies, rapid increases in demand for diversification, performance and cost reductions that make all stages of business difficult for a single company to perform, and the advantages to be gained in scalability through specialization in particular areas of the sector. Horizontal business development is especially pronounced in digital businesses such as the software, hardware, semiconductors and ICT companies.

Through the cases of global leaders Qualcomm, eSilicon and TSMC, this chapter looks at the value chain coordination of virtual vertical integration of these global partnerships through IBC formation, not only to promote the company's innovation activities, but to provide new value for customers' innovations within the horizontal structure of these corporations' manufacturing businesses. This chapter also describes hybrid innovation in Fujitsu as a 'New IDM' company in Japan through collaborative strategies.

4.2 Changing Value Chains in the Semiconductor Industry

Because of technological innovations, the structure of the semiconductor business has transformed from the old set development (system development) vertically integrated model consisting of design, manufacture (front-end/back-end), design tools and semiconductor manufacturing equipment, to a segregated, independent and open business

---

1   Intel, Texas Instruments, and ARM are vertically integrated IDMs specializing in development and manufacture of particular semiconductors (MPUs, DSPs, CPUs respectively), whose products are default standards worldwide.

structure consisting of these individual business elements. The modern semiconductor manufacturing industry consists of individual business elements including a diverse range of individual players who 'compete and cooperate' with one another (see Figure 4.1 'semiconductor sector business model').

In contrast, companies like Panasonic, Toshiba, and Fujitsu in Japan, and Samsung in Korea are vertically integrated semiconductor makers (called 'IDMs' – Integrated Device Manufacturers) that make semiconductors for their own systems (set products) and sell semiconductors to other companies. As well as the total set makers like Panasonic and Toshiba, there are also semiconductor makers that do not produce set products (Hitachi and Mitsubishi's joint company Renesas, or NEC Electronics (merged with Renesas in 2010) in Japan, or Texas Instruments and Intel in the United States) (see Figure 4.1 'IDM Model').

Furthermore, there are specialist semiconductor development businesses involved in LSI development, design and sales without actually having their own semiconductor production line (fabless manufacturers), and specialist design houses set up as design and development businesses. As well as those, there are developmental vendors called 'IP Providers' that focus on the intellectual property business accompanying the development and sales of semiconductors such as CPU cores and functional blocks (electronic circuits), without being involved directly in LSI products. And further, semiconductor vendors that deal with post-prototype LSI business (open foundry makers) are also on the rise in Taiwan and other places. Taiwan's leading foundry makers include TSMC and UMC (see Figure 4.1 'Horizontal Specialization Model').

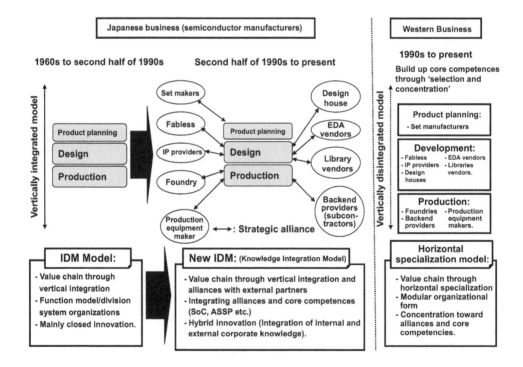

Figure 4.1   Semiconductor sector business model

During the 1990s, the demand for Application Specific Integrated Circuits ('ASIC' – specialized LSI) for certain customers outside of the PC market began to increase, and it became more important for semiconductor makers to respond to the demands of system manufacturing clients. Customer demand also meant that semiconductor makers had to improve precision and speed up development and manufacturing time, and provide customers (system makers) with cheap design tools and related design data. This 'sign off' concept was set up with clearly defined roles for the customer and the semiconductor maker so that there would be no occasions requiring redesign. In other words, a new business model emerged for more efficient design and manufacture of specialist LSIs.

It was during this period that semiconductor manufacturing began to become segregated. Design and manufacture in the semiconductor business is partitioned. Especially in the United States, fabless makers centered around Silicon Valley began to emerge (companies that don't have their own production line, and contract a foundry or IDM to produce a product once it has been designed, and then deal with sales of these products branded as their own – major companies like Qualcomm, Xilinx and NVIDIA in the US, or MegaChips in Japan). Design houses that specialize as design contractors also began to appear.

IP providers (intellectual property for design and manufacture) also emerged as new players during this period. These companies are involved in licensing core technologies for large-scale circuit blocks in microprocessors and specialized design technologies. They include ARM in the UK who provides MPU cores used with the SoCs (System on Chip – called system LSI) in a wide range of mobile phones, and Rambus who have a big influence on what goes on inside personal computers. Because of the increased levels of complexity and integration, reuse of proven IP blocks has become critical for quick completion of SoC design.

IP providers operate under a completely different business model to the design houses and fabless makers, and they have wide-ranging customers including IDMs and foundries, as well as fabless makers and design houses themselves. Because this business model enables start-up with relatively low capital investment in the same way as the fabless and design house companies, and because it has an inherently lower business risk, it is having a big impact on the modern semiconductor industry.

As well as for mobile telephones, SoC is becoming increasingly important for consumer electronics such as DVD players, digital TVs, and digital or networked household appliances. It's crucial to develop LSI's and get them into mass production as quickly as possible because of the shorter life cycles of this type of product. This especially means that since the demand for SoC consumer products is growing due to their inclusion in a diverse range of consumer products such as mobile phones, SoC production cycles are also speeding up.

Set and fabless makers actively seek out and deploy the intellectual property provided by IP providers to avoid prolonged design that would occur if the company had to design a new SoC product all by itself. While the implementation of intellectual property continues, a potential problem for SoC designers when a product using certain intellectual property is upgraded to create the next generation product with different architecture is that they have to dump their experience to date, and redesign everything from scratch. TSMC avoids this with a strategy that standardizes their design and manufacturing processes, and provides and promotes distribution of reusable IP based on common design rules or electronic characteristics. If we think about the background factors here, it is easy to see that consumer electronics manufacturers can increase speed and lower costs, and thus increase their competitiveness, by employing the services of TSMC, a high-tech, large capacity foundry, rather than design and manufacture semiconductors themselves, which in turn also creates a win-win co-evolution mechanism whereby manufacturing contracts to TSMC also increase.

4.3 Semiconductor Company Case Studies

4.3.1 QUALCOMM

The American company Qualcomm's main businesses are wireless communications technology R&D such as CDMA (Code Division Multiple Access), semiconductor and software development, sales and licensing. Qualcomm doesn't provide completed products such as mobile telephone handsets, but has specialized itself as an R&D company that offers a comprehensive range of technological developments for the wireless industry such as semiconductors, licensing, services and applications (specifically, cutting-edge technology for 3G mobile telephones – semiconductors, systems software, developmental tools and network development products). Notably, this fabless company has a near-monopoly on semiconductor chips for mobile telephones worldwide.

Qualcomm's business model includes a broad-based technological license-granting programme for manufacturers (suppliers of semiconductor chip sets, mobile terminals, infrastructure and testing equipment), and provides software and chip sets.

The company's technological policy places importance on technological innovation that serves to mutually and smoothly connect and complement functionality for the advancement of wireless technology, rather than competing technologies. Propelled by R&D, Qualcomm grants a wide range of technological licenses, and offers chipsets and software solutions to set makers that enable suppliers to bring infrastructure, testing equipment and mobile devices to the market more quickly and at a lower cost. This business model enables set makers to commercialize a mobile terminal and participate in the mobile phone market more swiftly and with fewer costs by eliminating the need for the company to spend time on chip set and software development.

The power behind Qualcomm's leap forward in recent years can be put down to the foundry members of their strong partnerships. If the fabless grows, the foundry also grows, and the companies co-evolve in a win-win relationship. Qualcomm's partnerships have grown from the traditional horizontal business model to full-scale technological alliances with the collaboration model involving all business processes from planning and design to mass production.

Qualcomm has taken up the so-called 'Virtual IDM' (Qualcomm calls this 'Integrated Fabless Manufacturing' – IFM) strategy through the alliances with the company's main foundry partners. Virtual IDMs are the strength of fabless makers and combine benefits with real-world manufacturing companies (IDMs). A key feature of Qualcomm's IDM strategy is the close communication and collaboration promoted across the whole supply chain through the boundary networks formed among the fabless, EDA (Electronic Design Automation), IP provider, foundry, assembly (back-end) and testing companies during the semiconductor development cycle, which brings about better performance, greater efficiency, lower costs, and shortens the development period (see Figure 4.2). The virtual

IDM has transformed the old foundry turnkey system (where the foundry company only provided Qualcomm with a completed product that it controlled from the wafer processing all the way to packaging) to a system where Qualcomm itself intervenes and administers at each juncture to manufacture and ship completed chipsets more flexibly in response to actual demand and orders. Because of this, the close collaborative strategies enacted across the IBCs formed between Qualcomm and its partners are of special importance (see Figure 4.2).

The second feature of virtual IDM strategy is the creation of a common platform among multiple foundry partners through the standardization of process technology. This enables an increase in suppliers such as foundries (in the US, Taiwan, Korea, China and Singapore, e.g.) that deal with mass production to stabilize supply and lower costs. To promote these two characteristics and ensure long-term line production capacity, Qualcomm assists in new process development through capital investment in its main suppliers. The company's collaborative strategies with its partners are a critical factor in realizing this type of virtual IDM, as is the formation, development and maintenance of IBCs and boundary networks across IBCs formed among its partners all the way from the up-stream to down-stream processes.

These IDM strategies enable Qualcomm to provide a steady supply of chipsets to mobile phone manufacturers, and quickly respond to constantly changing customer needs. Qualcomm's virtual IDM strategy does not only serve to advance the company's semiconductor technology and coordinate its value chain in the wireless semiconductor market, but also to take on a coordinator role in the finished-product mobile phone market because its mobile phone manufacturing customers use its chips.

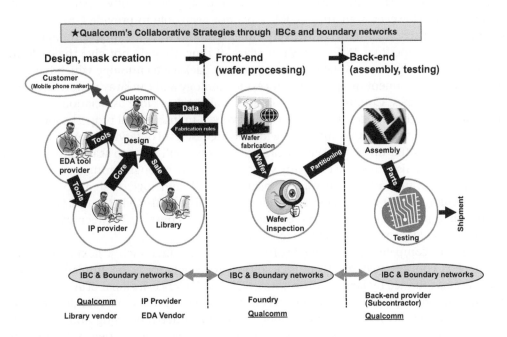

Figure 4.2   Qualcomm's IFM (virtual IDM) business model

Source: based on Qualcomm Publications

4.3.2 ESILICON'S INTEGRATIVE CAPABILITY

Along with Qualcomm, eSilicon is another noteworthy fabless company in the United States. Founded in late 1999 in Silicon Valley, eSilicon was the first comprehensive virtual IDM in the industry – a fully horizontally integrated ICT and semiconductor business involved in everything from semiconductor planning, design including IP procurement, to manufacturing and tests. As a fabless company with no actual production line, eSilicon oversees all processes in semiconductor manufacture – mask design, wafer manufacture, assembly and testing – for each ASIC (Application Specific IC) designed by specialized clients, and entrusts those processes to other specialized businesses. Just like Qualcomm, eSilicon is a company that offers total production by working to link up customers with the design departments in different manufacturers and semiconductor fabricators. In other words, eSilicon is able to provide its customers with optimized solutions by using its strength as a horizontal business involved in manufacturing to merge the knowledge held in the core competencies of various specialist companies.

When they entered the business, eSilicon recognized that the environment was one in which the different processes in semiconductor manufacture were becoming segmented into separate businesses, and formed close collaborations and coordination with top-class manufacturers and experienced professional fabricators to establish a flexible manufacturing supply system and provide many electronics companies with customized ASICs. One of the company's design achievements has been the ASIC for the iPod portable audio player.

eSilicon's virtual IDM differs from a real-world IDM because it realizes ASICs with a greater degree of design freedom, excellent cost performance and swift release onto the market. IDMs can also provide one-stop service for fully customized ASIC development. However, sometimes IDMs have not been able to provide a high level of customer satisfaction in terms of delivery time, cost and functionality. Although IDMs can develop competitive ASICs in a short space of time, they do not give the customer the ability to freely choose intellectual property, or package technology which has a big influence on component mounting or process technology and can sway performance and reliability outcomes. Countering this situation, eSilicon has close associations with top professionals in the semiconductor industry (involved in intellectual property, foundries, packaging and testing), and is able to provide the highest level of service to meet customer needs. eSilicon's full turnkey service means customers don't have to seal contracts with individual specialists, and the company's highly experienced engineering team provides comprehensive support all the way from choosing IP and logic design, to executing layout design to meet customer's various demands. eSilicon also lets the customer freely choose their interface level with the company (terms of contracts between eSilicon and the customer), depending on their circumstances.

The core competence that enables the company to offer such a flexible customer interface is concentrated in the unique knowledge assets found in human resources. eSilicon was founded by Jack Harding, former CEO of Cadence, a global EDA vendor, and Anjan Sen, former president of PulseCore, an IP provider. As well as its founders, eSilicon staff are all high achievers in semiconductor design, wafer processing and packaging, and have experience in strong global corporations such as Altera, Cadence, C-Cube and Quantum. The company has about 100 staff members all over the world, more than half of whom are engineers. As well as EDA tool specialists, the company consists of dedicated IP core teams and DFT (designed for testing) engineers, package and quality control experts.

There are back-end design and manufacturing engineering teams in the company, and each team is loaded with professionals highly experienced in the semiconductor industry. The company has established its own highly flexible and original design methodology to enable it to respond across a range of customer interfaces (contractual terms demanded by customers).

The back-end design team consists of seasoned engineers with an average of 18 years experience in ASIC design for personal information equipment, digital image processing, home networking, business networking, Broadband communications and other areas. These engineers have proven track records at Agere Systems, Bell Research Laboratories, Cadence, IBM, Intel, LSI Logic, PMC-Sierra, Synopsys, Sun Microsystems and others. On top of that, the manufacturing team has a wide range of technologies fostered through an average of 16-years applied experience in quality, reliability and production yield improvements, test program development, package fault diagnosis, supply chain management and customer service. The engineering team consists of staff with experience at companies like AMD, Intel, Cypress, KLA, Philips, LSI Logic, Xilinx, Adaptec Inc, National Semiconductor and S3. The top-class engineers of the back-end design manufacturing teams have realized collaboration strategies with the thousands of staff members in the specialized manufacturing companies that form their external partnerships.

Centered on the back-end design and manufacturing teams, eSilicon has strategic alliances with world-class design houses, IP providers, foundries, assembly and test houses. Forging these relationships with multiple corporations in all fields gives the customer the ability to choose the best vendor for the product or time. The company's IP provider alliances include major players such as Artisan Components, Virtual Silicon, InSilicon, and PalmChip. Other alliances include leading global companies such as Synopsys for design services, TSMC with its leading process technologies, and Amkor Technology Inc., a leader for assembly and testing. eSilicon does not just coordinate a straight and unified processing sequence to produce a completed device. The company also provides wide-ranging layout design utilities using ICT for customers who do the design themselves, and provides an ICT environment through which customers can select intellectual property and monitor manufacturing processes.

Different design and manufacturing knowledge boundaries exist at eSilicon between the back-end design and manufacturing team members. The key to providing customers with tailor-made LSIs is close dialogue and discussion within and between teams to solve problems that arise during the business processes right through from design to manufacture. This brings about knowledge integration of internal knowledge across the knowledge boundaries along the boundary networks within and between teams. The teams also form close and tight boundary networks to collaborate and coordinate with external partners and customers. In this way, eSilicon is able to create a deep sense of trust with its customers and external partners, absorb wide-ranging external knowledge and integrate it with the company's internal knowledge. eSilicon uses collaborative strategies to build an open service system and further reinforce its full turnkey service and support system to deal with diverse customer needs.

4.3.3 TSMC'S INTEGRATIVE CAPABILITY

TSMC's corporate vision is to be the biggest company providing the most advanced foundry service to fabless companies and vertically integrated device makers (IDMs). This vision was established after the company had already achieved a significant size as a foundry. Supporting its vision, the company has advanced technology to rival any major IDM, and offers services at the lowest possible cost that serve to maximize customer profitability. TSMC's fundamental values are grounded in the four concepts of integrity, commitment, innovation, and customer partnership.

TSMC was founded by its Chairman, Morris Chang. Before founding the company, Chang spent 25 years working for Texas Instruments, during the last six of which he was responsible for the company's global semiconductor business. He then went on to found TSMC after a request from the Taiwanese government who were taking measures to encourage semiconductor business growth. The company was initially a spin-off resulting from the government's industrial policy.

TSMC's 'platform solutions' is a platform that enables the manufacture of semiconductors produced to fulfill wide-ranging customer demands for fortification of applications with special specifications, and customized services for fabless, design house and IDM companies etc. Put differently, TSMC's 'platform solutions' is an easy-to-use environment for customers requiring foundry facilities, and provides the following three functions and services.

Firstly, the LSI design service. Through alliances with partners, this comprehensive design service offers design and manufacturing information necessary for customer designed LSIs (circuit design libraries and verified intellectual properties), and further provides EDA and LSI design services. TSMC is able to provide this excellent design service thanks to its design service alliances (DSAs) and close collaborations with design houses and EDA vendors around the world. This means, e.g. that TSMC can provide customers with a unique library from a library vendor combined with TSMC's own process technology. IP vendors can also use these libraries to develop their own intellectual property and offer it to customers. Furthermore, fabless and design house firms can use intellectual properties and libraries with their own unique LSI design services. TSMC also verifies EDA vendor design tools and process technologies using intellectual property, while EDA vendors can do the reverse, and verify design tools using TSMC's process technology and intellectual property. Because foundries, libraries, intellectual property and EDA all have complimentary relationships with each other, companies can add value to their own services and technologies through mutual collaboration with partners involved in these areas. Put simply, that's the idea of open innovation.

The second point is TSMC's LSI manufacture and turnkey services. These include prototype manufacturing, quality assurance, and semiconductor mask fabrication services (TSMC calls these their 'CyberShuttle' services) all provided to a range of business clients and colleges of engineering. This business model dramatically increases manufacturing yield, and greatly reduces production costs compared to other major semiconductor makers. TSMC is a certified partner of the Design Centre Alliance (DCA), an organization formed of leading global design houses and solutions providers, who also use TSMC's 'platform solutions' one-stop LSI turnkey service to design and manufacture system LSIs to meet their customers' requests.

The third point about TSMC is its unified approach to improving customer services, which enables customers to find out the processing status for their order at any time via the Internet – currently TSMC's customers include 400 companies around the world. To get customers to use the factory as if it were their own, TSMC makes full use of ICT to provide an easy-to-use virtual service in addition to its real-world face-to-face customer dealings. Customers need to be able to access information from anywhere in the world at any time. Through ICT with excellent information confidentiality, TSMC's virtually integrated supply chain provides customers with timely access to production yield management and progress status.

The most significant event in our history is quite possibly the creation of our foundry business model in the semiconductor industry. We have pursued a unified foundry approach since establishment 20 years ago. As a result of our success as a foundry company, many fabless semiconductor companies have been born, thus giving rise to the fabless industry and radically changing the semiconductor world. When our company was originally founded, we only manufactured semiconductors that we were requested to make, but as we began to develop cutting-edge semiconductor process technology, we also began to provide customers with a one-stop design environment and intellectual properties. Services have expanded in tandem with, and as a result of, sustained technological developments. As our manufacturing technologies and design capabilities improve, our relationships with customers have become closer with stronger elements of co-operation. We have extremely strong bonds with our customers these days. (Dr Rick Tsai, President, TSMC)

The strong bonds that Dr. Tsai talks about refer to the trust enabled through the formation of IBC's between TSMC and its customers.

TSMC's overwhelming share of semiconductor manufacturing is due to its ability to entice participation from companies with the technological elements needed to create advanced logic LSI's, such as fabless companies, design houses, IP vendors and manufacturing equipment makers. Providing core high-end technology, these partnerships serve to raise TSMC's competitiveness to a new level. The focal point of this competitive capability is the company's internal design and manufacturing specialization including Web services that enable mask manufacturing, examination, packaging and inspection through alliances brought about by virtual integration with partners including TSMC group companies. TSMC acts as the agent to coordinate the various companies engaged in processes, since the participants in these actual processes are not TSMC, but its group companies and partnerships.

TSMC has also created a flat and flexible organizational system featuring IBCs among and between the managerial layers across its business strategy, R&D, manufacturing, sales and marketing departments. TSMC's internal business processes are seamlessly connected through the boundary networks between these IBCs, and the company integrates its internal knowledge through this structure (internal knowledge integration), and also creates high-quality IBCs and boundary networks among its many partners from design support, prototype service, mask and wafer fabrication through to assembly and inspection, where it integrates external knowledge (external knowledge integration) and the company's internal knowledge to give rise to virtual vertically integrated value chains with its partnerships. Knowledge integration of this internal and external knowledge (merging of internal and external integration networks) gives birth to TSMC's hybrid innovation (see Figure 4.3).

TSMC's 'platform solution' creates a value chain as a high added-value virtual factory through the boundary networks between the IBCs connecting its partners, who consist of numerous fabless companies, design houses, IP, library, and EDA vendors.

> *We want to maintain our win-win relationships with our customers and partners, as well as further increase our market share and win the trust of even more customers. We are not going to change our customer focused and service oriented stance, and we are going to continue to provide superior technology and production. When our customers grow, we grow too. (Chenming Hu, CTO, TSMC)*

TSMC's collaborative strategies with various specialist partners create these win-win relationships and enable the company to provide customers with a wide range of complete and tailor-made LSIs.

Because of the encroaching limitations of Moore's Law – the increasing miniaturization of semiconductor processes – it is becoming even more difficult to deal with problems that arise with design and manufacturing. TSMC has transformed itself into a service business that provides a high-quality design environment offering cost benefits and shorter design cycles due to its strengthening of partnerships and alliances with customers and companies involved in everything from design to manufacturing. In addition to TSMC's

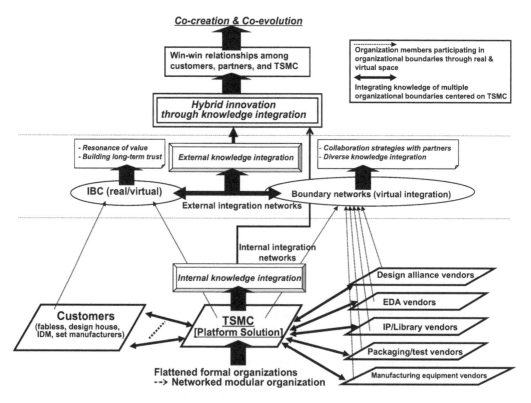

Figure 4.3   TSMC's hybrid innovation through knowledge integration

strength in the manufacturing field, the company has fortified its design and back-end services to realize a virtual, vertically integrated semiconductor business close to that of an IDM (the company offers solutions from design to manufacturing, like the virtual IDM mentioned earlier).

TSMC uses this new coordination and collaboration style with its partner companies to provide new products and services to its customers (fabless companies, design houses, IDM corporations, set makers etc.). For example, IP core and library development partners are customers for TSMC's leading technologies, so once the first semiconductor wafer has been developed for a new semiconductor manufacturing process, the library and IP can be verified. EDA vendors can use TSMC's technology to offer support to fabless companies and design houses for dealing with problems and issues that arise with design, as well as support for the IP and library designs. Or instead, EDA vendors can include script and design guidelines in their EDA toolsets to improve yields for cutting-edge semiconductor designs. This means that for customers who adopt TSMC's leading technologies early on, profits and value can be gained through the services offered by TSMC's third party alliance members (partners).

TSMC does not think it is enough to just provide high-performance technology and manufacturing capability to improve its partnerships with its end-user clients, but recognizes that it must provide the customer with integrated solutions closely linking the work all the way from semiconductor design to back-end services. This enables speedy product development and is an important profitability factor for both parties (a win-win relationship). This is why TSMC has widened its services to include upstream processes of design at the core of its manufacturing, and the back-end assembly and testing processes, thus functioning as a virtual IDM similar to a virtual and vertically integrated fabless semiconductor vendor (just like an IDM, the company deals with everything from design to manufacturing and final testing) (see Figure 4.4).

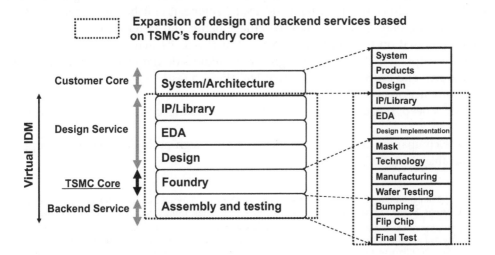

Figure 4.4 Changes in TSMC vertical boundaries – value chain integration
Source: based on TSMC Publications

TSMC's Senior Vice President Mark Liu said: 'Our technological alliances are also a way for us to distinguish ourselves from other companies.' To provide the customer with a total solutions package all the way from design through to manufacturing, TSMC broke free from its old business model and engaged in strategy transformation (transformation to a new integrated model) to become a virtual IDM business promoting collaborative strategies. In TSMC's interpretation, collaboration means moving from a traditional segregated model to an integrated model. In the traditional (i.e. prior to 90nm) model, there were clearly defined roles and responsibilities between foundries and their customers. Foundries were 100 per cent responsible for process technology, while ustomers were responsible for the design, including IP and library selection.

But in the new nanometer age, the responsibilities for integrated design for manufacturing, concurrent SPICE[2] model development, advanced design flows, library, IP optimization and production are to some extent shared across the relationship. The result is a new definition of collaboration – the TSMC definition of shorter time to market, greater customer product differentiation, accelerated defect reduction, and faster yield ramp (see Figure 4.5). In the past, TSMC's strategy was to fabricate semiconductor devices designed by customers using mature semiconductor processing technology from top semiconductor manufacturers (IDMs). However, these days the company applies the 'new integrated model' as a virtual IDM for close collaboration with customers all the way from process development through to circuit design and manufacturing.

One of TSMC's success stories is Altera, who have had a long-term collaboration strategy through this new integrated model. Altera[3] and TSMC have worked together in FPGA[4] technology since 1993. From design through tape out,[5] they are constantly refining the manufacturing process, resulting in chips that are rolled out successfully from node to node. Traditionally, foundries and their IC customers worked in their respective areas – manufacturing process development and IC design – somewhat autonomously. This resulted in longer time to market and higher costs. Through the new integrated foundry model as shown in Figure 4.5, Altera and TSMC engineers collaborate on manufacturing process development and IC design to achieve better and faster results, the benefits of which are passed on to customers. TSMC often checks its manufacturing process with Altera test chips. Test chips enable engineers to address design issues upfront, and verify circuit design and process characteristics. For Altera, a faster manufacturing ramp means a faster production cycle for devices.

TSMC's deep, broad collaboration with Altera assures customers' success from start to finish.

These companies' collaborations enable swift design problem-solving and supply of a predictable product.

---

2   SPICE (Simulation Program with Integrated Circuit Emphasis) is software that simulates analog characteristics of electronic circuits. Modern LSI circuit design involves simulations mainly using Spice for analog circuit design.

3   Altera Corporation is a pioneer in programmable logic solutions. They have contributed to the swift and cost-effective success and differentiation of market innovations by system and semiconductor corporate users. After developing the world's first PLD (Programmable Logic Device) technology in 1983, Altera continues to lead in programmable logic innovations.

4   FPGA is an abbreviation for Field Programmable Gate Array – an LSI programmable via the 'field' (a semi-custom LSI where the logic gates are arranged in an array).

5   LSI design is a word used to describe completed design. This expression has come to mean the magnetic tape that is output and handed over to the mask fabrication department once the LSI design is complete and the mask data has been created.

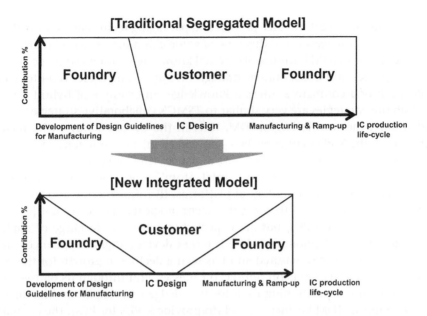

Figure 4.5   New integrated model in TSMC

In a broader sense, the 'new integrated model' provides a total solution 'turnkey service' to customers from design through to manufacture by virtue of these collaborative strategies with partners.

We will be continuing with our foundry business. However, to raise the profile of TSMC's brand, we would like to develop into a business that can offer superior value. One of our new business approaches will be the 'turnkey service.' Two or three years ago we were not able to offer this kind of service, but thanks to modern technological advances, we can now. (Dr Rick Tsai, President, TSMC)

This turnkey service that CEO Tsai talks about gives the end-user, i.e. the customer, the advantage of being able to order things from one company, because the company can offer the customer a total service all the way from LSI design to manufacturing. In this way, TSMC is transforming from its horizontal business model to a vertical business model through its strategies that include its diverse partners and customers, to unify and merge design and manufacturing due to the radical changes in modern technology. TSMC has had to change some of the specialized functions of the horizontal business model it has used to date, so that the company can meet the greater variety of demands for SoCs for future Broadband, ubiquitous and wireless communications that will accompany the frantic pace of technological change brought about by miniaturization. TSMC's business model shift to the 'new integrated model' means the same thing as Qualcomm's transition to the 'virtual IDM' business model discussed earlier.

The IDM business model itself is also gradually changing in response to business model changes like TSMC's. For example, Japanese IDM company Fujitsu Semiconductor Ltd (Fujitsu hereafter) have a basic agreement with TSMC for miniaturized process and packaging manufacture and development, for manufacturing 40 nm and 28 nm logic ICs, as well as a 28 nm high-performance process and packaging technology jointly developed with TSMC. One of the features of this type of value chain for semiconductor processing and manufacture in an IDM is the use of external knowledge through strategic outsourcing to other companies and collaborative strategies (Fujitsu calls these 'Fab-lite' strategies) and integration of a company's internal knowledge, an example of hybrid innovation. Fujitsu's 'Fab-lite' strategies are very similar to TSMC's collaborative strategies.

Furthermore, the world's largest IDM, Intel in the United States – who have an 80 per cent share of the MPU market for PCs – embarked on a comprehensive technological alliance with TSMC in March of 2009.[6] At a glance, this looks like the manufacturing agreement for the simple and low cost 'Intel Atom'[7] processor. However, this alliance actually covers all areas of technological platforms, IP, infrastructure and SoC solutions. The semiconductors produced through this technological alliance are not just products for net book and desktop PCs, but are expected to have a wide range of applications in devices such as smart phones, mobile Internet devices, digital appliances etc. Since the MPU for PC market has matured and has seen a decline in growth for the first time this century, Intel has its sights on non-PC businesses, and through its partnership with TSMC, the company is positioning itself for fullyfledged participation. This means that while Intel retains its IDM business model (to provide MPUs for PCs), the company also intends to bring about hybrid innovation by absorbing and utilizing external knowledge from other companies through collaborative strategies to incorporate the value chains in the company's internal knowledge with the value chains in new product territories.

The examples of Altera, Fujitsu and Intel are cases of hybrid innovation, as is TSMC's case with its move away from its simple foundry business model through collaborative strategies to absorb the external knowledge and design know-how of other companies and integrate them with its own internal knowledge to expand its value chain.

Foundries initially experienced growth because they were able to produce the semiconductors they were contracted to manufacture quickly and cheaply, but the expanding demand in recent years for SoC's with nano-level miniaturization has shifted the goal posts. As well as this, foundries require large capital investments for their production lines, and must be able to deal with user demands for small lots for a large range of products, and short turnaround times; which means that the older and simpler manufacturing contract business model can't really deal with customer needs or indeed maintain corporate profitability. What's more, nano-level miniaturization raises a whole range of technological hurdles[8] that are extremely difficult for a single company acting independently to overcome. This is another reason why companies have to form collaborative strategies across their various individual business areas (design/ manufacturing/back-end etc.). Viewed in this way, the boundary is no longer just a simple contract – the especially important business in developing and designing SoC's is in value chain upstream design support through close collaborations between the foundry and fabless and IDM companies. It has become even more important for foundries to deepen

---

6   However at the time of writing this work, concrete results for alliances relating to technology were unclear.

7   The Atom processor announced by Intel in March of 2008 is an energy-saving microprocessor best suited to submachine applications in a wide range of devices such as smart phones, handheld devices, tablet PCs, net books, simple desktop PCs and so forth.

8   Problems include increasing design complexity, crosstalk noise, higher mask costs etc.

the level of collaboration with fabless companies and IDMs all over the world so they can provide customers with the best solutions.

4.4 'Networked Modular Organizations' Realizing Virtual IDMs

Just like Qualcomm, eSilicon and TSMC, a characteristic of the organizational systems in the semiconductor industry is the segmentation of various specialized functions into individual professions across the whole value chain in the semiconductor market, in what has been termed 'modular organization' (Sanchez and Mahoney 1996, Lei, Hitt and Goldhar 1996). Accessing and combining the resources and capabilities of modular organizations dispersed within and outside a company enables it to provide products that meet diverse customer needs by merging a range of high-performance specialist technologies. Modular organizations with individualized professional functions are especially noticeable in industries such as computers where there are established areas of standardized technology or particular industrial structures in high-tech fields. The concept of merging a company's existing capabilities with a diverse range of external capabilities is important for these businesses.

Just like these cases, the semiconductor industry's accelerated horizontal integration has given rise to a new business model, where the foundry business is skilfully combined through collaborations and coordination across IBCs with the capabilities of these modular organizations – illustrated by TSMC's interpretation of its partners as modular organizations with capabilities (EDA, IP, library, back-end processing etc.) external to the company's own central foundry capability. On the other hand, companies like Qualcomm and eSilicon that have specialized their competencies in semiconductor design and manufacturing knowledge, without actually having semiconductor mass production facilities, interpret their design, IP, providers, foundry, assembly, and testing partners as modular organizations, and provided turnkey service to customers by merging their partners' capabilities across IBCs. In this way, TSMC, Qualcomm, and eSilicon have raised the level of modularity in their organizations amidst a complex industrial structure, and by designing an optimum way to interface capabilities between the modular organizations, they have been able to remain cost competitive in an environment of ferocious technological changes.

Existing research (Schilling and Steensma 2001) describes this connectedness between modular organizations as a 'loosely coupled organization' (Orton and Weick 1990), as opposed to tight vertically integrated organizations (e.g. IDMs). If business interfaces between all functions (design [fabless], manufacturing [foundry], assembly, and testing) are standardized or for mature technology (e.g. design and manufacturing process technology from the last generation), it can be said that there is weak interdependence between the individual functions – the fabless, foundry, IP providers etc. – and that they are loosely associated. However not all semiconductor commercialization relies on existing technology. In a world of rapid technical innovation and change with high levels of cutting-edge technological elements, semiconductor development is not carried out through this kind of loosely coupled organization system. In other words, modular organization based upon simple manufacturing contracts (Baatz 1999, Holmes 1986) (using old or mature technology), simple business operations or 'routine' outsourcing (Lepak and Snell 1999, Belous 1989, Davis-Blake and Uzzi 1993) do not adequately describe the current day model. By contrast, companies require strong interdependencies between the functions and modules in fabless and foundry corporations, and need to switch over to the 'Virtual IDM' or 'New Integrated Model' business models.

Qualcomm, eSilicon, and TSMC needed new meaning and strategic action to respond with technological solutions (existing technology? a mixture of existing technologies? improvements? brand-new technology? etc. ...) that merge and coordinate the capabilities of dispersed specialist technologies to satisfy more and more diverse customer needs (quality, functionality, delivery time etc.). For these reasons, these corporations have to share and merge different knowledge dynamically and in real-time with their partners and customers through the IBCs based on the virtually integrated (virtual IDM) or new integrated business models. Therefore, compared to the loosely coupled modular organization, these organizational systems (virtual IDM and new integrated models) should be called 'networked modular organizations' because the interdependencies across the organizations are much more tightly coordinated. In the semiconductor industry, where functional roles are assigned across fabless and foundry companies, interdependencies between different organizations vary, and fabless and foundry corporations adopt a modular organization or networked modular organization system according to the degree of interdependency required to commercialize a semiconductor product (with new or existing technology).

4.5 New Business Models and Organizational Systems in the Semiconductor Industry

Qualcomm, eSilicon and TSMCs' semiconductor industry business models involve strategies that skilfully use modular organization and networked modular organization structures to merge the knowledge dispersed within and outside their organizations. Information sharing and joint development with IP, library, EDA partners etc. about semiconductor design and processes for mass production encourages open innovation. To achieve this business model, it is important that a company specialize its field of expertise and capabilities (TSMC with its foundry capability, Qualcomm and eSilicon with their high-level design capabilities) and form IBCs and boundary networks for collaborative strategies.

In contrast, IDMs such as Japanese semiconductor makers Panasonic, Toshiba, Fujitsu and Renesas, American companies Intel and Texas Instruments, and Samsung in Korea are the complete opposite of the modular organization or networked modular organization systems of Qualcomm, TSMC, and eSilicon. An IDM is a vertically integrated structure where all functions (technological and organizational) are closely bound together within the organization to merge capabilities in a closed innovation business model. As mentioned in Chapter 1, closed innovation IDMs develop their own specialist technologies and pursue unified knowledge integration about design and manufacture within themselves to provide customers with all solutions. Important to the success of this business model is coordination and collaboration across the inter-organizational networks within the company (IBCs and boundary networks between IBCs), and for the company to be well versed in all its areas of specialization.

How then, have the Japanese semiconductor makers of the past been able to continue with this vertically integrated IDM model? One of the common reasons is 'unified development and manufacturing'. LSI technological innovations are extremely swift, and have been advanced many times with 'development design and manufacturing rules' to meet set products (systems) needs for higher functionality, LSI miniaturization for compactness, and lower power consumption requirements. Traditionally, companies in Japan that embarked on semiconductor businesses using the vertically integrated model accumulated experience and knowledge in development design and manufacturing, and developed new technologies through coordination and collaboration between development design departments and manufacturing departments, in addition to actively pursuing engineer training. Similar to technological innovation in the American model, Japanese semiconductor makers largely focused on accumulating resources of invisible tacit knowledge through technological capability accumulation and personnel training, rather than selling off businesses with low profitability and personnel restructuring. From the latter half of the 1990s, Japanese semiconductor makers began to shift towards strategic alliances with partners involved in particular specialist technologies and to promote collaborative M&A strategies to form 'hybrid innovation-based firms' called 'new IDMs' (a knowledge integration model) (see Figure 4.1 'New IDM model' and Figure 4.6).

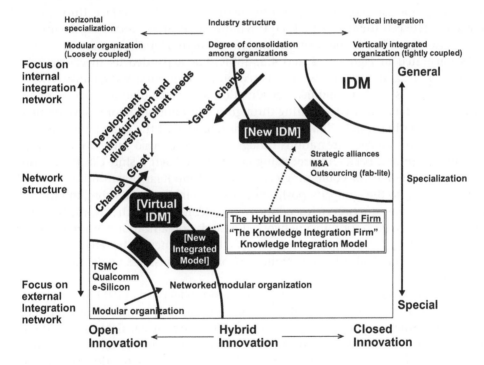

Figure 4.6   The new hybrid innovation-based firm in the semiconductor industry

Now in the twenty-first century however, LSI design, development and manufacturing has entered a new stage. The mass production age of standard generic semiconductor MPU and DRAM components is transforming into the SoC era of small production runs for diverse customized products (although mass production of many product types is still necessary), as Broadband and mobile phone service developments require even higher functionality, and converged communications and broadcasting applications, and LSI's for vehicles and so forth rapidly appear on the market. Accompanying all this are the fast-paced technological developments for higher levels of LSI integration and miniaturization, and thus the demand for even stronger linkages between semiconductor design and manufacturing process boundaries that were separated during the 1990s.

Engineers have especially had to start thinking about semiconductor designs that consider future manufacturing processes. Furthermore, simple optimization through data feedback between parallel processes in conventional semiconductor design and manufacturing is clearly insufficient for nano-sized compact LSI design. This is because conventional LSI design and manufacturing rules are undergoing a dramatic transformation. As mentioned earlier, foundries TSMC and UMC set up a business model with separated design and manufacturing, but the business model demanded by twenty-first century SoC development does not involve a simple interface through explicit knowledge between these areas; rather, it requires a business model that focuses on the mutual interdependencies between the design and manufacturing processes.

As illustrated in Figures 4.4 and 4.5, TSMC has expanded its specializations into design, support, and back-end services based on its core foundry capability. This means the company has further solidified coordination and collaboration with its traditional partners, deepened knowledge sharing through the promotion of joint development and information sharing, and built a new integration model. At the same time, the company has nurtured knowledge integration through its own internal integration networks to refine its design and back-end processing capabilities. Such a shift can be described as moving from the idea of combining capabilities of modular organizations specializing in various areas, to the company positioning itself to incorporate strong interdependent elements of various functions (closed innovation elements), in other words transforming from a modular organization to a networked modular organization with reinforced intra and inter-company convergence, as a virtual IDM (or new integrated model). These trends indicate a gradual shift away from the horizontal business model to a vertical one (see Figure 4.6).

The networked modular organization business model (virtual IDM or new integrated model) is able to provide individually customized solutions to meet customer needs. As Qualcomm, eSilicon, and TSMC have shown with their virtual IDM or new integrated business models for knowledge integration, bringing together elements of both closed and open innovation in this manner can be interpreted as hybrid innovation. The strengthening of these links with external modular organizations to form networked modular organizations means Qualcomm, eSilicon, and TSMC have shifted to become 'hybrid innovation-based firms' (the knowledge integration model) (see Figure 4.6).

However, TSMC does not perform all design and back-end services, and maintains its design centre alliances (DCA) and relationships with back-end service provider modular organizations, and intentionally changes the vertical boundaries through the new integrated model virtual IDM concept to respond to changing circumstances (thorough consideration of size of customer, degree of technological difficulty, price and delivery time etc.). Fabless companies Qualcomm and eSilicon have adopted the virtual IDM networked modular organization business model for the same reasons. Fabless and foundry companies scan over different technological areas surrounding their own business domains, and as discussed in Chapter 2, these companies raise the quality of their boundary vision to focus on flexibly adjusting their value chains.

Japanese IDM companies are also beginning to change their traditional business models in response to the miniaturization of semiconductor processes (Figures 4.1 and 4.6 'New IDM Model'). One is example of this is Fujitsu, who call this the 'New IDM', a company that has shifted to a business model focusing on external partnerships, and an IDM structure that doesn't place tight restrictions on function. This is because the limitations of total intra-company development have been reached (especially in regards to developmental costs) due to the rapid advances of integration in recent years, and the diffusion of highly specialized technologies such as IP, library and EDA. By contrast, since using IDM capability efficiently makes the best use of knowledge resources in other companies to satisfy customer needs, it has become important. Although external specialist organizations (fabless, design houses, IP providers etc.) are able to provide individual specialized services, in order to finally produce a system LSI (SoC) that customers want, the need for an integrated approach across the specialities in the IDM will most certainly arise due to those customers' demands and usage methods.

For instance in the highly specialized area of image processing chips, technological issues arise such as coordinating software functions and buffer memory, and coupling CPUs and other chips with integrated LSIs from other specialist companies. In such cases, the IDM has to function as the total producer, and play a coordinating role by intervening between the customer and external specialist companies. Moreover, interactive feedback is accelerating between specialist companies and all sorts of specialist departments (design, EDA, mask, manufacturing, and back-end processing departments) because of the ambiguous boundaries between design and manufacturing processes for miniaturization. Movers and shakers and organizations with initiative are required all the way from design through to manufacture to deal with these technological changes. Japanese corporate IDMs that have proven track records in making sufficient efforts to know about all the various specialist areas and use this strength are able to provide customers with a unified full turnkey service.

Accordingly, while Fujitsu maintains its traditional IDM function, the company engages in strategic alliances and M&A with external partners including Fujitsu group companies (design house, foundry, back-end process and sales companies) to intentionally merge internal and external integration networks to absorb external knowledge into the company, and swiftly meet diverse customer demands (through various contracts for set design, software, LSI design etc). Fujitsu's aforementioned collaboration strategy with TSMC through its 'Fab-lite strategy' for joint development of next-generation processing and packaging technologies is an excellent example of knowledge integration of internal and external knowledge. Both of these companies simultaneously use their core competencies for closed innovation, while aspiring to hybrid innovation with open innovation merging the expertise of partners.

The core frame of Fujitsu's business model shift from the IDM model lies in the shift from miniaturization processing and manufacturing to product development and IP focusing on developmental investment. The company consolidated and merged its upstream semiconductor processing lines (from a six inch line to a one inch line, an eight inch line to a three inch line) to streamline its manufacturing capability. While the company completely controls fabrication of logic ICs up to 45 nm, the company is in joint development with TSMC for processing and high-performance packaging technology for products smaller than 40 nm, and contracts some of its manufacturing to TSMC. Fujitsu's collaboration and Fab-lite strategies with TSMC create a business model for advanced and efficient semiconductor manufacturing.

Moreover, in product planning and IP development, Fujitsu focuses on developmental investment upstream in the value chain, and nurtures collaborative strategies with leading partners around the world while engaging in strategic M&A. As part of these policies, Fujitsu has set up its 'Graphics Competence Centre' in Germany for in-vehicle graphics technology development, and 'Fujitsu Semiconductor Embedded Solutions Austria GmbH' in Austria for software development. Fujitsu also bought up West Chip Star in China for microcontrollers designed for household appliance products, and has recruited development staff from Freescale in the United States for acquisition of RF license technology. As well as its collaboration with TSMC in Taiwan, the company teamed up with the 'Institute for Information Industry' to establish 'Fujitsu Global Mobile Platform Inc.' for development of WiMax applications.

Through these global alliances and M&As, Fujitsu has gradually been transforming its IDM model to a knowledge integration model with collaboration strategies focusing on the external knowledge of its partners. This means that with its changes to its business model in all business processes from product planning and design through to manufacture, Fujitsu also has become a hybrid innovation-based firm (knowledge integration model) that it calls a 'New IDM' with its shift from closed innovation to hybrid innovation (see Figure 4.7). This further means that the company's organizational system has transformed to the 'semi-structure' of a modular organization in the conventional vertically integrated organization (see Figure 4.6). The new IDM business model creates win-win situations for customers and partners and enables the realization of world-class customer value.

IDM, fabless and foundry companies like those above have to dramatically change the design and manufacturing rules to meet a diverse range of customer demands and deal with changes to technology such as miniaturization. For this reason, a new organizational system is required, not just the traditional vertically integrated or modular models. This will be a robust organizational system that can deal with the dynamic environment of changing markets and technologies, and includes the merits of modularity and convergence: the hybrid innovation-based firm (the knowledge integration firm). As mentioned in Chapter 1, skillfully creating and recreating dynamic IBCs and boundary networks between IBCs that include customers and partners both in and out of companies to incorporate a wide range of knowledge is the key to giving birth to this knowledge integration model. In other words, a knowledge integration firm is based on a corporate model that simultaneously promotes closed and open innovation.

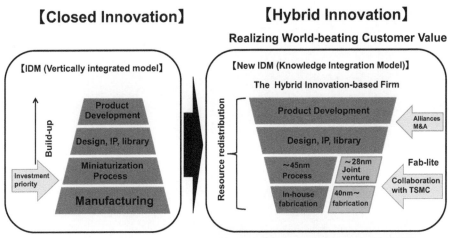

[Closed Innovation]

[Hybrid Innovation]

Figure 4.7   Hybrid innovation (the Fujitsu case)

Source: based on Fujitsu Publications

Chapter 4 Conclusions

1. The current day semiconductor industry is no longer based on the two fundamental theories of vertical or horizontal integration, but requires a flexible approach to meet changing circumstances that merges these two models to create a new business model (new IDM or virtual IDM).
2. High-tech networked modular organizations such as Qualcomm, eSilicon and TSMC use the virtual IDM model (new integrated model) to create virtual vertically integrated value chains and coordinate corporate supply chains.
3. Fundamental to the creation of virtual IDMs (new integrated model) is the formation of dynamic IBCs and boundary networks.
4. As leading IDMs, Japanese semiconductor makers are shifting over to the knowledge integration model (New IDM) that uses IBCs and boundary networks inside and outside companies to merge knowledge.
5. The new and virtual IDM models are corporate models that promote hybrid innovation through the merging of closed and open innovation, and give rise to 'the hybrid innovation firm' (knowledge integration firm).

5 *Chunghwa Telecom's Hybrid Innovation*

5.1 The Chunghwa Telecom Transformation

Following government liberalization policies effective from 1 July 1996, Chunghwa Telecom was inaugurated upon reorganization of the Ministry of Transportation Directorate General of Telecommunications. As a general communications company, Chunghwa Telecom currently employs about 24,000 people, with its main businesses in telephone line leasing, mobile telephones, and data communications, and offers other services including voice, network, and e-commerce services. Having a long history in the landline telephone business and close relationships with citizens, 99 per cent of households (12,370,000), use Chunghwa Telecom's lines, and the company also has a 60 per cent market share in the international telephone business. The company also performs strongly in the mobile telephone and data communications businesses, having more than 9,440,000 subscribers (40 per cent market share), and more than 4,070,000 users of its HiNet ISP service (50 per cent market share), with over 2,470,000 (50 per cent market share) ADSL customers. Moreover, the company has 1,850,000 FTTx subscribers.

Although the state-owned enterprise system of Chunghwa Telecom remained and the company was increasingly exposed to free competition from the private sector in the land-line and mobile telephone businesses, the company has managed to defend its position as a giant in the industry. The company's ability to control equipment and personnel costs, break into the ADSL and fiber-optic markets early on, grasp technology and provide a range of diverse services are factors ensuring its high market share and high profitability. Chunghwa Telecom began diversifying its main land-line telephone business into mobile and data businesses with the advances in mobile and Broadband communications.

As a state-run organization, Chunghwa Telecom was not able to form subsidiaries and affiliates as it would like, due to restrictions on capital investment.

However, about 10 years after privatization, the framework of the Chunghwa Telecom group began to take shape. After the liberalization of the communications markets in Taiwan, Chunghwa Telecom lost its monopoly over the telecommunications market and became more privatized. The company then had to be more dynamic in its activities to become more sensitive to customer needs and social demands.

Business environments of recent years have been fluctuating wildly due to the influence of ICT and globalization. Under these circumstances, Chunghwa Telecom has worked hard to strengthen its competitiveness and distinguish itself from competitors by continually striving to execute new strategies, reorganize and establish subsidiaries, and form alliances with other companies. For the company to remain as a flexible and protean corporation that 'changes itself before change is forecast', Chunghwa Telecom sticks to the following four fundamental principles:

1. Structural reform for genuine customer satisfaction.
2. Transformation into a collaborative business.
3. Internationalization with 'technological alliances, franchises, and retail alliances' etc.
4. Corporate social responsibility.

Undertaking structural reform to increase customer satisfaction means that management must specifically reflect changing circumstances as they happen in the fluctuating business environment around the company, and carry out organizational reform to ensure corporate competitiveness. Transforming the company into a collaborative company means promoting hybrid innovation to swiftly deal with a range of needs, by forming partnerships with many other companies, and by focusing on collaboration within the company in place of the older-style independent and closed innovation systems described in Chapter 1.

Internationalization through 'technological alliances, franchises and sales alliances' means deepening the company's level of globalization through the deployment of new supply chains and ICT innovations. Lastly, corporate responsibility involves recognizing the societal existence of a modern corporation as a public entity. Chunghwa Telecom has a corporate awareness that says if a company cannot be trusted, or cannot make people happy, it cannot justify its own existence.

Chunghwa Telecom offers a full basket of well-balanced services including landline, mobile communication and Internet services, and holds a 99 per cent share of the general telephone market. Just how was Chunghwa Telecom able to achieve such a turnaround leading to such high profitability? This chapter describes the IBCs Chunghwa Telecom formed within and outside the company that became the well-spring for the dynamic organizational capability at the core of its corporate competitive superiority. The chapter also presents the important network platforms that bring about hybrid innovation as a result of new knowledge created when knowledge embedded in groups or personal knowledge is integrated through IBC 'boundary networks' traversing the company's internal and external organizational boundaries.

5.2 Chunghwa Telecom's Organizational Capability

In 1996, telecommunications in Taiwan were greatly liberalized by the passing of three laws (the Telecom Act, the Directorate General of Telecommunications Ordinance Act, the Chunghwa Telecom Act). This was accompanied by the privatization of Chunghwa Telecom and the introduction of competitive markets to wide-ranging telecommunication businesses. As a leader in the Taiwanese communications field, Chunghwa Telecom holds a competitive edge in the areas of research and development, sales, distribution systems, and human resources compared to other companies.

It is often reported in the media that the success of Chunghwa Telecom is due to its ability to promote research and development based on its accumulated technological assets, its strong distribution system, its ability to introduce new services and its low-cost policies. These, however, are only superficial observations. There really hasn't been any thought regarding the success of Chunghwa Telecom much deeper than this. It is said that Chunghwa Telecom certainly holds the number one position in Taiwan in the area of telecommunications research, and big corporations in Taiwan have been restructuring in response to fierce market conditions. So what are the real factors behind Chunghwa Telecom's successful reforms?

5.2.1 CHUNGHWA TELECOM'S ORGANIZATIONAL REFORMS

When Chunghwa Telecom was a state-run public company, it was run with the idea that 'It's not good to make a loss, but we don't need to make a profit either' – similar to a non-profit organization. As a large-scale public utility, the company had deep-rooted conservative ideas and behaviors stemming from its long history and 'state-run company' habits and mentalities. However, in the ICT revolution and globalization of recent years, Chunghwa Telecom did not only have to improve the efficiencies of its traditional businesses, but it also had to change its strategic approaches to distinguish itself from other companies and fortify its competitiveness.

CEO Hochen Tan took the lead by formulating the concept of reform through 'collaborative strategies', and founded a business reform committee to strengthen management practices. Since its beginning, the committee, consisting of the CEO and Vice CEO, departmental chiefs, group officials and so forth, has held meetings every Monday morning from 10 o'clock for about an hour and a half. CEO Hochen Tan had this to say about the circumstances surrounding modern corporations:

> *Comparing past and present strategies, the biggest difference is that in the past, armed conflict was generally interpreted as something that occurred between nations, but now in the modern era, conflict isn't limited to countries. Nowadays small organizations consisting of perhaps only a single person can fight another country. We have already entered the world of 'asymmetric warfare.' Asymmetric warfare isn't a war of force against force, but surprise attacks against a country's weaknesses using new and unconventional methods to bring it to its knees.*

Hochen Tan has similar thoughts regarding competition between corporations. No longer limited to large scale corporations who succeed by virtue of their sheer size, it is quite conceivable that a small company or venture could come up with a highly inimitable core capability and win out, especially since the larger an organization is, the more difficult it is for it to move. To avoid this scenario, said CEO Hochen, communication between staff in different organizations needs to be encouraged, because the sharing and exchange of knowledge is extremely important.

An even more important issue for this unavoidable organizational reform, with the loss of market monopoly from liberalization, is that the competition for market share with other communications players is nothing less than a war of attrition, which is why CEO Hochen recognized that it was essential for his business committee to be able to fundamentally and thoroughly respond to change and bring about managerial and organizational reform on an even bigger scale. This committee pushed to transform Chunghwa Telecom from a government bureaucracy into an organizational network with collaborative management.

5.2.2 TRANSFORMATION TO THE NETWORK COLLABORATION BUSINESS STYLE

In a network collaboration business, people do their jobs based on close partnerships formed between people in different departments, or between people with different specializations and capabilities working through personal and organizational conflict. This does not mean a rigid partnership structure, but a new style based on dynamic collaborations and partnership diversity. Network collaboration business means working to bring about new value creation.

After privatization, the springboard for Chunghwa Telecom was the company's plan to re-create Chunghwa Telecom for the future; in other words, the company agreed on a corporate vision. In this vision the company stated their aims to form a highly profitable corporation through originality, high quality, and high efficiency; and to shift the focus from quantity to quality. Based on this reform management style with company-wide participation, concrete productivity targets and so forth were set for each department, and measures to fortify linkups between departments were actively carried out. This was especially achieved over a two-year period from 2003 to 2004 with the nurturing of perceptions to be shared among staff members. As a participatory system to bring about real reform, a specialized organizational structure was established to assign and transfer staff flexibly to reconfigure teams for quick response to project requirements.

To reconstruct Chunghwa Telecom's value creativity, in 2005 the company reorganized its sense of values to give rise to three mid-term managerial objectives for 'more and higher added value', 'diversification' and 'internationalization.' The company was able to extract issues relating to common organizational values, and adopt these into the reform process through the company's transformation to a network collaboration business during 2003–4. This process allowed the company to move away from its bureaucratic culture to the new corporate culture that it practices today. Furthermore, to reconstruct the corporate image and reform corporate culture, Chunghwa Telecom developed a thorough awareness of CSR, and formulated the idea of transforming into a globalized corporation.

Later on, through its process of network collaboration business reforms, Chunghwa Telecom was able to recreate itself as a customer satisfaction-based company. As well as formulating these critical corporate philosophies, the company established its 'working towards real customer satisfaction' long-term vision, and at the same time, as a customer satisfaction oriented business, Chunghwa Telecom established a customer service department. The mission of this organization is to rank the corporate driving forces of customer, society, and staff member satisfaction levels and to pursue overall customer satisfaction throughout society as a whole.

5.3 IBCs Between Organizations

Through its transformation to a network collaboration business, Chunghwa Telecom has formed various IBCs and multilayered and dynamic boundary networks between IBCs inside and outside the company. The following describes in some detail the important marketing and sales IBC, and the product and service development IBC, that lie at the core of Chunghwa Telecom's corporate strategy. Furthermore, this section will illustrate the process of establishing and executing new marketing strategies, sales strategies, new product and service development through integration of knowledge internal to the company with the external knowledge from partnerships via these IBCs and boundary networks.

5.3.1 THE MARKETING AND SALES IBC

It's easy to confuse marketing and sales – marketing sets the stage to try and increase sales, determines what type of users should be targeted, and decides upon market development strategies. Any company that has good marketing will have strong sales, without exception. Marketing and sales are closely interlocked – there are few examples of weak marketing power accompanied by strong sales. Aside from manufacturers engaging in direct sales systems, many companies rely on special retail agreements and dealerships, but take complete control of marketing strategies, while delegating wholesale functions to sales subsidiaries and so forth.

Marketing must ascertain changes in user needs and formulate sales strategies to deal with those changes, whereas sales must work to efficiently sell goods or services based on those marketing strategy proposals. The IBCs formed across Chunghwa Telecom's marketing and sales departments consisted of the internal 'marketing system IBC' and the external 'sales system IBC'.

1) Marketing System IBC

When attempting to increase market share in the communications business there is a tendency to get involved in price wars. Excessive discounting, even if it does serve to barely retain market share, can result in the company losing profitability and hence corporate clout. Initially, after the liberalization of communications, Chunghwa Telecom's performance was sluggish. The company first decided on a sales strategy to reduce fees, but this strategy didn't result in improved sales, and really only reduced its profits. This is because customers generally weren't interested in reduced fees so much as satisfying services and content. Making things cheaper and cheaper doesn't necessarily result in better sales.

This is when Chunghwa Telecom formed its marketing system IBC across the sales planning department, business development centre, and corporate planning department, as a project base to come up with superior marketing strategies targeting the 10 to 30 age bracket. This association didn't just formulate marketing strategies but also took on a leadership role with external organizations. The members of this IBC took charge of developing strategies for products and sales that featured unbeatable and clear selling points compared to competitors.

Chunghwa Telecom's penetration rate is about 90 per cent, and excluding the younger generation, most of this consists of replacement demand, which means that products do not become hits if they don't have plenty of features. In this mature market, Chunghwa Telecom sealed an exclusive supply agreement for animated content with Chun Shui Tang, and as a result of this product planning, the company produced its 'a-huei' hit mobile telephone brand.

One of the planners of the 'a-huei' product had the following to say:

It really doesn't matter how good an individual product is, if it doesn't suit the consumer it won't sell. In the present day mobile phone world, the first thing is to realize that a product won't sell if it isn't distinguishable or doesn't have individuality.

The a-huei was developed to become one of Chunghwa Telecom's leading hit products. The brand is named after a popular Taiwanese animation character, and the mobile phone offers a diverse range of related content. Young Taiwanese these days don't just use their mobile phones for calls, but are interested in important added values of design and content. There is another reason why the a-huei became a hit. The mobile phone terminal used was manufactured by Nokia, a hugely popular brand among young people, so the phone became a hot topic among the younger generation not only because of the rich content included with it, but also because of the popular terminal used.

If we think about the example set by this product, it is clear to see the importance of the capability of creating a product concept through trial and error and by deepening strategies with clever foresight into user needs and wants, and of deciding what sort of sales point should be emphasized, and what type of users should be targeted before releasing the product onto the market.

2) The Sales System IBC

Chunghwa Telecom's sales system IBC has participants from wholesale businesses and mobile terminal dealerships, as well as the general public. The company's business includes processes from development to wholesale activities, but it relies on mobile telephone retailers and specialist carrier outlets for sales. Nevertheless, the company does take charge of nationwide advertising and marketing activities for sales planning, demand and key products. The mobile phone retailers and specialist carrier outlets then mostly focus on the sales activities. Chunghwa Telecom's mobile telephone sales are generally divided between the 'Chunghwa Telecom shops' and 'other dealerships' sales channels.

Mobile telephone retail businesses deal with handset sales and carrier subscriptions. The carrier retail outlets are exclusive franchises set up by dealerships contracted with the carrier. Compared to Japan, the difference here is that the Taiwanese carriers sell national brands such as Nokia and Motorola handsets fitted with their own SIM card, whereas the Japanese carriers all sell their own exclusive mobile phone brands.[1]

Also, dealerships operate as commercial IT entities in addition to their mobile phone dealership businesses. Another feature is that the uniquely branded mobile phones are sold as supplied by OEMs, which combined with rewards from the carrier secures earnings. Chunghwa Telecom is always searching for information about sellable goods and soaking up information about user needs through the retail outlets. The company has a symbiotic relationship with retailers that enables the company to provide details about selling points, new product information and so forth.

The sales system IBC also functions as a communications forum with customers to enable Chunghwa Telecom to receive enquiries about products or deal with complaints

---

1   This means that the Japanese mobile telephone business model is unique; however, after 2012 the SIM lock release system will begin in earnest in Japan.

via mail or phone, and amass all of this information. The objective of this system is to promote swifter responses to customer feedback and improve customer service. Having 30,000 items of user data input each year means there is a constant exchange of information between users and retailers, and manufacturers.

For Chunghwa Telecom, this system of business and service activities closely linked with customers is a valuable source of clues for improving a range of products, because it contributes to the company's ability to put themselves in the position of the user, enabling it to speedily grasp market information and develop products accordingly. Further, because Chunghwa's enquiry system deepens communications with customers, it also deepens customer trust towards the company.

A market is a place where products and the general public meet. Not only is it important to listen to people's opinions about products, but it is also important to analyze their attitudes and behaviors. Of course, in modern times 'the citizen' is not something that can be understood as a uniform entity as diversification and individuality continue to become more pronounced. As mentioned earlier, Chunghwa Telecom's a-huei brand is a successful combination of Nokia – the number one brand in Taiwan – and content targeting the youth market. When young people purchase goods, they look past the price for the value found in diversity and individuality in a product.

Because Chunghwa Telecom has IBCs within and outside itself, it can create dynamic forums (also known as a 'ba') as needed to identify wide-ranging user needs, and consolidate the wisdom that exists in the internal marketing system IBC and external sales system IBC. Chunghwa Telecom achieves knowledge integration through the internal and external IBCs to solve the various problems and issues that arise with market and product development. Its internal marketing system IBC and external sales system IBC are examples of the internal and external integration networks for hybrid innovation described in Figure 1.12 in Chapter 1.

3) Boundary Networks – Networks Between IBCs

Chunghwa Telecom's marketing system IBC decides the outline aims and objectives for its marketing strategies, and functions to crystallize those aims and objectives. The marketing system IBC has three strategies – 'product strategies' and 'sales strategies' targeting mass users, and 'communication strategies' for particular groups. The two IBCs form the base for these marketing activities. The three marketing strategies have a profound relationship to the linkages between the internal marketing systems IBC and the external sales systems IBC, in other words, the network between the IBCs – the boundary networks.

'Product strategy' places a strong emphasis on how well the features of the product are articulated. Since the central issue is achieving high sales in the marketplace, Chunghwa Telecom's marketing strategies require that the company make use of its technological resources to develop products of distinguishable quality, performance, and functionality compared to their competitors.

Chunghwa Telecom's communication strategies serve to raise the profile of the company's products. By appealing to customer satisfaction through uniqueness and a wonderful array of usage applications – features that appeal to the owner's individuality – Chunghwa Telecom can raise products from just simply being 'things,' to being 'things that have meaning'. As already mentioned, a-huei is a product designed to offer this kind of new value to the user.

A critical part of the sales strategy is selection and retention of sales channels. Distinguishable products are purchased by certain types of customers. For example, a sales channel operating near a school would have to provide products appealing to students, and at prices compatible with student budgets. Refining sales channels in this way brings efficiencies in logistics management for stable supply and efficiencies in customer service and promotions. Also, streamlining by stocking original products that other outlets in the area (e.g. mass retailers) do not sell contributes to improve sales and customer retention, which in turn enables the gathering of valuable customer data.

Chunghwa Telecom sees the intelligence gained through the diverse information coming through the various markets as very important. That's why the company focuses on interactive information sharing between the customers, the retailers, and the company itself. In support of this, Chunghwa Telecom has set up an Intumit[2] customer data management system, into which all items from retail shops are input to help the company to get an idea of which products are not selling, product features, customer feedback and so forth. The company uses this system in its activities all the way from devising new sales strategies to providing specialist consulting and new customer services.

Not only is this an excellent information sharing mechanism that allows easy access to retailer information from a computer, but it also enables the company to grasp the state of sales in retailers all over the country in real time, and analyze trends in sales for each of their products. This makes it easier for Chunghwa Telecom to respond to changes swiftly. The information gets shared with staff throughout the company, and enables integration of various departments including the business development center, corporate planning department, sales planning department, and with retailers and dealerships to propel business by acting as a single organization formed by the complementary relationships between the different sections. This is the thing that seals the linkage between the internal marketing systems IBC and the external sales systems IBC, in other words, the network between the IBCs – the boundary network.

Apart from the information system, another important aspect forming the linkage between Chunghwa Telecom and the retail outlets is a mutual awareness of 'retaining customers by focusing on customer convenience'. Without this common awareness the relationship, in other words the linkage, would not work so well. Customer convenience is critical because communications markets have matured and are slimming down, which means even fiercer competition in the coming years. Important to the company's sales strategies is the recognition that more than ever customer retention will be inextricably linked with customer satisfaction, which is why the company is expanding its existing product lineup through alliances with retailers etc., across a national network focusing on customer convenience. Specific joint Chunghwa Telecom business initiatives include support to, and regular meetings with, retailers and distributors to discuss and confirm progress of projects and to provide latest product information in a timely manner, as well as joint seminars and presentations etc.

---

2   Founded in 1999, Intumit Inc. pours its efforts into software development and system convergence centered on Java technologies. The company is very flexible and scalable, and provides application solutions for high efficiency knowledge management. In 2005 Intumit passed CMMI Level 3, international specialist recognition for product development in the spirit of service processes emphasizing quality control.

Chunghwa Telecom promotes communications and information sharing between its organizations and retailers through these real-world business activities and virtually, through the Intumit customer data management system. This enables the two IBCs to be networked, and contacts and values to be shared to build mutual trust and raise the level of access to information and knowledge, which in turn serves to generate hybrid innovation for new product development.

For successful marketing and sales strategies, Chunghwa Telecom has to use collaborative strategies through IBCs formed with external partners to integrate their knowledge with its internal knowledge and promote hybrid information. Realization of the linkage – the boundary network – between the internal marketing systems IBC and the external sales systems IBC is critical to this (see Figure 5.1).

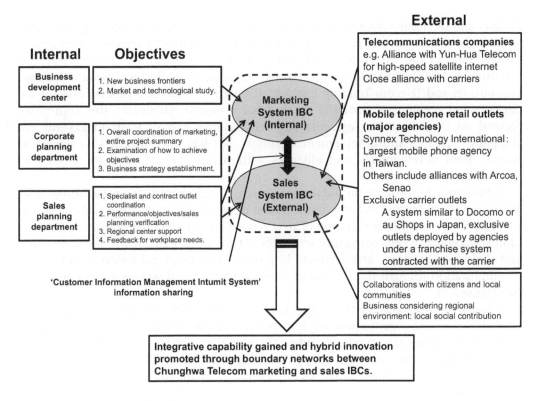

Figure 5.1 Marketing and sales system IBC

5.3.2 PRODUCT/SERVICE DEVELOPMENT IBC

When it comes to the number of engineers involved in development, the number of departments and manufacturers involved, or the developmental costs for products and service development, Chunghwa Telecom is in the top class of telecommunications carriers. To get hit products onto the market quicker than competitors and recover the large capital expenditure involved in service and product development, Chunghwa Telecom is caught up in furious competition where telecommunications carriers are simply risking fate. New product and service development just gets tougher and tougher, with demands for more and more speed and lower and lower costs.

1) The Product and Service Development IBC (Internal)

Product and service development based on the company's unique technology continues at Chunghwa Telecom, and is the responsibility of the company's Telecom Laboratories. Internal product and service development is carried out through the company's Network department, Mobile Business Group, Data Communications Business Group, Telecom Laboratories and Telecom Training Institute. Chunghwa Telecom's 'product and service development committee' generally meets once a month. Originally, this committee focused on considerations regarding research facilities and so forth to expand the company's research and development capability, but has since widened its agenda to include joint developments and alliances with partner corporations to respond to technological innovations.

Chunghwa does not use the old linear research – development – manufacturing – sales business process, but instead employs a system of parallel and concurrent advancement that contributes to the speeding up of new service and product development. This is a unified approach where marketing and sales get involved right at the initial research and development stage, and business is promoted through collaboration and close communication through the company's internal product and service development IBC (see Figure 5.2).

Chunghwa Telecom's research department is separated into specializations. Individual laboratories in the organization are further divided into even more detailed areas of research. To oversee the company's internal research groups in each R&D domain, five separate departments have been set up. They are: Telecom Training Institute; Telecom Laboratories; Network department; Mobile Business Group; and Data Communications Business Group.

Having such a fragmented organizational structure in the various research fields is certainly not optimal for mobilizing personnel in response to a project. Strong leadership in top management is indispensable to most effectively deploy talent across the organization. If you don't have strong leadership at the top, research department chiefs and laboratory directors tend to hold back their best talent for their own research projects.

To overcome this kind of sectionalism, Chunghwa Telecom radically changed its appraisal system for its research and development department. The company established a system whereby credit is given not only to individual achievers, but also to the directors of the research department and laboratory to which those people belong, that contribute to big projects on which the fate of the company is riding. Chunghwa Telecom is able to

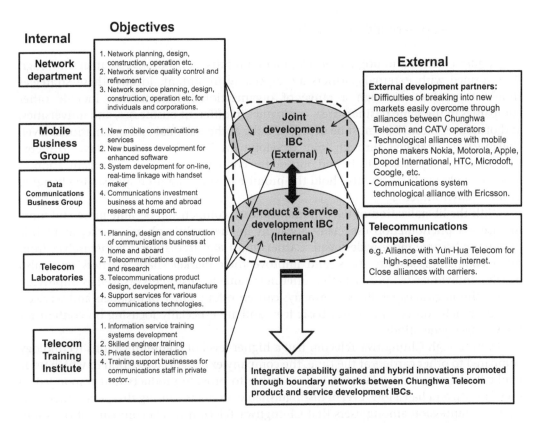

Figure 5.2   Product/service development and Joint-development IBCs

advance with this cross-organizational project team system for research and development. Themes for this system are adopted at the company's monthly 'general technology meeting' and project teams are formed to work over periods of one or two years.

Mobilizing talent from the five research areas for rapid response to projects is definitely not easy. To ensure easy organizational movement at Chunghwa Telecom, the CEO handpicks project leaders for emergency projects and assigns those leaders responsibility for choosing and summoning the best personnel. In this way, team leaders appointed by the CEO can optimally designate and assemble the best R&D specialists from within the company's five R&D units. The cross-organizational project team system enables strong leadership at the top, and successful mobilization of personnel across the various organizations.

Chunghwa Telecom uses this cross organizational IBC (product and service development IBC) to create a forum where necessary (a 'ba') to absorb a wide range of opinions, gather together the wisdom of engineers from various departments, solve a range of problems, and create highly competitive technology. The close communication and collaboration of these project teams enable Chunghwa Telecom to produce leading products in response to the changing times, and this kind of product and service development IBC is a source of the company's core capability (see Figure 5.2).

2) Joint Development IBC (External)

To produce creative and original developmental results, collaborative strategies through IBCs formed with external partners are especially important. Ideally, these strategies should be realized through a range of organizational systems that include other companies in the same business area, companies in different businesses, and universities, and of course, these IBCs must be deployed both at the national and international level. Collaborative strategies through joint development IBCs do not only serve to merge various knowledge from within and outside the company and enable an organization to accumulate know-how, but also hold the promise of speeding up responses to changing business environments.

With the liberalization of telecommunications, competition became more and more intense – a phenomenon especially apparent in the mobile phone market as mobile phone use became more widespread. Carriers must aim to distinguish themselves from other companies, acquire users, and improve their market share. Carriers must also develop individualized products that offer new value to customers, as well as improving their technological capabilities. Nowadays carriers offer a range of products and services, including rich content and lower basic fees, and are especially focusing on content for the younger generations.

Even though Chunghwa Telecom had a higher level of communications technology compared to other carriers at the time, the company experienced a period in which users gradually migrated away because it was unable to provide products that responded to users' needs, and had a low level of distinguishable products. During this period there was a strong impression among users that Chunghwa Telecom was 'a company of tradition, but slow to respond to the market'.

To improve this situation, Chunghwa set up technological alliances with external partners to augment its technological capability at the time, and embarked on strategies to reinforce its brands, services, quality and so forth. This was a process of strategy transformation to move from closed innovation to hybrid innovation, as illustrated in Figure 1.12 in Chapter 1. One of the measures Chunghwa Telecom undertook was to form an alliance with Ericsson and the company's 'emome' mobile portal system technology and content management business.

In Taiwan, where the mobile Internet business is growing rapidly, emome is the first and biggest wireless mobile portal – the Taiwanese version of i-mode (NTT DOCOMO's world-first mobile telephone and Internet access service). Mobile Internet content (information services and e-commerce in the areas of lifestyle, leisure, social networking, MMS (Multimedia Messaging Service), Java, finance etc.) frequently changes, which means carriers must have excellent tools to efficiently stay up-to-date on the content front.

Important to Chunghwa Telecom's services dealing with end users, the company absorbed and merged a range of elements with its own technology to provide personalization of Ericsson's WAP/GPRS services, communications gateways and content management systems, and shared services. The IBC for collaboration strategies with its external partners enables the company to produce products that distinguish it from others. Also, Chunghwa Telecom's wireless mobile portal business model has created win-win relationships with its external partners such as end users and content providers (cp);

in other words, the company has used its 'platform thinking' capability to bring about co-evolution businesses such as emome.

3) Boundary Networks – Networks between IBCs

Products are not created by single technologies, but consist of various elemental technologies bundled together. Chunghwa Telecom's product and service development process consists of the following three technological elements: 'Basic Technology,' 'Key Technology,' and 'Complementary Technology'.

Here, 'basic technology' refers to Chunghwa Telecom's long history of research and development capability with telecommunications technologies, its ICT equipment and works, multimedia and network technologies, communications facilities design and construction etc. This basic technology element is especially important for Chunghwa Telecom's incremental and sustained innovations.

On the other hand, to produce distinguishable and competitive products, 'key technology' and 'complementary technology' are crucial. These two technological elements provide methods for designing ways to introduce products with completely new functions into an appropriate market, or technological methods to change the basic properties such as quality and cost without changing basic functions, or methods to increase the range of models through design, color and size etc., without changing the basic properties of the product. The 'architectural thinking' that includes the 'architectural innovation,' 'modular innovation,' and 'radical innovation' described in Chapter 2 is required for these types of technological strategies to successfully create distinction from other companies.

Chunghwa Telecom has to use collaborative strategies through the IBCs formed with external partners to integrate their knowledge with its unique knowledge to promote hybrid information for the success of these types of differentiating technological strategies. It is also important to realize the linkages (the boundary networks between IBC networks) between the product and service development IBC within the company and the external joint development IBC (see Figure 5.2).

Chunghwa Telecom promoted strategic alliances with a number of companies to encourage the formation of a joint development IBC. One of these was a contract sealed with Nokia to provide a comprehensive end-to-end multimedia messaging system (MMS) for Chunghwa Telecom's high-performance wireless network. Nokia offers a range of end-to-end multimedia messaging solutions including Nokia MMS Center, Nokia Multimedia Terminal Gateway for mobile terminals that don't support MMS, Nokia WAP Gateway, Nokia Multimedia Email Gateway, and Nokia Profile Server. Nokia also provides a personal album application for long-term message storage.

Chunghwa Telecom CEO Hochen says 'we are really happy to be able to further reinforce our association with Nokia. Nokia's big strength is its demonstrated capability and vision to provide customized solutions and services to bring about next-generation services.'

'Nokia's cutting-edge MMS solutions, strong content and applications support ensure Chunghwa Telecom's capability to provide end users with excellent services.', says James Lin, Vice-General Manager of Asia-Pacific Business Development for Nokia's Network Department.

Thanks to this, Chunghwa Telecom users can experience an innovative and easy-to-use multimedia service that supports Chinese language for the first time, and enjoy richness in their messaging with text, imaging, graphics and voice.

Different technologies need to be combined for new product and service development in the communications businesses of today. The question is, how can the knowledge and know-how scattered all over the world be merged? Corporate alliances are co-operations between companies based on conscious and intentional agreements, and as well as being a fundamental strategy, they also provide an important basis for decision-making about 'selection and concentration'. The knowledge integration process is an important consideration for promoting hybrid innovation, as it enables decisions about where, when and to whom business resources should be distributed, and what types of cooperative associations should be formed for merging and complementing resources and functions.

This means that right from the beginning of the process, nurturing careful awareness of development policy and close communications with joint development partners is critical for joint developments involving B to C (business to consumer) or B to B (business to business). To this end, Chunghwa Telecom set out five strict steps for its joint development processes:

1. The 'development vision' step: in this step, strategic targets are set through mutual understanding of strategic values and developmental vision via close communications. It's important to thoroughly examine the necessity of a development, regardless of the source of notions about joint development. Since it is not possible to cancel a development once started, decisions on whether to embark on development shouldn't be taken lightly. Bad decision-making results in wasteful development and visible failure. Therefore, the important thing for planners and developers is 'systems thinking' using the 'top-down approach' business design capability for boundary vision described in Chapter 2.
2. The 'market analysis' step: firstly, in what area is there leeway or potential to get into an existing market? Emerging needs and market place competition must be analyzed. Secondly, explore hidden, non-existent needs and the possibilities of finding new market opportunities in the current market. At this point systems thinking is needed using the top-down and bottom-up approaches linked to the development vision decided upon in the previous preparatory stage.
3. The 'strategy establishment' step: Chunghwa Telecom and its joint development partners use the results of market analysis to think about specific methods of executing a plan and examine whether product commercialization is possible. The most hopeful option is selected from among those judged to have potential, and a concrete joint development plan is established.
4. The 'strategy execution' step: the partners collaborate according to the joint development plan and hold regular meetings to check on progress of the project.
5. The 'deployment' step: both parties establish a deployment plan, and execute it accordingly.

In terms of these five joint development steps, the processes along the boundary networks between Chunghwa Telecom's product and service development IBC and the joint development IBC with external partners are of extreme importance. Hybrid innovation mutually improves synergies of the best knowledge, and enables lowering of risks and costs associated with research and development.

The boundary networks across IBCs are communities that promote the merging of knowledge and technology etc. to speed up hybrid innovation However, the power of these IBCs cannot be harnessed if the IBCs are not properly linked up, regardless of how many IBCs are created internally and externally. New knowledge integration is difficult in an isolated IBC because of the limited amount of knowledge and information flow within it. Therefore, 'linkage capability' between internal and external IBCs is a necessary item for generating core capability.

When observing Chunghwa Telecom and its external partners it is clear to see that there are a great number of multitiered IBCs in existence. The following illustrates the linkages between IBCs through the example of the 'Dopod CHT9000' mobile phone developed by Chunghwa Telecom. Since alliances with other organizations are indispensable for the development of new products, the Dopod CHT9000 was jointly produced by Chunghwa Telecom, Microsoft, Dopod International,[3] and HTC, and is Taiwan's first 3G mobile phone featuring the '3G mPro pro business service' designed for business people.

Manufactured by HTC of Taiwan, the Dopod CHT9000 (Dopod is a brand name of HTC, CHT is the product vendor – Chunghwa Telecom) is a smart phone installed with Windows Mobile 5 that supports W-CDMA/GSM, and is 112.5x58x22 mm in size with a sliding QWERTY keyboard on the left-hand side. The display is a 2.8 inch QVGA LCD, and the device supports Bluetooth and wireless LAN IEEE 802.11 b/g peripheral connections. The device links with Microsoft Exchange Server to push mail and to synchronize schedules, and even supports document viewing including Microsoft Word, Microsoft Excel, and PDF files.

Chunghwa Telecom's 3G mPro business service with the Dopod CHT9000 delivers business news through Push-mail or RSS feed, and offers easy access to the customer centre and financial information. The service screen also provides access to a telephone book and schedule.

The Dopod CHT9000 development was led by a cross-organizational project team. Of course leadership and initiative are essential, but if there hadn't been alliances between departments within the company and with external partners to bring about the design, problems with the process right from the factory floor may have arisen. There could also have been practical problems with the sales department, or failure to satisfy customer needs. The way to solve these potential problems and issues before they arise is to establish close communication and collaboration between different departments in the company and external partners, beginning at the development and design stage.

Core personnel were mobilized from the Telecom Training Institute, Telecom Laboratories, Network department, Mobile Business Group, and Data Communications Business Group, and an internal IBC was formed to develop the Dopod CHT9000. Even though a group of experts in their fields was formed consisting of joint development

---

3   Dopod International Corp. Ltd. operates as a mobile communications company integrating mobile communications with information system technologies. The company offers digital products, including seamless mobility products and solutions, such as smart phones, PDA phones, and accessories. Its handsets offer Internet and other applications, as well as audio-visual functions. The company sells devices to mass consumers in the retail segment in Asian countries, including China, Hong Kong, Indonesia, Malaysia, Taiwan, Thailand, and Singapore. Dopod International Corp. Ltd. has a strategic partnership with High Tech Computer. The company was founded in 2004 and is based in Taipei, Taiwan. As of May, 2007, Dopod International Corp. Ltd. operates as a subsidiary of HTC Corporation.

partners (Microsoft, Dopod International, HTC) and project team members, a range of unforeseen problems and issues arose during the development process. However, if these technological difficulties and issues had been faced solely within the company itself, all that could have been done would have been for people to return to their vertical duties, hold discussions with specialists in the same field about solutions or try to find some sort of useful clues. By contrast, interactive development staff can absorb knowledge and know-how from horizontal organizations in cross-organizational projects, as well as absorbing knowledge and know-how from staff belonging to formalized vertical organizations, and thus pile up even more problem-solving capability.

To generate the most successful outcome for the Dopod CHT9000 development joint-venture between Chunghwa Telecom, Microsoft, Dopod International Corp, and HTC, Chunghwa Telecom formed a joint-development IBC between all the partners to pool together the best knowledge through concentrated communications and collaboration in accordance with Chunghwa's five joint development steps described earlier. The company also strengthened the close synergistic linkages between the two internal and external IBCs to mutually share and merge knowledge. Thus, the Dopod CHT9000 is an excellent example of new hybrid innovation born of boundary networks formed through strong linking of IBCs both in and out of a company (see Figure 5.2).

5.3.3 BOUNDARY NETWORKS CREATING VERTICAL VALUE CHAINS

An IBC is a community that encourages the merging of knowledge and technology to accelerate hybrid innovation, but it is not possible to harness the full power of IBCs unless they are properly networked. New knowledge integration is difficult in an isolated IBC because of the limited amount of knowledge and information flow within it. Therefore, IBCs must be networked to generate core capabilities for entire companies.

In the 'a-huei' product development case described earlier, a vertical value chain was created from boundary networks formed across the various IBCs set up for research, product planning, development design, sales and support business processes within Chunghwa Telecom. A source of Chunghwa Telecom's competitive strength lies in its vertical value chain. Just like Chunghwa Telecom, any company that is faced with intense changes due to shifting market structures and technological innovations, and is constantly looking for new strategies, needs to form IBCs and boundary networks as an organizational system to enable value chain integration (see Figure 5.3).

The a-huei success was overseen by the Corporate Planning Department. To respond to issues and action items, flexible IBCs were formed to enable close communication and collaboration between the Corporate Planning Department and others such as the Sales Planning Department, Business Development Center, Customer Service, Mobile Business Group, and Telecom Laboratories. Multitiered individual IBCs were formed inside and outside Chunghwa Telecom including the R&D IBC, product development and manufacturing IBC, product planning IBC, sales promotion IBC and IBCs with partners. Communication and collaboration through and between these IBCs enabled Chunghwa Telecom to integrate its core knowledge and technology with that of its external development partners and produce a unique and difficult-to-duplicate product.

In Chunghwa Telecom's development system, the project team appointed by the CEO is empowered to nominate and call together the best R&D talent from the five R&D units. Technology, knowledge, and results born through activity in each IBC were exchanged

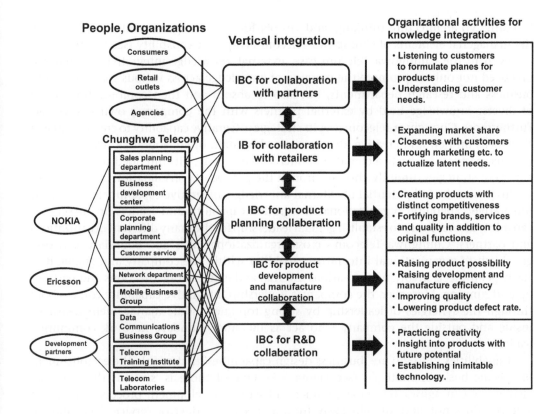

People, Organizations

- Consumers
- Retail outlets
- Agencies

Chunghwa Telecom

- Sales planning department
- Business development center
- Corporate planning department
- Customer service
- Network department
- Mobile Business Group
- Data Communications Business Group
- Telecom Training Institute
- Telecom Laboratories

- NOKIA
- Ericsson
- Development partners

Vertical integration

- IBC for collaboration with partners
- IB for collaboration with retailers
- IBC for product planning collaberation
- IBC for product development and manufacture collaboration
- IBC for R&D collaboration

Organizational activities for knowledge integration

- • Listening to customers to formulate planes for products
- • Understanding customer needs.

- • Expanding market share
- • Closeness with customers through marketing etc. to actualize latent needs.

- • Creating products with distinct competitiveness
- • Fortifying brands, services and quality in addition to original functions.

- • Raising product possibility
- • Raising development and manufacture efficiency
- • Improving quality
- • Lowering product defect rate.

- • Practicing creativity
- • Insight into products with future potential
- • Establishing inimitable technology.

Figure 5.3   Creating vertical value chains with boundary networks

and coordinated by collaborations with other IBCs, which enabled understanding with external partners to be deepened, and collaboration between organizations to be even more productive. The a-huei product development case is an excellent example of vertical integration of knowledge dispersed through IBCs achieving hybrid innovation.

5.4 Chunghwa Telecom's Seven Boundary Vision Capabilities

Chunghwa Telecom uses collaborative strategies formed through the internal IBCs, and IBCs with external partners to integrate their knowledge with its unique internal knowledge to promote hybrid information. A key factor in promoting hybrid innovation is the realization of boundary networks linking the internal and external IBCs, while the boundary vision of practitioners plays a vital role in deciding what kind of IBCs to form, and how they should be converged. Now, let's consider Chunghwa Telecom's seven boundary vision capabilities.

As mentioned in Chapter 2, there are seven capabilities required to improve the boundary vision of corporate leaders and managers to promote hybrid innovation. They are: i) external knowledge integrative capability; ii) strategic integrative capability; iii) organizational integrative capability; iv) leadership integrative capability; v) systems thinking; vi) architecture thinking; and vii) platform thinking. Capabilities i) to iv) are the managerial elements of Chunghwa Telecom's corporate capability (see Figure 5.4).

Even in the Chunghwa Telecom case, external knowledge integrative capability is practiced not only to promote the merging of knowledge across various specialist fields, business and research departments, but also to absorb and then combine the wealth of diverse knowledge held by external partners with the company's own knowledge. Furthermore, Chunghwa Telecom uses its strategic integrative capability to create strategies that focus on new and creative ideas conceived by staff, or collaborative strategies with external partners to create a climate conducive to merging of its intended strategies with emergent strategies carefully chosen through the process of consolidation and selection.

To realize the full potential of external knowledge integrative capability and strategic integrative capability, organizational integrative capability and leadership integrative capability are necessary to establish general leadership for the many different organizations and partners. Chunghwa Telecom's cross-organizational IBCs and boundary networks give birth to organizational integrative capability within the company and enable it to easily get projects involving the various internal and external organizations and partners up and running. Moreover, the company's leadership integrative capability comes about through the synergies of leadership by strong top and middle management dispersed inside and outside the company who act as IBC and boundary network community leaders.

Capabilities v) to vii) are 'business design capabilities' that enable the establishment of specific business strategies (see Figure 5.5). One of those is 'systems thinking,' an element of Chunghwa Telecom's product and service development process. Chunghwa Telecom does not start straight away from a specific product or service development, but first fosters thorough understanding among development team members to establish a shared vision. Through close dialogue, team members gain mutual understanding of each other's strategic values and set macro strategic targets. Then, members decide upon macro development visions (the top-down approach) which become established as they are incorporated into specific strategic plans.

Conversely, the company also uses the bottom-up approach of merging its knowledge with the knowledge of external partners to verify that the target developmental vision is realized. Systems thinking using the top-down and bottom-up approaches for product and service development is a core competency of Chunghwa Telecom's development team.

To develop distinctive hit products and maintain competitiveness, Chunghwa Telecom also bases its technological philosophy on the three ideas of 'basic technology,' 'key technology,' and 'complementary technology'. Not only does Chunghwa Telecom advance its basic technology to ensure incremental and sustained innovation based on its core knowledge accumulated throughout its long history, but the company's developmental staff and developmental community IBC also use 'architectural thinking' with the technological design concepts of 'key technology' and 'complementary technology' to bring about new architectural, modular, and radical innovations.

The company further uses the final business design capability – 'platform thinking' – to create win-win relationships with end users and external partners and realize co-evolution businesses. Hybrid innovation was a trigger to create a new 'network platform,' brought about through collaborative strategies across IBCs with external partners integrating Chunghwa Telecom's internal knowledge with external knowledge to develop e-businesses and mobile phone services.

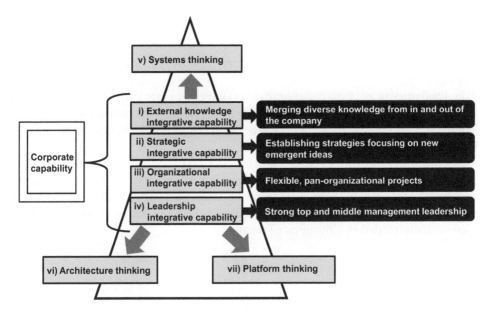

Figure 5.4 Chunghwa Telecom's corporate capability for boundary vision

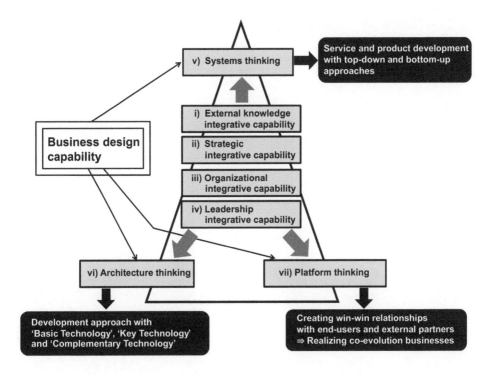

Figure 5.5 Chunghwa Telecom's business design capability for boundary vision

Chapter 5 Conclusions

1. Chunghwa Telecom's core corporate strategy is network-based collaborative management.
2. The fundaments of this collaborative management are the IBCs and boundary networks formed within the company, and with its external partners.
3. These IBCs and boundary networks give rise to Chunghwa Telecom's unique hybrid innovations.
4. The corporate capabilities that improve boundary vision and promote hybrid innovation – i) external knowledge integrative capability; ii) strategic integrative capability; iii) organizational integrative capability; iv) leadership integrative capability; v) systems thinking; vi) architecture thinking, and vii) platform thinking – are well embedded in Chunghwa Telecom.

6 HTC's Strategy Transformation – Strategies for Building a Company Brand

6.1 Strategy Transformation in Taiwanese EMS Businesses

EMS[1] businesses are a major part of Taiwan's electronics industry. One of the features of EMS industries is that they do not have their own brands – they act as specialist design and manufacturing subcontractors for brand makers from all over the world. Not releasing their own branded products serves to shield EMS businesses from competitive markets. However, a look at the 'smiling curve' for value chains sets (curves that indicate value added in the PC industry)[2] shows that specialized manufacturing business profitability ratios are comparatively lower than for other businesses (e.g. R&D or services).

In these circumstances, a company brand strategy is one of the first available choices that Taiwanese EMSs have for transforming their business, although these strategies have a low level of success. Taiwanese EMS businesses have been following this OEM ODM OBM developmental path.[3] Acer, Lenovo and Asus have all evolved through this model (and still use it).

In the past, OEM/ODM contract manufacturing was a central factor in Taiwanese economic growth. However, to sustain innovation now and into the future, Taiwanese corporations are expanding from the OEM/ODM contract manufacturing model to the OMB model to produce their own branded products. In support of this, the Taiwanese government introduced a seven-year plan in 2006 called 'Branding Taiwan Plan' to

---

1   EMS means 'Electronic Manufacturing Service' – a contract manufacturing service for electronic devices. In general terms, the EMS business model is defined as a batch service which contracts from product design and prototyping, to manufacture, shipment and maintenance on behalf of the product maker. Most EMS businesses are contracted to make ITC equipment, computers and mobile telephones, and are able to do this because of the high level of generic parts common to different products regardless of the manufacturer. Buying parts in bulk lowers manufacturing costs. Because of this, EMS factories can produce the same types of products for different makers on dedicated production lines.

2   Former chairman of Acer Stan Shih, advocated the smiling curve for Taiwan's computer manufacturing industry. This U-shaped (like a smiley face) curve illustrates added value in the computer manufacturing industry where value is shown by the vertical axis, and manufacturing processes (from left to right – R&D, component design, assembly, distribution) are indicated on the horizontal access, thus indicating the low level of added value in assembly (at the middle of the curve). Put differently, the smiling curve shows that higher value added areas are in key upstream areas of R&D and device design, and downstream distribution (this includes branding, sales, service and logistics).

3   Refer to Hobday (1995). OEM: Original Equipment Manufacturing (contract manufacturing of a particular product brand), ODM: Original Design Manufacturing (contract manufacturing and design of a particular product brand), OBM: Own-Brand Manufacturing (manufacturing the company's own brand).

foster an environment in which Taiwanese companies can engage in business with company-branded products. Since then, Taiwanese businesses have adopted the OBM business model one after the other, in line with the government objective of raising the international competitiveness of Taiwanese manufactured and branded goods.

However, while this has been going on, Taiwan's dominance in OEM/ODM contract manufacturing has been slowly eroded away by China, Korea and the ASEAN countries, which is forcing more and more Taiwanese makers to focus on the OBM model. Acer's founding CEO Stan Shih Chen-Jung is also an advocate of company-branded product businesses:

> Because of the low value added in OEM/ODM contract manufacturing, Taiwan has to go to both ends of the smiling curve. In other words, Taiwanese corporations have had to get out of OEM/ODM contract manufacturing and evolve into higher value added businesses that offer branded products and services or are involved in innovation and intellectual property says CEO Stan Shih Chen-Jung. (Global Views Monthly 2004)

Because of the decline in assembly business profitability in the computer industry value chain, Acer intentionally moved the focus of its business to the high profitability upstream component manufacturing and downstream distribution (creating its own brand, establishing sales channels and streamlining logistics), and has achieved continued growth with its own branded products and services. Acer, along with other Taiwanese major manufacturers, are shifting over to this higher value added business model – motherboard manufacturers Asus and Gigabyte are other examples of companies that have reformed to produce their own brands and services. In spite of this trend, there are a still lot of EMS businesses in Taiwan that continue to use the OEM/ODM business model.

Even though modern Taiwanese EMS businesses have good technological and manufacturing capabilities, successful examples of transformation through company brand strategies are thin on the ground. Nevertheless, there are a few cases of these EMS companies that have grown up in the same environment and have achieved global success with their own-branded products. PC makers Acer and Asus just mentioned are examples of successful company brand strategies and are recognizable all over the world. This chapter considers the issues behind the big differences in success of EMS companies' own brand developments, even though they are in the same business environment.

With the exception of HTC (High Tech Computer), there are hardly any mobile phone Taiwanese EMS makers who have succeeded globally with their own brand. HTC was founded in 1997 by Cher Wang (Chairman) and Peter Chou (CEO). HTC is involved in PDA and smartphone[4] development, manufacturing and sales, and boasts an 80 per cent share of the worldwide Windows Mobile handset market. The company has close ties with more than 50 operators and carriers all over the world, and strong partnerships with Microsoft and Qualcomm.

The company also has a long list of 'world-first' achievements in the PDA and smartphone market. This includes the world's first palm sized PC, wireless PDA phone, color wireless PDA phone (O2 Xda), smartphone (Orange SPV), 3G PDA phone, CDMA2000 1x

---

4   Smartphone is a mobile phone/PHS merged with a PDA mobile information terminal. Smartphones do not only have individual voice and mobile telephone functions but also include network functions combined with the schedule functions of PDAs and diverse functions for personal information management, multimedia access and so forth.

EV-DO smartphone, 3G smartphone (MTeoR), tri-band UMTS smartphone (HTC TyTN) – all made by HTC: clearly, a world leader in the smartphone market. Familiar to PDA users, HTC was OEM for the world's first PDA – the 'iPAQ' manufactured by the then Compaq.

HTC has made many devices for major carrier brands, and currently has solid partnerships with major mobile brands including the five largest European companies and the four largest American companies, and is establishing links with numerous carriers in the rapidly growing Asian region. While HTC continues to put products on the market through its OEM partnerships with global majors, the company first announced its own brand products in June 2006.

HTC is one company that has achieved rapid growth in the mobile sector with remarkable business results in the last two years. The American *Business Week* magazine ranked HTC as number two in Asia in 2007 among technology companies that produced excellent operating performances. Also in 2006, the company was rated third in the world. Since HTC began to sell its own brands, the company has improved its global visibility.

HTC was the first Taiwanese mobile telephone EMS corporation to successfully release its own brand onto the world market. Fundamental to HTC's successful global expansion beyond its national borders is the company's excellent hybrid innovation based on diverse IBCs formed through the company's excellent boundary vision.

This chapter will illustrate the strategy transformation undertaken by HTC through the formation of IBCs. Characterized by management that has built superior competitiveness in today's smartphone market, the company went on to form IBCs with its developmental and carrier partners to develop its range of world-first mobile terminals such as PDA phones and smartphones as it expanded from its PDA subcontracting specialization.

6.2 Corporate Management at HTC

Firstly let's look at an overview of the development of the company since its establishment to understand the essence of HTC's evolution; then we can draw some conclusions about its value-based management and alliance strategies.

6.2.1 THE CURRENT STATE OF HTC AND ITS DEVELOPMENT

Since its establishment in 1997, HTC's manufacturing orders for the Palm PDA saw it become one of the fastest-growing companies in the rapidly developing mobile telephone market. The company now sells Windows mobile and android PDAs and smartphones all around the world.

Through its partnerships with Microsoft and major mobile communications companies, HTC has achieved a reputation as a pioneer in the smartphone market.

As well as strategic partnerships with Intel, Texas Instruments, Qualcomm and others, the company has established partnerships with major telecommunications carriers such as Orange, O2, T-Mobile, Vodafone, Cingular, Verizon, and Sprint, as well as NTT DOCOMO, SoftBank Mobile, EMOBILE and au in Japan.

The HTC name is widely known for innovation. HTC continues to expand its product spectrum with product developments powered by new form factors[5] and applications designed to respond to the increasing needs of its partner customers. All HTC products feature excellent solutions for wide-ranging mobile multimedia sourcing with enjoyable operability for flexible wireless Internet access.

At the beginning of 2006, the company announced its groundbreaking form factor high-powered 'HTC Advantage' product. The HTC Advantage features a 5-inch screen with a detachable qwerty keyboard – a mobile office unique on the world stage. Then at the beginning of 2007 the company announced the 'HTC Shift'. This Windows Vista product features an excellent 7-inch widescreen touch display with a 40 GB hard drive.

HTC engages in sustained R&D, and with their belief that 'fingertip control that requires no manual would offer more intuitive operation', the company announced the HTC Touch™ in July 2007, and the HTC Touch™ 3D in May of 2008. The revolutionary HTC Touch™ features the company's TouchFLO™ for easy access to functions such as frequently used addresses and content just by running a finger over the screen. HTC continues to develop smart and innovative new products that enable users to enjoy more freedom in their lives.

As the company pursues designs with higher value added, they also expand and grow smartphone technology and functionality. It is HTC's mission to be a leading mobile information and communications device maker with world-class manufacturing, delivery and service capabilities. Since establishment, the company has continued to attract attention for its persistent pioneering innovation and design achieved through its efforts to strengthen its R&D capability as Telcos all over the world announce advanced operator branded PDA telephones and smartphones. As well as having an excellent R&D team consisting of 25 per cent of its staff, HTC focuses on global level mass production systems (and those in Taiwan).

HTC's growth can be classified through the four following steps (Wu 2007):

Step 1: PDA (May 1997 to February 2001)

Because ODM computer market growth was expected to reach its limitations in future, HTC devoted itself to PDA manufacture. Chairman Cher Wang says 'unlike the PC business, we started out with the aim of developing devices small enough to hold in the palm of your hand that can achieve a wide variety of things.'

Step 2: Entering the PDA Market in March 2001, Smartphones Released from March 2001 to 2003)

At this stage the company concentrated on smartphone R&D based on know-how and knowledge accumulated in Step 1. Following that the company released the world's first smartphone into the marketplace.

---

5   'Form factor' is a collective term describing the factors that affect decision-making about hardware shape and size. Specifically, this includes external dimensions and screw holes for attachment etc. for memory devices such as hard disks, motherboard placement, peripheral connectors and so forth. Just like IBM's PC/AT that have an overwhelming share of worldwide products and became the default standard for component specifications, there are many cases of companies using form factors. Using standardized form factors for products helps to avoid incompatibility between components and regularizes mounting.

Step 3: 3G Smartphones (2004 to May 2006)

Amidst a growing tide of next-generation mobile phones, the company focused on strategies to popularize 3G smartphones. At this step the company transformed itself to focus on the smartphone ODM business.

Step 4: Company-branded Smartphones (from June 2006)

HTC had already grown to hold a one per cent share of smartphone ODM business. At this point the company embarked on strategies to develop their own brand. In 2006, the company acquired Dopod International to make use of its sales channels. Then HTC began to develop their brand strategy through strategic alliances with European and Asian telecommunications companies.

6.2.2 HTC'S VALUE-BASED MANAGEMENT

In the ITC industry, it is crucial to come up with innovations ahead of other companies to meet the demanding economies of customer value and speed. That being said, HTC's top management focuses priorities on enacting value-based management, which cannot be characterized as a simplistic efficiency-based Western-style management with a strong tendency to focus on shareholders. The late Peter Drucker said – 'Excellent managers pierce through the bad habit of not considering whether things will be beneficial for customers, although it is also common knowledge that thinking about business in the long-term also means big profits for shareholders in the end.'

The managerial levels in HTC always throw issues at company personnel. Specifically, these issues are related to what kind of products can be developed to improve customer value while improving value for HTC. HTC does not consider it important to just invest in R&D to develop products, or win some competition to pursue profits. The company has a deep sense of the value embedded in its employees, and top management is characterized by its devotion to finding ways to create new value for its customers. In concrete terms, this means that the value of the corporation is born through the corporation's unique and creative management style, and through the company having technology not found anywhere else in the world to provide customers with highly individualized products.

Unlike leading American 'excellent companies' (Peters and Waterman 1982) or 'visionary companies' (Collins and Porras1994) that succeed in generating continuous profits, management in Western family businesses (Miller and Breton-Miller 2005) (companies like Wal-Mart, Cargill, Estée Lauder, Levi Strauss, in the US; Porsche, BMW, Fiat, Hermès, Ferragamo, Michelin, and Sparr etc. in Europe) doesn't focus only on profit pursuit as a top priority to please shareholders, but rather considers investments in R&D and employee education and motivation to be the most important elements. In short, companies with good business results think (O'Reilly and Pfeffer 2000) that the most valuable asset they have is their personnel.

HTC also could thoroughly rationalize costs and efficiencies to generate short-term profits, but the more they did this the more they would cheapen customer value. Although it's certainly possible to achieve profitability in the short-term with cost reductions and restructuring, excessive restraints in investments in R&D, production technology and personnel training just to achieve short-term profits can erode staff morale (Osterlof and

Frey 2000) and bring about the collapse of the organizational platforms in IBCs and boundary networks between people and teams, and the coordination and collaboration between organizations.

Since HTC's R&D activity is working towards future business development, such tactics would nip new innovation in the bud (Vogel 2006, Handy 2002). In reality, HTC doesn't run after short-term profits, but instead takes a long-term view and continues to focus investment in customer and partner satisfaction through 'value-based management' – management that enables competitive superiority through sustained innovation.

As part of value-based management, HTC's top management does not only invest in long-term R&D strategy and personnel training strategies, but makes serious efforts through meaningful dialogue to share the company's values, visions and missions, and business achievements with its customers, partners and staff members.

In today's world of fierce competition and rapid change, companies have to invent their own unique corporate styles just to survive. More specifically, companies have to create a unique, open and challenging corporate culture based on meaningful communications and dialogue between staff members. Management at HTC believes that creating an original corporate culture is certainly not only up to decision-making in top management, but requires common ways of thinking that are spread out among all staff members.

At inception, HTC had difficulty creating this kind of corporate culture, but once management began to encourage meaningful communication between staff, its R&D department, customers and partners, they were successful in embedding HTC's original corporate culture in all employees. Firstly, HTC staff consider how they can offer value from the perspective of HTC itself. Then they also consider what kind of value others can offer the company by looking from the point of view of their counterparts' positions. Then, through the process of meaningful dialogue both in and outside the company, they are able to mutually discern issues and problems and solve them, and take specific action to create value for HTC and its stakeholders across the board. You could say that this practice is an educational method that opens people's eyes to new value creation processes.

Encouraging creative and productive dialogue between staff members, between the company and its partners, and between the company and its customers enables the sharing and resonating of values among participants and hence builds trust. It also raises staff motivation and commitment levels, and encourages the formation of IBCs and boundary networks inside and outside the company with customers to reinforce coordination and collaboration. These kinds of actions are the seeds that build co-creation and co-evolution business systems that include all stakeholders.

For 10 years since its establishment, HTC has been developing products through strong partnerships with Microsoft, who provide Windows Mobile, and also with chipset vendor Qualcomm and well-known mobile telephone businesses T-Mobile, Chunghwa Telecom, NTT DOCOMO, SoftBank Mobile, BT and Vodafone in the UK, as well as Verizon Wireless in the United States. Chairman Cher Wang says he thinks of HTC as a human body. The combination of the vital roles played by each different part mean that if one part is missing, the whole won't function properly.

CEO Peter Chou had the following to say on the 10th anniversary of the company:

HTC is only a small company – there are limitations to what it can achieve by itself. Fortunately, however, we have the support of major mobile telephone businesses around the world, and we hope to continue to learn from our partners for the next 10 years, one step at a time.

HTC's ambitions are not simply to become a global giant like mobile telephone makers Nokia or Motorola. The company has specialized in the smartphone field and aims to continue to be a leader in this area. CEO Chou says he wants his company to be 'Small, but very cool' like Audi or BMW.

6.2.3 HTC'S ALLIANCE STRATEGIES

As its business model, HTC encourages strategies to develop its own brand, but at the same time also encourages alliance strategies with partners focusing on its main smartphone ODM/OEM business. The relationships with its alliance partners are mainly in the areas of technology and sales.

Firstly, the technological area is divided into hardware and software. Put simply, smartphones are just devices that merge data processing functions of computers and PDAs with the communications functions of mobile phones. There are many more parts in a smartphone than in a conventional mobile telephone or PDA, and the relationships between the parts are much more complicated.

To solve the hardware problems that arise with parts development and the interdependencies between parts, HTC puts effort into parts development and R&D through collaborative strategies with a range of developmental makers. For example, the company is involved in joint development with Qualcomm in the United States for the chipsets that lie at the heart of the smartphone, and encourages joint development with suppliers for other parts such as camera lenses and keyboards.

Furthermore, in the software area, HTC produced the first smartphone to use the Windows Mobile OS developed by Microsoft. In manufacturing this Windows smartphone, HTC engaged in joint development with Microsoft to manage and coordinate between the hardware and software sections. HTC also invested resources into developing smartphones using Google's Android OS, and the company is also the first maker in the world to achieve a smartphone using Android.

HTC develops and manufactures smartphones using two types of operating systems from among the four types used in the current world smartphone market. Moreover, HTC leads the world in smartphone developments using the Windows Mobile and Android systems. The Google-branded Nexus One smartphone is also an OEM product from HTC. Google chooses to use HTC because of HTC's technological and development capabilities and the companies' long trusting relationship.

HTC also promotes alliance strategies with telecommunications carriers for its sales channels. The company has partnerships with NTT DOCOMO, au, SoftBank and EMOBILE in Japan, and an alliance with Chunghwa Telecom in Taiwan. Furthermore, the company has ties with AT&T, T-Mobile and others in the United States, as well as European Vodafone and T-Mobile (Germany's biggest telecommunications business), and Orange (France's biggest telecommunications business). HTC does not only offer sales rights for its products through these alliances with carriers, but also offers the carriers design and manufacturing tailored to individual needs and order-made operator-branded smartphones.

The pioneering spirit of HTC's partnership capability is one of the drivers behind the achievement of its own-branded products. As well as pursuing high-value R&D activities, the company works to fortify its whole value chain on a global level from productivity through to product delivery and service capabilities as part of its mission to become a leading mobile information and communications terminal manufacturer. The capabilities in HTC behind these accomplishments lie in its R&D team that consists of 25 per cent of its staff, as well as its global level mass production system.

6.3 Encouraging Strategic Alliances to Create New Value Chains

6.3.1 BUILDING NEW VALUE CHAINS THROUGH 'UNIFIED PRODUCT PLANNING, R&D, PRODUCTION, SALES AND SUPPORT'

Up to now, EMS businesses have pursued profitability in mass production through cost leadership based on economies of scale. However in recent years as consumer tastes have greatly diversified and demand structures have shifted towards products with more individuality, and with the fierce competition coming from Asian countries such as Korea and China, the end of the road for OEM businesses that just simply manufacturer and assemble products has begun to appear. In response, EMS makers have to move to spread themselves to both ends of the smiling curve, in other words transform themselves through company branded strategies by fortifying their R&D and innovation, sales and support businesses (see Figure 6.1).

Even though EMS businesses recognize the value added potential illustrated by the smiling curve, Taiwanese EMS companies continue to focus on OEM/ODM business. This is because of the large capital investment required to develop new products technologies and innovations, the higher risks involved, and the fact that there is no guarantee that releasing company-branded products will result in success – there are many cases of new products that disappear off the market as soon as they are released. Also considering the average scale of Taiwanese EMS businesses, these companies have far fewer resources than famous brand makers in developed countries. If we take a look at the structure of the worldwide electronics industry of the present day, famous global brand makers in the developed countries in the European Union and the developed countries of Korea, America, and Japan pool their resources into new product and technology development, and contract product manufacturing and assembly mainly to Taiwanese EMS businesses. Developed country brand makers also lead in product sales and brand strategies. This is why Taiwanese EMS businesses have a tendency to stick to the OEM/ODM business model. HTC however, decided to put its efforts into contracts for PDA products when the company was established. But for a company that had only just been founded, how were they to acquire orders from PDA makers? The company answered this question by producing high-quality products with more sophisticated levels of technological capability. At its beginning, HTC only concentrated on manufacturing technologies for PDA's, but later on acquired developmental capabilities for other PDA related technologies. When HTC was formed, the computer business was the most popular industry in Taiwan. So why then, did HTC choose to focus on PDA products? At the time, HTC's management accurately predicted that the dominance of the desktop and notebook computer market could not be maintained.

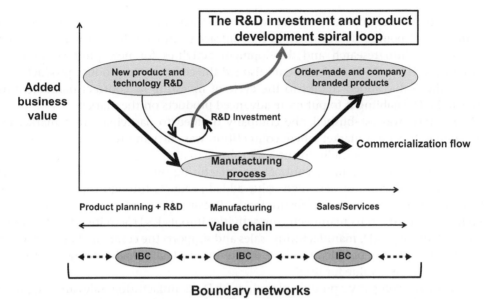

Figure 6.1   HTC's value chain

They saw that the demand for real-time information for corporate users and business people would increase with the advances in globalization. Naturally, handheld PDAs are easier to carry around than notebook computers, which is why HTC's founders decided to set themselves up as an OEM maker developing PDA production technology. This choice can be interpreted as the so-called 'blue ocean strategy'.[6]

The blue ocean strategy refers to undeveloped markets in which a company is able to dig up new demand that holds the promise of new profit generation. Even though there were many uncertainties[7] surrounding the PDA market at the time, HTC aimed to produce a new product based on PDA technology. Eventually, HTC was able to successfully combine PDA data-processing technology with conventional mobile phone voice communication technology to develop the new smartphone product and release it on to the market.

HTC did not only have to advance their production technology to achieve this, but also recognized the importance of improved R&D capability for new technology to bring about new product ideas, and so encouraged unification of product planning, R&D, manufacture, sales and support. This is why HTC was able to increase its competitiveness with sales of its own-branded products in a highly competitive EMS business environment.

---

6   'Blue ocean' refers to an un-pioneered market that is essentially devoid of competitive entities. Blue ocean strategies to pioneer markets use both low costs and product differentiation, and place great importance on value innovation to deliver high-value at low-cost to the buyer. These strategies must not include cost-cutting competitive elements considered normal in business. Raising value for buyers means introducing elements that are unknown in the industry. Over time, economies of scale begin to work with these strategies to further reduce costs when sales improve as buyers are attracted by the superior product value. Refer to Kim and Mauborgne (2005).

7   Apple failed with its 'Newton' product. NTT DOCOMO in Japan also failed with its 'infogate' PDA Internet portal business.

HTC needed development capital for its R&D activities. To secure these business resources, HTC poured its profits from its contract manufacturing activities for global brand makers into research and development activities for new products and new technologies. HTC's R&D achievements also led the company to produce products with much higher value added thanks to the cycle of investing its contract manufacturing profits in R&D, enabling it to put more advanced products on the market.

When HTC was established, the company decided to participate in a market free from competitors (or a market where competition was soft) and thus was able to secure an important position as leader in the smartphone market. Moreover, the company was able to acquire capital from its contract manufacturing business, and establish a cycle of sustained production of new high value added products through capital investment into R&D for new products and technologies. Because HTC encouraged investment of capital gained through its manufacturing activities into its R&D activities, (unification of product planning, R&D, manufacturing, sales and support) the company has been able to commercialize its own branded products based on new technologies developed through R&D and create new value for itself.

To unify the company's product planning, R&D, manufacturing, sales and support in this way, the company formed strong linkages between the members of those specialist organizations through the formation of IBCs and boundary networks both inside and outside the company. As well as being formed within a company, IBCs and boundary networks are formed between different organizations, and thus are also born of the relationships with external development partners and telecommunications carriers. These internal and external IBC and boundary networks give rise to a flexibility that enables product planning, research and development, manufacturing, sales and support systems to develop the company's own brand as well as the order-made products for carriers (see Figure 6.1).

In the process of commercializing a line of goods, product innovation enables the release of a wider variety of distinguishable products which in time accelerates diffusion and market acceptance. Eventually in this type of market situation, some product will emerge as a dominant product – a 'dominant design' (Utterback 1994) – a product that becomes a standard in the marketplace (e.g. the model T Ford with its dominant design specifications, or the Windows PC. More recently, a dominant design for the much talked about electric vehicles may be emerging). A dominant design serves to take market penetration to a new level. Furthermore, the emergence of a dominant design continues standardization of product functions, accelerates process innovations on how to more efficiently produce performance and quality, while increasing productivity.

In short, the key to the company's productivity model is its cost competitiveness. EMS corporations pursue cost leadership through the use of highly standardized production systems, and although higher efficiencies are found when routines become embedded in manufacturing methods, excessive focus on production efficiency in the horizontal businesses in America and Taiwan can disadvantage product innovation, and cause 'productivity dilemma' (Abernathy 1978) for manufacturers. This means that the flexibility of the manufacturing system is gradually lost, making it difficult to upgrade the production line with new manufacturing technologies and develop new products, thus retarding ability to generate new product innovation due to the company's diminished capability to respond to the changing external environment. This trade-off between technical innovation and productivity is called the 'productivity dilemma'. According to the smiling curve, it's easy to fall into this productivity dilemma if the company concentrates its resources only in R&D while neglecting its manufacturing functions.[8]

However, a common thread among the leading vertical integration business models adopted by Japanese makers is invariably the use of a unified R&D and manufacturing approach (of course, this also means a unified approach to product planning, sales and support). This unified approach has the effect of giving birth to new product innovation when technologies advance. New technologies or design rules affect existing production technologies and production rules, and the reverse is also true – new production technologies affect existing technologies and design methods. For this reason, IBCs and boundary networks are vital for engineers, designers and manufacturing technology specialists to dynamically and mutually share highly specialized knowledge and information.

One of Japan's top brand makers had the following to say about the unified approach to R&D and manufacturing:

Running a manufacturing business with its development and manufacturing sections disconnected is dangerous. For example, with the DVD recorder, the cellular production team examine manufacturing processes, provide the set department (development and design department) with specification counterproposals, and the designers quickly take these up. Development and manufacture should be unified. At Utsunomiya TV, there is a tradition of passing on the tacit knowledge that cellular manufacturing processes are a combination of development and manufacturing. (Panasonic CEO Kunio Nakamura)

Just like Panasonic, organizational systems for digital appliance development incorporating cutting-edge technologies are created with a high level of vertical integrity across and between all functions and specializations therein. Canon CEO Fujio Mitarai emphasizes the same thing – 'that development and manufacturing should be integrated and unified'. Canon does not only unify its digital camera development and manufacturing, but actually has its lens development and manufacturing organizations physically located in the same place as a permanent IBC for developing and producing critical lens components common to cameras, printers, and photocopiers etc. This IBC brings about synergies between development and manufacturing through a unified approach to merging organizations and knowledge boundaries to trigger the engineer creativity needed to advance new development and manufacturing rules.

6.3.2 SKILLFULLY EXECUTING STRATEGIC ALLIANCES BETWEEN CORPORATIONS

Established as a specialist contract manufacturer of PDA terminals in 1997, HTC is now a global leader in the smartphone market, having brought a number of world-first terminals onto the market including the world's first PDA phone and the world's first smartphone. As a company founded in Taiwan, it has not been easy for HTC to establish its position as one of the world's top five smartphone brands over the last decade. The reasons behind HTC's extraordinary results in such a short space of time must surely

---

8   Ikujiro Nonaka refers to the value curve for unified R&D and manufacturing as the 'Samurai Curve'. This is because a samurai never smiles – his mouth only forms a horizontal line. Different from the Smiling curve that describes the IT industry, the samurai curve is valid for describing industry groups such as Japanese corporations with their overwhelming strength. IT industry corporations Panasonic and Canon also practice samurai curve management.

be the inter-corporate networks over which the company enacts its strategic alliances to bring about the process of unified product planning, R&D, manufacturing, sales and support mentioned earlier.

Aside from HTC, all the world's top smartphone brand makers – Nokia, RIM, Apple – are European and American companies, and Nokia has traditionally dominated the worldwide mobile phone market. Looked at from the point of view of brand profile, HTC was initially an unknown, but through the creation of value chains by unification of product planning, R&D, manufacturing, sales and support, at the same time as forming strategic alliances with carriers in Europe, America and Japan, HTC shot into the ranks of world's top five smartphone makers. In other words, the networks between corporations formed by these alliances are a factor of HTC's successful OEM ODM OBM strategic business model transformation.

The corporate networks formed by HTC's strategic alliances are not limited to global telecommunications carriers. The company also has strategic alliances with leading developmental partners around the world to advance its R&D capability, especially since modern mobile telephones have a much more complicated product architecture than the older PDAs; and because of this, HTC must involve itself in broad-based development for the components required to build smartphones, and the integration of those parts. Therefore, the company has joint ventures with Qualcomm to build the chipsets that lie at the heart of the smartphone, and with Microsoft and Google to create the operating systems. These alliances have given HTC a vital leading role in the development of smartphones using Windows Mobile and Android.

The right side of the smiling curve where value added is high represents product sales and support, and thus the offering of company-branded products. HTC has moved into this area of company-branded business. HTC has expanded to the left and right sides of the smiling curve through unification of product planning, R&D, manufacturing, sales and support by pouring efforts into its company-branded product development strategies, while maintaining its alliance strategies.

In the process of carrying out its OEM/ODM business in the past, the company recognized that user needs were changing with changing generations in the European communications market. When the European mobile market shifted from 2G to 3G, demand exploded for computer-like data communications and processing with mobile phones, and demand for smartphones from European corporations and business people also began to rise. HTC took advantage of this situation and began to provide order-made smartphones to European carriers.

These relationships also provided an excellent opportunity for the company to develop product strategies for the HTC brand, because obviously a relatively unknown company like HTC would have had great difficulty selling its own-branded products in the European mobile telephone market at the time, and so the order-made smartphones for carriers gave HTC the opportunity to release 'co-branded products' with the HTC brand added to the carrier brand. HTC was also able to expand its own-branded smartphone business through carrier sales and distribution channels.

HTC did not only make use of the carrier sales routes, but was able to absorb carrier product planning knowledge and know-how through the development of order-made carrier-branded smartphones and to learn product planning and marketing capabilities. HTC has R&D capabilities for new products and technologies as well as manufacturing capabilities, while carriers have sales planning capabilities, product sales routes and communications technology. On the other hand, core technologies needed to realize product architecture for smartphones is held by HTC software and component development partners (Qualcomm, Microsoft, Google etc). HTC's relationships with carriers and development partners have mutually complementary functions, in which all companies involved are in 'co-creation and co-evolution' win-win business relationships with each other.

HTC continues to form multitiered IBCs and boundary networks through its strategic alliances with carriers and development partners to absorb and study knowledge and know-how that it does not have, and merge it with its own core knowledge by intentionally building long-term organizational relationships. This knowledge integration of the company's knowledge with other companies' knowledge creates core capability of the company's value chain through unification of product planning, R&D, manufacturing, sales and support and achieves hybrid innovation for the company's own-branded products (see Figure 6.2).

Since establishment, HTC has especially continued to grow through its strong partnerships with Qualcomm and Microsoft. Leaders of both companies have stated their intention to continue their close collaborations to develop technology to make mobile telephones that are even smaller and lighter with more sustainable batteries and better performance characteristics. HTC and Qualcomm will continue to create new technologies and products through their win-win co-creation relationship and intend to promote hybrid innovation that realizes even better device development in line with their corporate visions.

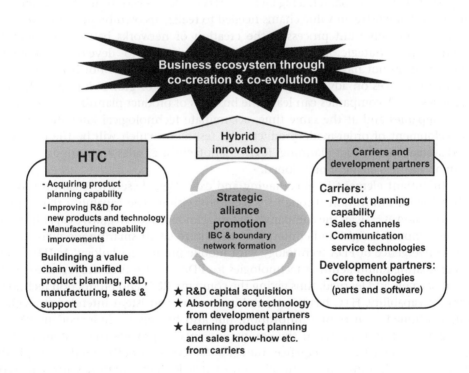

Figure 6.2   HTC's alliance strategies

As mentioned earlier, Chairman Cher Wang sees HTC like a human body, which is similar to the concept of an ecosystem. He recognizes the important role that HTC plays in the smartphone and mobile phone industry. This is why HTC works to continue and develop mutual collaboration and co-evolution through these ecosystems with its various alliance partners (see Figure 6.2). The key is the IBCs and boundary networks formed among all stakeholders in the business ecosystem.

6.4 Encouraging Hybrid Innovation through Boundary Vision

This chapter has discussed the successful strategy transformation that HTC underwent to change from an EMS business to a global brand manufacturer in the smartphone market. This case illustrates that it is possible for an EMS maker to produce its own-branded product and succeed on the global market. However, the key to company brand strategy success here is the encouragement of hybrid innovation through excellent boundary vision, and the two business processes described below.

The first process is the creation of a set of value chains through the unification of product planning, R&D, manufacturing, sales and support. EMS companies must recognize their competitive capability and make decisions about how to use that capability in the product area, and what kind of specific products they should make. Then, the company has to create its own unique blue ocean market through building a set of value chains that unify product planning, R&D, manufacturing, sales and support. As a pioneer in the smartphone blue ocean market, a big factor of HTC's success was its quick creation of the upstream and downstream value chains needed to realize its own-branded product.

The second important process is the creation of networks between corporations through global strategic alliances. For EMS companies to develop own-branded products that do not have any brand profile or sales routes, it is not beneficial to use up limited resources on advertising and sales promotions or pioneering sales channels. Nevertheless, EMS companies can learn the business of product planning and sales from brand companies and at the same time, accumulate technological know-how through the development of order-made products, the results of which will be the completely unified system for product planning, R&D, manufacturing, sales and support – the first important business element mentioned.

An important element in encouraging and executing these two business processes is HTC's hybrid innovation through its boundary vision. The capability that supports boundary vision at HTC, is the company's 'external knowledge integrative capability', that gave the company insight and contact into the future latent smartphone market, based on the convergence of PDA technology with mobile phone technology. As HTC started by accumulating manufacturing technologies for PDAs, it absorbed the knowledge of its external partners and learned, thus giving the company R&D and production technology integrative capability. HTC has the capability to enact consistent intended strategies to pursue continued smartphone innovation, but also focuses on independent R&D for an imaginative future in which the company wants to provide the customer with 'a place for new experience'. Emergence strategies that come from this kind of imaginative thinking can be legitimized as official product development strategies through HTC's strategic integrative capability and executed as one of the companies consistent intended strategies.

To realize the full potential of external knowledge integrative capability and strategic integrative capability, organizational integrative capability and leadership integrative capability are necessary to establish a general leadership for the many different organizations and partners. HTC's flexible IBCs and boundary networks in and out of the company make it easy to seamlessly create open and flat organizations for cross-organizational projects, thus giving the company its organizational integrative capability. The organizational integrative capability of these seamless organizations enables the flexible sharing and merging of knowledge dispersed in different specialist organizations through the IBCs and boundary networks within the company and with external partners. Moreover, HTC's leadership integrative capability comes about through the synergies of leadership by strong top and middle management dispersed in and out of the company who act as IBC and boundary network community leaders. These external knowledge, strategic, organizational and leadership integrative capabilities are the corporate capabilities that support boundary vision.

HTC also incorporates business design capabilities into its boundary vision. HTC uses 'systems thinking' to focus on product planning and development for future smartphone and mobile telephone businesses, and uses a 'top-down approach' to move from the macro product visions and concepts down to the detailed specifics of design and product specifications. HTC also has a number of research themes related to smartphones, including voice recognition and interface technology developments using a 'bottom-up approach' to integrate individual technological development themes into macro product concepts.

Based on systems thinking, HTC uses architecture thinking for product innovation aiming for high-performance, high-quality and miniaturization. HTC does not only aim for version upgrades for its products, but has strategic objectives that include potential radical innovation through existing technical breakthroughs as well as engaging in modular innovation and architectural innovation to produce innovative core technologies and product developments. The company's product development processes with architectural thinking are a factor in raising the level of its business design capability.

The company also uses the aforementioned 'platform thinking' as a boundary vision capability to improve its business design capability for new business models. It can be said that HTC itself plays an important functional role in the formation of the business ecosystem of the larger mobile telephone industry. This is an example of 'business platform thinking' required to construct an ecosystem for the industry as a whole. While HTC makes use of its developmental partners' product platforms (hardware and software), the company also develops its own product platforms merging these, and uses 'product platform thinking' to create a developmental environment in which there is a diverse flow of applications and contents.

As previously described, HTC's boundary vision based on these seven capabilities is a key driver that encourages collaborative strategies with other companies (developmental partners and telecommunications carriers). HTC continues to learn and absorb external knowledge for R&D, product planning, sales and support and integrate it with its own internal knowledge, and accumulates knowledge and know-how in its upstream and downstream value chains. These consistent value chains unifying product planning, R&D, manufacturing, sales and support through the collaborative strategies with other companies are closely linked to HTC's ability to bring about hybrid innovation.

Chapter 6 Conclusions

1. Important elements of HTC's corporate innovations are found in its value-based management style and strategic alliances.
2. Collaborative strategies through strategic alliances encourage HTC to create value chains that unify product planning, R&D, manufacturing, sales and support.
3. HTC achieves these consistent value chains by collaborations within the company and alliances outside the company through IBCs and boundary networks.
4. These IBCs and boundary networks promote HTC's unique hybrid innovations.
5. HTC's boundary vision based on the seven capabilities is closely tied in with the company's ability to bring about unique hybrid innovation through consistent value chains and collaborative strategies fostered with other companies (development partners and telecommunications carriers).

CHAPTER 7

Technology Integration through Boundary Vision

7.1 Innovation through Technology Convergence

There is a constant demand for new innovations in today's world of rapidly changing markets and technologies. Engineers are required to merge and integrate different technologies across the different high-tech fields of industrial machines, medical, nanotechnology etc., as well as ICT technologies used with mobile telephones and the Internet, digital products and vehicles. This involves deep searching vertically through established technological areas while at the same time, expanding and merging horizontally into unfamiliar and different fields to create new technologies. Innovation with horizontal technological integration does not only require development of traditional components and modules, but especially demands development of total product and design architecture. To respond to these demands engineers must have the capability of bringing about mutual effects across a range of different technological areas.

Technological integration requires engineers to have diverse knowledge and capabilities. Discussed in Chapter 2, these are the corporate capabilities described as knowledge, strategic, organizational, and leadership integrative capabilities, and the business design capabilities described as systems, architecture and platform thinking. Corporate and business design capabilities serve to forge the boundary vision needed to give engineers the insight into creativity to bring about new technology and product systems realized through merging and integration across diverse technological areas.

Some examples of this 'convergence' involving merging and integration of different technologies are given in Chapter 1, and like the representative example describing converged mobile telephone services illustrated by Figure 1.3, the merging of ICT with many other fields of industry (automotive, industrial equipment, information appliances and broadcasting etc.) is accelerating. Case examples in a wide range of new product areas such as the merging of PC and NC (numerical computing) technologies (Shibata and Kodama 2009) in the industrial equipment field, the combination of gyro sensor and digital camera technology to bring about the anti-shake digital camera (Ohshima 2010), Toyota's development of the hybrid car, and the combining of PC and mobile telephone technology to create the smartphone talked about in Chapter 6, all suggest a common technological trend in a wildly fluctuating and accelerating market environment.

All of this means companies have to search for solutions to produce new products and business models at the same time as concentrating on their core competencies to win out and survive in the ferociously competitive business environment of convergence. This diversification of business models and integration of different technologies means companies are coming under more and more pressure to merge diverse knowledge scattered within themselves and outside. The knowledge merging process is one of the key issues for corporations. They have to reinforce the boundary vision of engineers in different professional areas across a range of knowledge boundaries.

On the other hand, the speeding up of net businesses, segmentation and specialization in technological areas and more divisions within organizations that all make organizational boundaries more complex forms the current business environment. In spite of these challenges, it is along these boundaries between different areas of knowledge and organizations where innovation is born. Although boundaries are by their nature places of friction between organizations and contradictions between specialist knowledge, they are also the breeding ground for innovation, which is why invigorating communications and collaborations across boundaries can act as a strong inducement to bring about new and imaginative products and technologies.

Through the examples of Sharp's world-first camera phone developed in Japan, and the company's One seg Aquos mobile telephone innovation, this chapter discusses cases of technological integration across the boundaries between different organizations and technologies. In diagnosing these cases, it becomes apparent that new product developments were carried out through close collaboration via creative dialogue across voluntarily formulated IBCs and boundary networks among formal and informal multitiered project teams within the company.

7.2 Case studies

7.2.1 PRODUCT DEVELOPMENT – THE MOBILE PHONE WITH BUILT-IN CAMERA

Although a major Japanese appliance maker (the company's 'Aquos' large-screen LCD TV is a globally famous brand), Sharp only became involved in mobile telephone development and sales about 10 years ago, comparatively late compared to other companies, but has successfully expanded its share of sales into the present day from its beginnings as the world's first developer of mobile phones with built-in cameras. After assuming office as Sharp's CEO in June 1998, Katsuhiko Machida predicted the profitability of the mobile phone business and began concentrating resources into it. At the outset, Sharp's Communications Systems HQ in Hiroshima became the main centre for these developments, and the company also embarked on a collaboration strategy with J-Phone (later Vodafone, SoftBank Mobile).

As a generic manufacturer, at the time Sharp thought including a camera module in a mobile phone could be a hit with teenage Japanese girls, who were frequenting the highly popular 'purikura'[1] ('print club' photo-booths), and that the camera-in-phone could become a portable version of this. There was also other logic behind the idea. Looking back at the state of mobile telephone advancement at the time, it was already possible to use handsets for voice communication, as well as mail and text exchange; the i-mode mobile Internet had progressed and services for ring tone and video download were also available. Against this backdrop, it was natural to think that customers would want a camera in their phones to take pictures. Since the digital camera culture had already established itself, if pictures could be taken with a mobile phone camera, these

---

1   Print club ('*purikura*' in Japanese) is the name of a popular photo booth system in Japan that enables users to take a picture of themselves or with friends and print decorative stickers of the photographs.

could be stored in the camera and enjoyed later, or attached to mail and sent to family and friends. Sharp was certain these devices would sell.

At the same time, J-Phone's mobile terminal development chief Keiji Takao was thinking the same thing – about a camera phone[2] – an exact match with Sharp's idea, and so the companies teamed up in a joint development. As project leader for the built-in camera phone joint development with Sharp once it got under way, Takao had to seriously consider the coordination within J-Phone of the company's business planning, sales, equipment and maintenance departments, while working to strengthen the collaboration with Sharp's development project. Camera phone sales from Kyocera's 'visual phone' PHS were also hot on J-Phone's heels, which had created negative sentiments within the company about developing a mobile telephone with a built-in camera. Nonetheless, Mr. Takao was able to get the understanding and support of his direct superiors, and worked on leaders and managers in the related departments to get consensus within the company for the new development. The whole of J-Phone was also fearful of competition from NTT DOCOMO and KDDI, but it was this fear that spurred J-Phone to action on the mobile phone with built-in camera mobile project, and a spirit of challenge flourished throughout the whole company.

Meanwhile Sharp, in their undertaking from J-Phone, got on with the job of formulating a development project with all the company's various departments to develop a compact camera module that could be installed into a mobile phone (see Figure 7.1), which was accompanied by much discussion about the concepts involved (IBC-0 in Figure 7.1). Through the sharing, contact with and creation of knowledge, Sharp used this IBC to ascertain its customer's (J-Phone) needs and ideas, such as specific product functions and specifications, so Sharp's personal communications division could get down to the business of specific design based on details discussed with J-Phone (the whole system, architecture, hardware and software, individual module level elements), and discussions took place among designers and research department staff as required (IBC-1 in Figure 7.1: IBC for knowledge sharing, contact with and creation in the context of product planning).

At the focus of all this interaction lay the miniature camera module to be developed. Engineers in the personal communications division were experts in communications technology for mobile telephones, but lenses and image processing were outside their sphere of knowledge, in spite of the fact that the communications technology and lenses and image processing chips had to be merged and integrated to create the device. Fortunately, though, Sharp had released the PDA product 'Zaurus' and LCD 'Viewcam' video camera, both hit products, and so already had quite a bit of accumulated imaging and camera technology. Straight away, the engineers in Hiroshima accessed the CCD division at the company's IC HQ in Tenri in Nara Prefecture.

---

2   The 'Sha-Mail' concept was triggered by the following episode: Keiji Takao's parents came to Tokyo from Kyushu. Takao went to Hakone, a famous Japanese sightseeing area, to take a break and spend some time with his parents. While the three of them were on a cable car enjoying the wonderful view, something else caught his eye … 'hello, hello? – dang, it is out of range. How do you send mail with this thing?' It seemed that a woman in the cable car was trying to send an email to someone from her mobile to share the beauty of the view, and wasn't quite sure how to make it work. What's more the phone didn't have a camera, so she couldn't take any photographs. It was at that point that it came to Takao in a flash 'Ah! that's it!' he thought – 'If mobile phones had built-in cameras, people could quickly express their emotions and excitement to their friends or family with photographs attached to an email sent from the phone.' This experience gave birth to J-phone's 'Sha-Mail' concept.

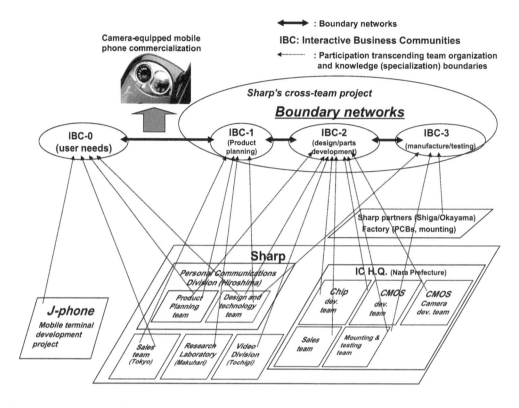

Figure 7.1 Boundary networks at J-Phone and Sharp

These engineers from the personal communications division and the CCD division held a number of meetings at the H.Q. The main issue to overcome was how to develop a compact camera module (a unified image sensor, lens and image processing chip) small enough to be inserted into a mobile phone, without having to change the current phone size. Through these discussions, the members of this group dynamically progressed with examination into new low-power image processing chip development, compact CMOS camera module development and ways to mount the new components (IBC-2 in Figure 7.1: IBC for sharing, contact with and creation of knowledge in the context of design and component development).

Sharp engineers encountered a number of problems in the development process due to the short development period requested by its customer J-Phone, such as figuring out how to make an all-in-one CMOS sensor and lens, and deal with noise problems for the CMOS sensor, but through co-operation across organizational boundaries, the professionals in these different specialist areas were able to solve a range of issues, and remarkably, come up with a camera module roughly half the thickness of the module used in Sharp's hit 'Zaurus' PDA device.

However, the new device also required technology to mount some 50 parts including the miniature camera module and special chip on a compact circuit board. The IC H.Q. mounting and testing team entrusted circuit board parts mounting to Sharp's partner company in Shiga prefecture, Sumitomo Electric Printed Circuits. Since new flexible PCB technology had just started to be used in the industry for mounting parts, the circuit patterns that formed the electrical signal paths didn't look very neat after surface processing, and only 20 per cent of them were any good – an extremely poor result. There was no way the company could have gone ahead at this pathetic level of capability, especially since they expected to sell 10,000 mobile telephones every day. So to deal with this problem, the mounting and testing team from IC HQ, and the manufacturing supervisors from Hiroshima assembled at their partner Sumitomo in Shiga Prefecture to reconsider quality-control standards and surface processing, and through trial and error, this team was able to gradually reduce the number of defective products.

But then another problem occurred. After mass-producing the PCBs, the circuit patterns broke during the process of mounting the multitude of tiny parts due to heat distortion during the soldering process. Even in countering this serious problem, Sharp cooperated across different departments (with support from the mounting specialists in Hiroshima) to find a solution and take high-density component mounting capabilities for mobile phones to a level never before seen in the industry (IBC-3 in Figure 7.1: IBC for sharing, contact with and creation of knowledge in the context of manufacturing and testing).

Mobile phones with built-in cameras only became a possibility because these problems were overcome. An important point in forming a project team across different organizations is the realization that there are always informally formed teams that share knowledge across various contexts in boundaries between organizations, and between people in different professional fields (knowledge) to solve problems, and these informal teams share this kind of knowledge and context through contact with each other via their IBCs. Sharp also has boundary networks (project networks) between different companies linking IBC-0 to IBC-3, which includes their client J-Phone in IBC-0.

This is how the joint venture between Sharp and J-Phone was able to produce the 'J-SH04' mobile telephone in November of 2000 – the world's first camera phone, and made in Japan. J-Phone named their service that enables users to send e-mail attached with photographs taken by the camera 'Sha-Mail', and with this bundled service, the camera phones sold like hot cakes. J-Phone's marketing and sales team did not only aim the Sha-Mail product at consumers, but engaged in a number of different experiments to develop usages targeting corporate users across a range of different businesses, advertised the camera phone heavily and achieved excellent sales.

7.2.2 PRODUCT DEVELOPMENT – THE AQUOS MOBILE PHONE

Thanks to the unprecedented demand for Sharp's hit product – the mobile phone with a built-in camera – the company managed to grab the number one share of the mobile telephone market in Japan, and continued to advance with more and more mobile telephone innovations converging technologies, notably the Aquos mobile released in May of 2006.

This mobile telephone is designed to support terrestrial digital broadcasting which also commenced in April of the same year – now a standard function in most models widely used indoors and outdoors regardless. The Aquos mobile was the first manufacturer-branded phone, and was named after Sharp's Aquos LCD TV brand (manufacturers who developed mobile phones were not known to brand their products at the time). The device features the 'cycloid' LCD screen that can be mechanically rotated through 90° to offer the user a new viewing style.

Just like the camera phone, the Aquos mobile development involved a number of new approaches, not only the merging of LCD and communications technology, and demands for new technological developments for LCD and mounting, along with a compact tuner design; but was a mobile phone created with intent, especially from the marketing end. Having contributed to Sharp's hit products and product concepts, Sharp's Creative Lifestyle Focus Centre (Currently the One-of-a-Kind Products Planning Center in the One-of-a-Kind Products and Corporate Design Group) also contributed greatly to the development of the Aquos mobile phone. The One-Of-A-Kind Products Planning Centre's mission is to hold hearings with leading users and exchange opinions with different businesses to collect and analyze various information to plan new products, and steer new technology developments in the right direction through close link ups with all business divisions.

Product planning staff at the centre began intra-company discussions regarding TV broadcast for mobile terminals about three years prior to the One seg mobile commercialization. Through a variety of market research, the centre was able to determine a high marketability for mobile telephone TV viewing for multiple mobile devices. More specifically, the product planning staff conducted questionnaires, hearings and group-focused interviews and found that high-quality TV broadcasts viewable on handsets would generate demand from business people, who were their main target users.

Pivotal user comments that influenced this development were that most users said they watched TV at home when they wanted, but had different comments about viewing while out of the home or office. As far as viewing while out of the home was concerned, the centre found that there was potential high demand for viewing availability while on the train home from work, while waiting, or while killing time in cafes and so forth, as well as demand for a handset that could be easily operated with one hand during train travel; and of course, users wanted a mobile phone unaffected by noise with a much higher picture quality than the older-style analog reception versions. These latent users also hoped that they could view long recordings of missed programs at a later time. The product planning staff analyzed these latent user needs and summarized them as core product specifications to pilot the product plan.

The first of these specifications demanded from the marketing end was the need for a liquid crystal screen that would enable viewing in sunlight just as clearly as normal television. The second demand was for a lightweight and compact device with low power requirements. The third demand was for a device capable of recording long video segments, and fourthly, for a wide and sharp-looking LCD screen just like the Aquos TV, with a human interface that could be operated with one hand. The company's designers came up with a number of suggestions for this human interface, and finally decided upon the 'cycloid' design. The cycloid design allows the user to rotate the screen 90° thus transforming the terminal into a T-shape, giving the product a distinctive feature compared to other company's devices. The product planning staff took the pilot plan for the One seg mobile phone around the company, and after a getting consensus from officials in the related divisions finally submitted it to top management who simply commanded 'Proceed with commercialization!'.

After that, top management also instructed the technology division to establish one of Sharp's 'Urgent Projects' for the plan (discussed in more detail later). On this point, the Aquos mobile phone commercialization plan was a different story to the development for the camera phone, because it originated at the marketing end (the product planning department in the company not directly involved in sales).

Meanwhile, the technology division had fortunately already set out on a technological road map into fundamental research for a compact TV tuning device for elemental mobile technology, and immediately set about producing a One seg mobile phone tuner module. And so began the detailed commercialization for the Aquos mobile telephone, okayed as an 'Urgent Project' by top management.

At Sharp, they define an 'Urgent Project' as a new product development project under the direct control of the company CEO. Under the umbrella of this Urgent Project, specialists in various segments of the company gathered including staff from the One-Of-A-Kind Product Planning Centre, Technology HQ, Design HQ in Osaka, engineers from Communication Systems HQ in Hiroshima (mobile telephone development division), video processing engineers from Makuhari and others.

These teams in the urgent project were confronted with a range of difficult technological issues in the process of commercializing the Aquos mobile, but forged ahead regardless. Members engaged in thorough and creative dialogue based on the specifications demanded from the marketing end. All urgent project members worked in geographically separated offices, and apart from engaging in face-to-face meetings in real space, they also actively used IT tools to build a virtual place for creative dialogue, and held videoconferences when necessary (one TV conference every two weeks to discuss administration and issues of the whole project and share issues and problems), thus the IBC for the Aquos urgent project served to encourage the sharing, contact with and creation of knowledge across a range of different contexts in real and virtual space.

The engineers in these IBCs were able to overcome a whole host of technological issues and come up with yet another of Sharp's one-of-a-kind technologies, consisting of the compact tuner module, the cycloid design, and mobile ASV liquid-crystal display for clear viewing in bright outdoor light. Over and over again, the engineers involved in mobile telephone picture quality received instruction from television picture quality engineers and engaged in discussions to improve the image. The product was approved as a one-of-a-kind product by the company's one-of-a-kind product strategy planning group formed from top management, and over a two-year period, the urgent project team's efforts paid off, the world's first One seg 'cycloid' mobile phone was commercialized and sold, originally through SoftBank.

7.3 New Insights and Implications

7.3.1 TECHNOLOGY INTEGRATION AT SHARP

The camera phone and the Aquos mobile are the result of technology integration brought about by combining various specialized technologies held by engineers in different fields. The camera phone is the result of merged core technologies in Sharp's organizations dealing with communications, information, liquid-crystal, video processing, and semiconductor technologies, while the Aquos cycloid mobile is the result of combining development of a high-quality liquid crystal display panel and a compact video tuner with the technology to mount these in mobile phones.

A mobile telephone consists of complicated system architecture and a range of hardware and software. These devices require high-performance software technology for their operating systems, middleware and applications for high-speed processing of rich content such as high-performance games, music and video distribution, as well as videophone and the so-called wallet functions designed for financial transactions and so forth. On top of all that, mobile telephones also have high-performance camera and display components combined with advanced battery technology developments. This means the devices demand profound technological innovation both in individual specialist fields and in convergence across all of these different fields. Any high-tech corporation working in ICT like Sharp needs engineers with highly specialized knowledge in individual areas of hardware and software, and as the key to creating revolutionary technological innovation and unique products, these various different technological fields must be converged. As well as vertically integrating to turn unique devices into one-of-a-kind products with high added value, engineers need to horizontally integrate their core technologies across video, communications and data processing fields.

While Sharp makes the best use of the technology it has accumulated over its long history, it is also a company that has a successful track record of accurately grasping changing times and fluctuating competitive environments through cross-organizational collaboration between people in different divisions, and merging of specialist technologies, regardless of the framework of those individual technologies.

This organizational capability of merging technologies found in Sharp's DNA comes from the pioneering spirit of manufacturing embedded in the company by its founder Tokuji Hayakawa, who was among the first to successfully commercialize radio and television products. Hayakawa's original philosophy of creating products that 'other companies will want to imitate' is an unbroken tradition upheld by all of Sharp's engineers and is central to current management's blackbox strategies and their philosophy of creating 'one-of-a-kind technology that other companies cannot imitate'. The cornerstone of Sharp's R&D and commercialization efforts for its one-of-a-kind strategies lies in the company's 'Urgent Project' teams.

Product development at the heart of Sharp's one-of-a-kind technologies and blackbox strategies doesn't just happen overnight. Sharp's Urgent Projects are undertaken by teams directly formed by the CEO from preferred experts in development divisions in the range of specialist fields to commercialize important products as quickly as possible. These projects are authorized top-down from the CEO and official management after original bottom-up proposals from middle management (and of course, there are cases where the Urgent Projects initially originate from top-down leadership).

Sharp's Urgent Projects originated in the early part of the 1970s when the company was embroiled in bitter competition with Casio in the calculator market. To win out in this battle, the company formed a cross-organizational team consisting of researchers and engineers from its calculator and liquid crystal display divisions, and within a year, this team had developed the world's first LCD calculator. Triggered by these circumstances, the Urgent Project system was properly established in the company in 1977.

Depending on the theme, these project teams are configured by mobilizing engineers from within the whole company (a project may have anywhere from ten people to several tens of people involved) to commercialize a product in a limited period of time.

Sharp's Urgent Project system has given birth to a whole stack of hit products including the frontloading VTR in 1979, electronic notebooks, the 3-inch color LCD television, the LCD Viewcam, the color Zaurus PDA, the Mebius PC, as well as the Aquos mobile discussed in this chapter (see Figure 7.2).

As one of the company's eventual successes, development for Sharp's leading Aquos LCD TV began in earnest when Katsuhiko Machida took over as the company's CEO in 1998, and decided to pour business resources into LCD technology through strong top-down leadership and bring together elite engineers from the company's television and liquid-crystal divisions to develop the large-screen Aquos TV. There is also a historical background to this development.

Even though Sharp is a time-honored appliance manufacturer, the company had often been teased as a second-class company or a company that produced inferior goods. This was due to the fact that the company had not been able to properly establish its own company brand. Sensing a crisis, CEO Machida made the astonishing policy announcement in 2000 to scale back its semiconductor business and pour resources into LCD technology. Sharp had developed LCD technology 40 years prior, and CEO Machida strongly felt that the time had arrived when LCDs would become indispensable in society. Machida commanded the whole company to 'Lead the world with LCD' and 'Become a top brand in eight years'; thus the Aquos development project was born (Kitada 2010).

Just as with the camera phone, engineers in different specialist areas collaborated to clear a number of technological issues and leap forward into today's era of LCD television. The liquid-crystal, television and LSI engineers doggedly persisted with their adjustment of the image processing technology to bring about the responsiveness needed for contrast and snappy movement in the LCD screen and create a thoroughly high-performance product with a commitment to quality.

Figure 7.2   Hit products created through 'urgent projects'

Source: based on Sharp media publications

In 2000 the 'Tatami Project' was formed in the company – a project to produce the glass substrates needed to manufacture LCD televisions the size of the tatami mats used in traditional Japanese houses. This project enabled the company to set up the world's first factory to produce everything from the LCDs themselves through to completed LCD televisions.

As the backbone of its technology and R&D, Sharp's technology HQ pursues originality and the spirit of entrepreneurship as central R&D policy. The company simultaneously engages in long-term and short-term technological strategies in pursuit of one-of-a-kind technologies and products full of originality that must also bear fruit as business. Supervised by technology HQ, Sharp's Urgent Project teams are decided upon at the department's regular monthly technology conference, and at any one time the company usually has around 10 teams at work on different projects (development proposals are also screened at research director meetings in advance, and proposals that pass this process are discussed at the monthly technology conference). Project leaders are selected by middle management, and authority is given to freely assemble resources (personnel and capital etc.) across the boundaries between various business and research divisions as required.

Constantly aiming at plans for products that will sell, project teams always include personnel from the product planning department so that the marketing knowledge from the point of view of the customer can be included. Urgent Projects at Sharp involve personnel reshuffling within the company. As well as that, chosen leaders and officials responsible for submitting development proposals to the monthly technology conference have to commit to the development schedule and content that the conference decides. Sharp also uses this system to raise motivation levels in the company by forging a competitive spirit between departments, since departments with higher rates of proposal adoption are looked upon more favorably by management, although no cannibalization or battling goes on between divisions for product development.

Sharp's urgent project system serves to provide temporary authority for projects to transcend the organizational knowledge boundaries (specializations) within the company, and plays an important role in training the company's staff. Once projects have been disbanded and staff returned to their regular departments, the new knowledge forged through the urgent project system leaves staff with more motivation to accept further challenges, and becomes a driving force for personal growth. The more capable engineers are, the more often they will be called up for urgent projects. There are many cases where engineers have been called into new projects straight away once one is finished. Sharp staff members who have grown through the urgent project system and graduated from it are now active as the company's departmental and divisional chiefs. There are also staff members who have repeatedly offered up new development proposals as urgent projects, and who have repeatedly worked as project leaders and project members. CEO Machida had the following to say about the urgent project system:

When the urgent project system was initially formulated, it presented quite a few difficulties. A lot of departments were reluctant to let personnel jump across the walls between organizations. However as years passed, staff gradually deepened their understanding of the system and reinforced interdepartmental exchange, and since the engineers picked for urgent projects are always of a high caliber, and those people have gone on to become our departmental and divisional directors, they are quick to understand new urgent projects as they come along. This has created an atmosphere of congeniality across our organizational boundaries.

That explains the higher level of understanding that staff at Sharp have regarding urgent projects – a culture that has become well embedded in the company over the course of its history. Sharp's project management characteristically recycles the tacit knowledge and know-how that staff have accumulated through completed projects into new projects, and staff members continue to hone and develop new skills through this spiral project learning entrenched throughout the company. This type of project training seen in the case of Sharp offers a different viewpoint to that suggested by existing Western research into project management (Kodama 2007c).

Mobile telephone development is not always carried out through the urgent project system, but is also undertaken through development processes in the regular business sections of the company. For example, Sharp's camera phone development wasn't the result of an urgent project. However, the Aquos mobile development was an urgent project triggered by a pilot plan originating from middle management that was later structured with the top-down approach, even though the camera phone development could be interpreted as something close to an urgent project, since it was conceived as a highly innovative product that merged different technologies. This commercialized product was achieved through informal and voluntary dialogue and collaboration encouraged by the company's communication systems department and the IC Department supervising the camera module. In other words, the camera phone was the result of staff members voluntarily sharing and merging knowledge and technologies across the boundaries between organizations and specialist areas, as part of their daily routine activities in their various departments. Sharp is a company that has this kind of hospitable and cooperative organizational culture and teamwork attitude enmeshed within itself.

7.3.2 SHARP'S BOUNDARY VISION

Sharp's Corporate Capabilities – External Knowledge, Strategic, Organizational, and Leadership Integrative Capabilities (see Figure 7.3)

CEO Machida stresses the importance of mastering the depth of technology in the vertical dimension and its breadth in a horizontal dimension. This is what brings about 'creative reactions' within the company. When thinking about the merging of knowledge, technological depth in the vertical dimension comes through understanding of knowledge in individual areas of specialization. For example, engineers involved in communications, computer, software, imaging, lens, semiconductor, high precision mounting and production management technologies and so forth have to thoroughly learn and approach their individual fields of specialization with an enquiring mind. Engineers who have pursued an understanding of a single technology in the vertical dimension aim to acquire new knowledge through learning technical areas that lie in the horizontal periphery of their own specialization.

This could mean that engineers involved in imaging learn about semiconductors and software, or communications technology designers learn about the design of home appliances, or digital camera and digital video design specialists learn about communications equipment design etc. The technological convergence made possible through the linking up of horizontal technologies such as in the case of the camera phone, is an enabler to bring about products based on brand-new concepts through original and previously unknown 'creative reactions'.

Simply put, these 'creative reaction' mechanisms are the measures that Sharp takes for its innovation processes. CEO Machida had the following to say about these creative reactions:

> It's important for engineers to try and broaden the scope of a technology while they work to search out a single thing, because in future, more and more new products will be created through the merging of different technical capabilities. These creative reactions are just like chemical reactions, like the reaction between hydrogen and oxygen to create water, and just as with chemical reactions, it's important to realize that when different technologies are merged the product is something of an entirely different nature than its original ingredients. If companies want to forge new markets and demand, they will have to create new products in this way, by merging completely different technologies.

The 'creative reactions' that CEO Machida talks about and the actual processes behind them can be thought of as the external knowledge integrative capability – one of Sharp's boundary vision corporate capabilities that has enabled the company to release such a long string of hit products over the years. Products such as the camera phone, the Aquos mobile phone, and the large-screen LCD television are all imaginative products that have come about through Sharp's 'creative reaction' processes. These products are examples of engineers searching deeply through different areas of expertise and integrating knowledge across the horizontal boundaries of their individual specializations. Sharp's boundary networks between its different divisions feature multiple IBCs, and the business people working along these boundary networks merged different IBCs (networking) to integrate knowledge and eventually produce the camera phone (see Figure 7.1). Sharp is a company imbued with dynamic chains of these formal (urgent projects) and informal IBCs to enable creative reaction processes to take place.

As a feature of Sharp's strategy generation, this system enables the company to flexibly introduce new product ideas into the organizational lines among divisions etc. for product commercialization and development plans. Product commercialization at Sharp can either originate from the company's One-of-a-kind Products Planning Center, or from ideas that flourish on the shop floor in different departments. This system highlights Sharp's strategic integrative capability, as the company merges these new emergent product ideas ('emergent strategies' discussed in Chapter 2) by incorporating them into, and establishing them as 'intended strategies'. This strategic integrative capability is one of the boundary vision elements of corporate capability, and is a notable feature of Sharp's strategy generation.

The case of the mobile phone with built-in camera is an example of a bottom-up project triggered by middle management. Being surrounded by various related departments in the company, middle management has to practice 'middle up-down leadership' (Nonaka 1998). In this scenario, top management plays a supporting role for a project, and the important point here is for middle management to foster a climate in which informal projects can be executed voluntarily across different departments.

This type of organizational activity among Sharp's staff is the company's organizational integrative capability – a boundary vision corporate capability – that encourages them to engage in creative dialogue across the boundaries between different organizations and knowledge specializations, and is a driving force in the creation of IBCs and boundary networks. Sharp uses its organizational integrative capability to share its one-of-a-kind management vision with all staff members – who are always willing and delighted to cooperate by offering support and suggestions, or by lending a hand to help people in other departments deal with issues. This is also a driver behind the 'leadership integrative capability' that the company's staff members practice. The company encourages creative abrasion and productive friction in its IBCs and boundary networks to deal with new issues as they arise.

Behind all of Sharp's one-of-a-kind technologies and black boxing are people interacting with one another, and Sharp's expert engineers are always willing and ready to team up and work together. CEO Machida continued:

> *I believe Sharp is a company that runs on the 'power of harmony.' This is a very important thing for me. 'Harmony' suggests technological convergence. Skilful merging of devices created the camera phone and its 'Sha-Mail' service. Nokia and Motorola only had communications technologies, but by mixing up communication and imaging technology we were able to create the camera phone and Sha-Mail, and through combining word processor and information processing technologies we also produced Zaurus. Things can crystallize out of chemical reactions, and I think new products are born by a similar principle.*

> *How do we go about causing these reactions? Well, the idea of harmony is very important in Japanese culture and thus has a special power for the Japanese people. To explain this more clearly let me give you an example – One day someone is supervising cutting-edge semiconductor technology in the next day they are put in charge of household appliances. Normally, you would think such a person would quit, but at Sharp we believe that it's possible to find harmony through being introduced to unfamiliar things. This is because we have an environment in which these creative reactions can take place and crystallize into something new. To encourage this to happen, I do not advocate the usual company system. The old-fashioned company system does not enable convergence, and as technology becomes more and more complicated, and individual engineers reach the limits of how much they can actually know, ideas about combining technologies to produce products are becoming more and more important.*

The harmony that CEO Machida talks about here can be interpreted as a feature of Sharp's organizational and leadership capabilities. Staff come together in pursuit of unique technology, maintain their culturally important idea of harmony and pool together each other's wisdom to work as a team. That is the basis of Sharp's management style.

As part of their corporate vision based on the idea of harmony, Sharp staff are committed to 'sincerity and creativity' which they describe as follows: 'Sincerity is a virtue, put your heart into your job and the power of harmony will bring strength. Find unity and trust with each other, and show gratitude and respect to each other, for courtesy refines us. Creativity means to advance, and innovation and improvement give the courage to progress, and courage is the foundation of a rewarding life, even in times of difficulty ...'

These DNA-level values – sincerity and creativity – are infused into every member of staff; they promote resonance of values and collaboration, and trigger creative reactions and team work across the different organizations within the company. Furthermore, as the basis for Sharp's organizational and leadership integrative capabilities, external knowledge and strategic integrative capabilities, the 'power of harmony' is a vital element of the company's boundary vision to realize its one-of-a-kind technologies, products and management.

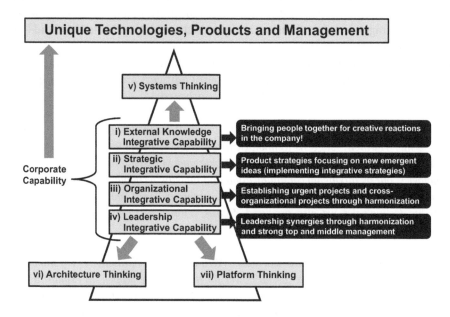

Figure 7.3   Corporate capabilities for Sharp's boundary vision

(2) Sharp's Business Design Capabilities – Systems, Architecture and Platform Thinking (see Figure 7.4)

A company's 'business design capability' is crucial for specific product developments. As one of their business capabilities, Sharp's 'systems thinking' involves the company putting itself in the shoes of ordinary citizens to develop products. Sharp's product planning department doesn't provide technological leadership; rather, staff in the department focus on human lifestyles and think about what kind of businesses and product planning can be conceived in that context.

Sharp's product planning originates from observations the company makes of people's lifestyles, and survey data the company collects through communication with ordinary citizens to extract needs and wants and think up product concepts for actual usage scenarios, and concepts that will deliver a high level of customer satisfaction. The company then takes the needs and market values that they discover and transfers them to actual product planning and design through the top-down (ordinary citizen's viewpoint functional viewpoint) and bottom-up (functional viewpoint citizen's viewpoint) knowledge integration approaches described in Chapter 2. Sharp matches needs and technology through this interactive trial and error process oscillating backwards and forwards between a grand design and micro designs to create new products and services. This systems thinking approach of matching market opportunity with business strategy is a feature of Sharp's product planning capability and has given birth to a range of hit products.

The second point of business design capability is architecture thinking – and the characteristics of this begin to appear if we observe the product architecture of Sharp's hit products. New products that Sharp creates are commercialized under the motto of 'one-of-a-kind products'. This is not 'incremental innovation' involving modifying and improving existing technology; rather, Sharp focuses on technology integration through architectural innovation. As mentioned, the camera phone and the Aquos mobile phone are both the results of the ingenious combining of different technological elements while simultaneously focusing on black boxing to bring about architectural innovation. The company also achieved radical innovation with unique technological methodologies where other global companies had failed – in the area of liquid crystal television development. Sharp also focuses on its own unique process architecture for unified development and manufacture all the way from the development and design stages through to the manufacturing for its liquid crystal televisions and mobile telephones.

The third point about business design capability is 'platform thinking'. Even though Sharp is particular about its own technology, the company does encourage collaboration and platform strategies with other companies. In October of 2008, Sharp linked up with NTT DOCOMO, Renesas and Fujitsu to start up a joint-venture for single LSI chip development for a mobile phone platform for HSUPA/HSDPA/W-CDMA (3G/3.5G) and GSM/GPRS/EDGE (2G) systems. By using this platform, Sharp and other mobile phone makers will be able to shorten development times and bring down costs because they won't need to independently develop basic mobile phone functions, which will make it easier for them to engage in product strategies that enable more distributed business resources that focus on developing unique functions or model lineups, and enable these companies to come up with more distinguishable and unique mobile telephone handsets.

In April of 2010, Sharp also announced a six-company collaboration with the four companies above in addition to NEC and Panasonic to form a joint venture to develop a new application platform for the Linux and Symbian operating systems. This means that companies won't have to independently develop basic functions for application processes in mobile phones, which will also reduce costs and development cycles, and enable different makers to focus on developing their own unique functions. By providing this platform not only in Japan but across mobile telephone markets globally, these companies also plan to support the Android open operating system and others in the future. This platform strategy through collaboration among Japanese mobile telephone makers is also a countermeasure against competition from companies like Samsung, LG Electronics, Nokia and Motorola, who hold leading positions in the global market. Sharp's platform thinking through collaboration with other companies is an example of merging and integrating core knowledge with partner knowledge to encourage hybrid innovation.

Also in recent years, since the introduction of Kindle and iPad, a platform competition for digital content delivery such as e-books has begun to emerge all over the world. Tackling this, Sharp has an ambitious proposal to create a unique format called 'next-generation XMDF' to deal with multimedia including audio and video, rather than just a simple strategy to offer some kind of terminal. Based on this format, Sharp hopes to provide newspaper and publishing companies with e-book authoring and delivery systems. The company also has strategies for future international expansion with its content delivery platform, and is currently negotiating alliances with Verizon in the United States and Vodafone in the UK.

Sharp's strategic systems thinking at the heart of its imaginative product design and technological development capabilities, and its architecture and platform thinking, are important elements of the company's business design capability that enables it to create new and innovative products.

Sharp is a company that makes good use of its corporate and business design capabilities through its boundary vision, and takes the insights gained to engage in dynamic development projects and urgent projects through the company's unique IBCs and boundary networks, based on a corporate culture rooted in 'the power of harmony'. Moreover, the company's boundary vision triggers the integration of unfamiliar knowledge and sparks off creative reactions in the company, thus enabling the company to realize one-of-a-kind technologies, one-of-a-kind products, and one-of-a-kind management.

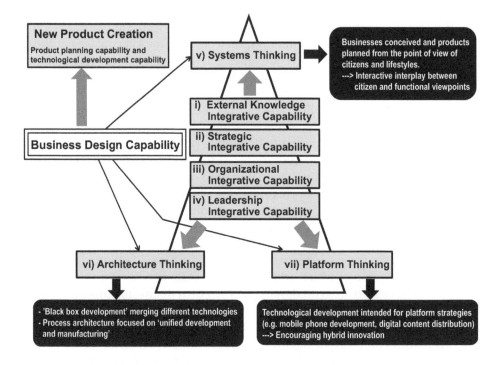

Figure 7.4   Business design capabilities for Sharp's boundary vision

Chapter 7 Conclusions

1. Sharp pursues new business models and products through the integration and convergence of different technologies. Twenty-first century high-tech businesses have to merge multiple points of view across boundaries in and out of companies to continually create new knowledge to meet their objectives.
2. The organizational capability at the core of innovation is born through interaction among professionals in different specializations in various organizations inside and outside corporations. 'IBCs' formed as boundary networks merging the many boundaries in and out of companies, in other words networking, encourage knowledge

integration that enables the establishment of organizational capabilities and business models which give companies a competitive edge.

3. The 'power of harmony' enriches boundary vision corporate capability and gives rise to the organizational systems of urgent and cross-functional projects, and encourages the merging of technologies within companies.

4. 'Systems thinking' is at the heart of imaginative ideas and concepts for product design and technological development capabilities, and architecture and platform thinking are also important elements of business design capability to bring about new products.

PART 3

Discussion and Conclusion

8 IBC and Boundary Networks Lead the Way to Innovation

8.1 Innovation Through Dynamic Knowledge Created by Boundary Architects

There is a strong tendency for new knowledge, and hence creativity, to emerge along the boundaries between different fields of specialization. Companies are segmented into specialist departments, business units etc., and furthermore there are a great many divides between corporations, industries, and business sectors, and there are innumerable visible and invisible boundaries between these macroscopic and microscopic partitions. As illustrated by many case studies of companies operating in highly volatile and competitive businesses, many corporations must execute strategies to merge wide-ranging knowledge across various boundaries within their own companies and between companies, and between companies and their customers. Certainly, knowledge is the primary source of a company's competitiveness, but it is worth considering that as well as the sectionalized organizational boundaries between business people in companies, there are also knowledge boundaries at the micro level due to the different values, specializations and backgrounds that business people possess (see Figure 2.1). These kinds of mental models and knowledge path dependencies that are entrenched in practitioners can be a hindrance to innovation (Kogut and Zander 1992, Nonaka and Takeuchi 1995, Leonard-Barton 1995, Brown and Duguid 2001, Spender 1990, Carlile 2002).

There are many business people who are aware of the 'invisible walls' that exist within companies, between companies, and between companies and customers. Uneasiness and complexities surrounding new businesses, and problems and issues arising due to relationships with external partners and customers far outweigh those in a company's own internal context. Is it possible for business people to overcome knowledge and organizational boundaries and manage diverse knowledge to create new knowledge?

As described in Chapter 2, business people who share knowledge to create new knowledge (called 'boundary architects' in this book) engage in network behavior patterns that demonstrate the 'boundary vision' needed to bridge the various boundaries inside and outside companies. Boundary vision is a way of thinking and discernment that enables corporations to design diverse boundaries and configure their vertical and horizontal boundaries ('boundary architecture' – see Figure 2.3 in Chapter 2). Boundary architects do not only adjust their company's boundaries to meet changing business and market environments, but also intentionally change boundaries to create new markets and businesses and bring about boundary innovation, and as an important factor for sustained corporate innovation, these concepts and skills should not be limited to top corporate management, but acquired at all levels of management throughout companies.

The formation of internal and external integration networks as IBC and boundary networks is crucial to achieving wide ranging innovations including hybrid innovation. Establishing these networks enables value chains to be optimized and new knowledge to be created, because the dynamic structuring of IBC and boundary networks based on this boundary vision dynamically changes a company's horizontal and vertical boundaries. This chapter illustrates the concepts behind IBCs and boundary networks in the context of the corporate cases described up to now, and also discusses the frameworks required to generate new innovation by managing and merging leadership patterns and diverse collaboration network systems through the 'leadership integrative capabilities' of boundary architects.

8.2 IBC Concepts – Three Dynamically Changing Characteristics

So far, this book has presented a number of case studies of high-tech corporations in the US, Japan and Taiwan that have achieved sustained innovation through the formation of diverse IBCs and boundary networks both in and out of their companies. This chapter describes three inherent characteristics of IBCs that transform dynamically in response to changing business environments, and their managerial aspects. Typically, leading global high-tech companies such as Apple feature organizational structures called 'boundary teams' (described in detail later) that play the central role in product development. There are four identifiable characteristics of these structures.

8.2.1 BOUNDARY CHARACTERISTICS AND ORGANIZATIONAL SYSTEMS

Business people are aware of a range of boundaries in their daily business activities. Chapter 2 provides an overview of the various boundaries that exist in and out of corporations (see Figure 2.1), but discussed in more detail, these boundaries are as follows. Firstly, there are organizational boundaries between official organizations within a corporation. These are examples of the organizational boundaries that formally exist between different business areas and functions such as research, development, manufacturing and sales. Based on the limitations and nature of their occupations, practitioners perform their daily business while adhering to the rules of their individual places of work. Formal organizational boundaries serve to delineate the territory for a business person's job, and in time, these formal organizational boundaries also transform into 'communities of practice' (Com.oP hereafter)[1] that correspond to the nature of the work and function of the business within those boundaries.

The second type of boundary is related to the first type, and is a boundary that sets out the hierarchical authority structure for the organization. In this type of boundary, official

---

1   A 'Com.oP' (community of practice) is a community group formed from actors in the same areas of specialization or business functions within a corporation. Com.oPs are basically associations of the same type of specialists (e.g. groups of managers, developers, who have the same type of knowledge), often formed as study communities (Lave and Wenger 1991; Brown and Duguid 1991; Orr 1996). Com.oPs are not dependent on particular personal knowledge. Members create common knowledge through sustained cooperation and coordination with each other over time. The knowledge gained through continual learning in a Com.oP aids the growth of an organization.

positions of authority are assigned to individual business people within an organization, and boundaries emerge as hierarchies of the powers held by those individuals (Thompson 1967, Pfeffer and Salancik 1978).

The third type of boundary is also related to the official positions in the first type, and is rooted in the specializations of business people involved in areas such as research, layout, manufacturing, product planning design and so forth. These boundaries can be called 'knowledge boundaries'. Knowledge boundaries separate the unique 'thought worlds' or mental models of individual business people, and are the borders that define uniform opinions about various issues and serve to establish the domains of occupations and tasks. Confrontation between marketers who focus on things to do with marketing, and engineers who concentrate on technologies occurs along these knowledge boundaries.[2]

As well as these boundaries, there are also a range of boundaries that exist between different corporations. Apart from the organizational and knowledge boundaries among business people, there are for instance, boundaries that are inherent in the various customs and practices of different types of businesses or business functions, as well as knowledge boundaries that are rooted in the individual strategic intentions of different corporations.

In the mass production model, organizational and knowledge boundaries promote efficiency in stable business environments, and provide an effective framework for business people to carry out their routine occupational functions within the individual official organizations in which they have been granted authority. In hierarchical (or bureaucratic) organizations, business people have clear boundaries defined for them in advance, and managers place importance on top-down leadership for their strategic planning. The mass production model demands systematic efficiency to meet central operating targets for product commercialization through routine business processes that have already been decided via hierarchical organizational structures and established development and manufacturing methods. The main purpose of these individual boundaries (organizational, hierarchical, knowledge) is to bring about efficient and productive business processes with a focus on rules, regulations and company procedures such as business and operation manuals for information dissemination and business interaction between organizations. Boundaries like these, which require business people to follow procedures for transferring knowledge and information among themselves have been called 'syntactic or information-processing boundaries'.[3]

By contrast, in organizations that have responded to fluctuating market and business circumstances, a different sort of boundary to these syntactic boundaries arises among business people. These different boundaries are formed among players to enable new ways for knowledge to be interpreted and new meanings to be created, and are called 'semantic boundaries'(Shannon and Weaver 1949, Jantsch 1980, Carlile 2002, 2004). Semantic boundaries serve to promote action to gradually (incrementally) improve and

2   For more details about 'knowledge boundaries', 'thought worlds' and 'mental models', refer to Brown and Duguid (2001), Dougherty (1992), Spender (1990) and Grinyer and McKiernan (1994).

3   The organizational 'information processing model' describes new product development and streamlined business processes in formal organizations within a company, or through communication and alliances among business people in different companies. For example, see 'differentiation and integration' in Lawrence and Lorsch (1967), 'adequate information processing capacity' in Galbraith (1973), 'coordination theory' in Malone and Crowston (1994) and others – existing research that describes the optimization of information processing in syntactic boundaries within and between organizations. For more details about the characteristics of these three boundaries, refer to Shannon and Weaver (1949), Jantsch (1980), and Carlile (2002, 2004).

reform existing business processes as well as development and manufacturing methods. Semantic boundaries focus on rules and regulations and company procedures in the same way as syntactic boundaries, but also promote ongoing organizational learning to advance a company's best practice, Total Quality Management (TQM) and so forth for corporate reform and improvement.

As previously mentioned, the formation of a 'Com.oP' brings about the creation and sharing of new meanings among business people along the semantic boundary to promote organizational learning and best practices. Founded on the sharing, empathy and resonance of values among members,[4] Com.oPs promote mutual learning along semantic boundaries as business people deepen their understanding of each other's contexts and values, and thus bring about the sustained creation of new knowledge. As the membership of business people active on the semantic boundaries gradually becomes more established, there is increasing impetus for organizational learning to give birth to new contexts for their targets and missions. These semantic boundaries that promote organizational learning are the first foundations on which 'boundary teams' (BTs hereafter) and 'collectivities of practice' (Col.oPs hereafter) are formed, discussed in more detail below.

8.2.2 COL.OPS AND BTS – PRAGMATIC ORGANIZATIONAL SYSTEMS

Innovation boundaries (new product and service development, new business model development etc.) with a high degree of novelty, or boundaries where uncertainty arises, demand the creation of new knowledge and exchange of existing knowledge that goes beyond the organizational learning and creation of new meaning in Com.oPs with their shared contexts. These kinds of boundaries are called 'pragmatic boundaries' (Shannon and Weaver 1949, Jantsch 1980, Carlile 2002, 2004). These correspond to the realization of completely unconventional business concepts, such as product and service developments to achieve new business models, new component and technological architecture developments and big changes in rules that accompany new developments and manufacturing methods, and therefore there is high potential for new knowledge to be born as a source of innovation along these pragmatic boundaries.[5]

Various frictions and conflicts occur at pragmatic boundaries.[6] To achieve new and unconventional targets and solve problems as they arise, business people take action to advance existing knowledge through the conflicts and frictions among themselves and political leverage in these communities. Because these three types of boundaries are mutually dependent upon each other, their characteristics can change drastically with

---

4   For more about the 'resonance of values' process, refer to Kodama (2001).

5   Much of the existing research to date regarding cross-functional boundaries behind successful new product development (e.g. Allen 1977; Tushman 1977; Tushman and Nadler 1978) suggests the need for smooth communications, or the need for the so-called 'boundary spanner' (Brown and Eisenhardt 1995). The central concept of these theories is an information processing model that focuses on the efficient processing, transfer, storage and retrieval of large amounts of information and knowledge in syntactic boundaries. Of course, the information processing approach is also required for corporate procedures based on regulations, efficient project management and the execution of business processes. However, because innovation tends to occur along the boundaries between different business people in different areas of specialization or organizations with distinctly different rules (Leonard-Barton 1995), the information processing approach with its focus on efficient knowledge and information processing cannot adequately describe the innovation process.

6   For more about creative abrasion and conflict, see Leonard-Barton (1992). For details about political negotiations, refer to Brown and Duguid (2001).

changing circumstances (customer needs, market competitiveness etc.), the emergence of uncertainties, and the interests and intentions of the people involved. Especially with innovation and corporate reform, with changing circumstances and people's intentions working even stronger, a shift towards these pragmatic boundaries occurs in the relationships between business people (syntactic boundaries semantic boundaries pragmatic boundaries) (see Figure 8.1).

All kinds of conflicts, frictions and contradictions arise among business people working along pragmatic boundaries. Not only is this due to sectionalism among business people in corporations separated by organizational boundaries, but also due to differences in personal values, backgrounds and skills along knowledge boundaries. The reasons for these conflicts are the dominating path dependencies and personal mental models that business people gain through their different backgrounds and experience, which results in them expressing uneasiness or resistance when faced with new or unfamiliar knowledge at their organizational boundaries.[7]

Temporary or informal project organizations consisting of people from a range of different specializations formed to deal with issues characterized by high levels of uncertainty and novelty have the characteristics of these pragmatic boundaries, because they contain large knowledge boundaries that cause friction and conflict. In contrast to the Com.oPs in the semantic boundaries mentioned earlier, these types of project organizations that bring together personnel with knowledge in diverse specialist fields are called 'collectivities of practice'[8] (Col.oPs hereafter), a term coined by European Scholars of Business Studies. These are not the same as Com.oPs with their collective and organization knowledge and infrastructure based on knowledge common among the members in those organizations, because Col.oPs are organizations of loosely bound personal knowledge that do not retain the knowledge shared in project organizations.[9]

---

7   Just as history has taught, corporations and organizations who are dominated by rigid mental models and cannot overcome competency traps (Levitt and March 1988; Martines and Kambil 1999), or core rigidities (Leonard-Barton, 1992, 1995), run the risk of losing opportunities for innovation due to their path-dependent knowledge (Christensen, 1997).

8   As Wenger (1998) states, a project is clearly not the same as a Com.oP. Because Com.oPs consist of actors in the same field of expertise or business function, the boundaries between them are small, and they possess similar thought worlds and mental models. Since these communities are also focused on routine work, they do not encounter the large degrees of novelty or uncertainty inherent in project work, and therefore do not experience much conflict or friction between actors. Com.oPs derive new meanings from regular work practices, and deeply share this among their members to promote learning and incremental improvement and reform. The Com.oP theory has limitations and cannot be applied to all business contexts. For more details, see Roberts (2006).

9   Lindkvist (2005, p. 1190) described project organizations as 'Collectivities of Practice' and stated the following in this regard: 'Typically, such temporary organizations or groups within firms consist of people, most of whom have not met before, and who have to engage in swift socialization and carry out a pre-specific task within set limits with respect to time and cost. Moreover, they comprise a mix of individuals with highly specialized competencies, making it difficult to establish shared understandings or a common knowledge base.'

     Projects are highly autonomous in their objectives. Because projects often have to meet their targets within strict time limits, team members cannot afford to adequately share and accumulate knowledge through learning in the same way that Com.oPs can take time to share new contexts for developing new actions. Therefore, in carrying out project tasks, project members are highly dependent on their own personal knowledge and capabilities. Project teams do not depend on the sharing of common knowledge and values in the same way as Com.oPs; rather, they carry out their jobs based on the highly dispersed personal knowledge of the team members involved. For this reason, it is especially important for project leaders to coordinate and integrate (combine) particular knowledge or capabilities of individual team members. Then, once a project is complete and the team disbands, individual members can walk away with the new know-how that they have gained as a result of their involvement in the project. However, it can be difficult to share or exchange this knowledge with other projects or other existing organizations. Furthermore, big knowledge boundaries and different individual thought worlds exist between the different specializations and business functions of members of

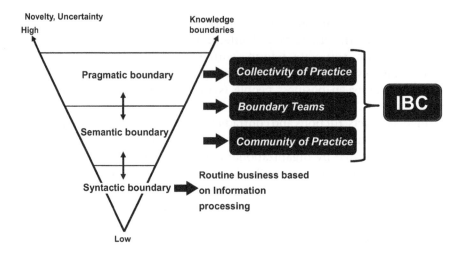

Figure 8.1   Forms of IBCs in boundaries for three levels

Note: this figure was generated based on Kodama (2007a)

This is a good place to introduce examples illustrating the difference between a project organization and a Com.oP. Having research and business centers in 21 countries, Buckman Laboratories International is a company that contracts R&D from its main paper manufacturing business and has a network-based forum for the sharing and creation of knowledge that it calls 'Techforum'. Staff in any of these countries can access Techforum and rapidly search for advice from people with specialist knowledge from anywhere around the globe. Not only does this transcend the boundaries of international borders, but also crosses over the boundaries that lay between different areas of knowledge and organizations, and when many of the participants in the forum are in agreement with each other, autonomous project organizations form. Staff bring their own knowledge into the various projects born on the network, and exchange discussion with each other while proceeding with their R&D tasks. Including specialized paper manufacturing technologies, there are several tens of new technologies born every year through this project system.

CEO Buckman calls the Techforum an 'issue-driven community' and says it has different characteristics to a Com.oP (Buckman 2003). The point about the 'issue-driven community' is that it forms informal and dynamic teams consisting of members in different areas of specialization to rapidly respond to issues. The speedy nature of this context and the variety of specializations involved is characteristic of Col.oP dynamic human networking and collaboration that brings about new and novel knowledge (or it is close to a BT, discussed next).

Because of frequent tradeoffs and logical compromises however, there are cases of project organizations on pragmatic boundaries that don't always achieve genuine innovation. This is because idea creation and execution processes end up dominated by logic and rational dialogue among participants. In contrast, merging the characteristics of

---

Col.oPs. As well as that, there are large elements of novelty and uncertainty in projects which can result in frequent and serious conflicts and frictions.

shared value in Com.oPs as semantic boundaries with the collection of (or simultaneous use of) different kinds of specialized knowledge in Col.oPs as pragmatic boundaries does not only promote rational decision-making, but also raises the potential for a shift to more productive innovation through creative dialogue among members.

The teams of business people with diverse knowledge formed along boundaries created from the merging and combining of these two semantic and pragmatic boundary characteristics, are referred to as 'boundary teams' (BTs) in this book (see Figure 8.1). BTs are organizational bodies that merge and combine the characteristics of both semantic and pragmatic boundaries and bring about 'creative collaboration' (discussed later) that promotes creative abrasion and productive friction among team members.

IBCs are formed from these Com.oPs, BTs, and Col.oPs – three distinct 'human interaction' organizational systems. IBCs can be dynamically adjusted among these three types of system to meet changing business circumstances (novelty or uncertainty, or the level of knowledge boundaries and so forth).

In BTs and Col.oPs, a range of arguments and battles arises because they often include contexts that negate the existing mental models or experience of business people. Furthermore, BTs and Col.oPs that include certain customers present a range of customer demands, issues and problems, although to achieve innovation, especially in BTs, creative abrasion and productive action must be induced through creative dialogue among participants. Moreover, simple BTs and Col.oPs are not enough for innovation in all cases, and a number of them may be merged within companies (between departments, businesses, management levels etc.) and between companies (partners and customers) to form boundary networks. The more complicated a business model proposal, the greater the pressure on participants to form BTs and Col.oPs and network these together. The author believes that the new knowledge born through these IBC and boundary networks formed from BTs, Col.oPs and Com.oPs existing in and out of companies is also a source of organizational capability.

Especially, the thinking and action of business people who merge new knowledge born of IBCs formed in and out of companies that include partners (in other words, merge IBCs that exist inside and outside the company) is a source of innovation that also ties in with the organizational capability needed for sustained competitiveness. These Boundary networks are the creation of 'boundary architects' who link together and merge various IBCs in and outside their companies (see Figure 8.2).

To create new knowledge and bring about innovation in industries involved in fiercely competitive and volatile markets, boundary architects form IBC and boundary networks across a wide range of boundaries in and between companies including their customers, to merge all kinds of knowledge to execute their strategies. This book has presented a range of case examples of high-tech corporations that respond to the rapid pace of technological innovation and fluctuating markets and continually execute product development strategies by not only engaging in deep collaboration across diverse boundaries between different technological areas to converge technologies, but also by creating collaboration networks that simultaneously include marketing, sales, technical and production sectors (see the case of Chunghwa Telecom in Chapter 5, and the case of Sharp in Chapter 7).

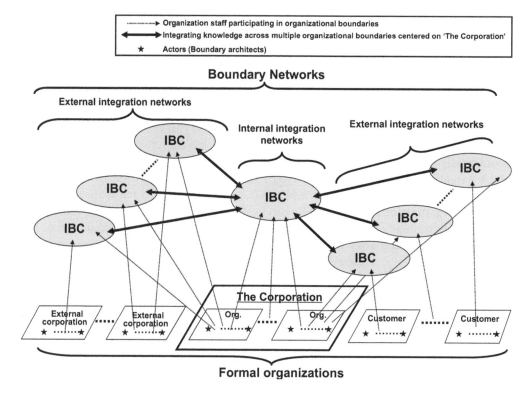

Figure 8.2 IBC and boundary networks

Members of these IBCs work hard across the borders between sectors to understand technological trends and product development road maps from the points of view and ways of thinking of a range of different areas of specialization through the act of constant sharing. Not only does this apply to technological innovation, but also to innovating new business models – IBC and boundary networks that are formed within companies as well as across different industries and businesses, and include customers and partners (see the cases of NTT DOCOMO, Google, and Apple in Chapter 3, and the cases of Qualcomm, eSilicon, TSMC and Fujitsu in Chapter 4).

Panasonic President Fumio Ohtsubo suggests the importance of forging what he calls 'undersurface competitiveness' (Ohtsubo 2006):

> *A company's 'surface competitiveness' can be seen in its sales, its market share, the ranking of its brand image – indexes that customers can easily understand. The problem is the 'undersurface competitiveness' that customers do not easily see is an essential part of manufacturing. This 'undersurface competitiveness' forms the main foundation on which staff members perform their daily tasks and engage in teamwork. It's important to regroup the businesses of design, development, manufacturing and quality control like a single chain. If you take a look at western IT corporations, they are often strongly colored by distributed business functions. Personnel is personnel, design is design, development is development – departments are independent of each other and tied together by powerful leadership. However in Japan, designers get down onto the manufacturing floor, and manufacturing professionals make requests to developers. There*

is always some degree of information overlap between different business functions, which greatly empowers the whole company. This is the character of Japanese manufacturing, the duty of Japanese manufacturing. Most Japanese corporations have this culture of collecting and combining wisdom across their design, manufacturing and resource sectors.

Adding to those comments, former NEC President Kaoru Yano suggests the importance of innovation through teamwork (Yano 2006):

Currently, our slogan is 'One NEC', which says that everybody in our company should express unity. Teamwork is very important to us. Adjacent organizations that are always aware that they are working together can open up any number of new possibilities. Actually, we have advanced our cooperative relationships across organizational barriers quite substantially ... Japanese people are especially good at teamwork. If we forget teamwork, how are we to compete globally? Overseas corporations are beginning to imitate Japanese-style teamwork, which is our strength. So, I think now as much as ever, to break through the 'growth barrier', it's important to continue to team up and cooperate with each other.

These two business leaders' comments do not at all reflect something that is limited to Japanese companies, but point out an opinion held by corporations throughout the world. Just as Messrs. Ohtsubo and Yano say, IBC and boundary network formation brings out the power of teamwork across departments and organizations with simultaneous structuring of business processes and value chains, which enables the embedding of organizational capability within a company – what Mr. Ohtsubo calls 'rear competitiveness'.

8.2.3 BT CHARACTERISTICS – THE FOUR 'MEAN POINTS' OF CREATIVE DIALOG

Boundary teams (BTs) encourage creative dialogue. The fundaments of creative dialogue lie in dialectical thinking.[10] Dialectics are characteristically good at enabling people to grasp logical solutions to problems, because they incorporate both the intuitive and the analytical. In general terms, the process of problem solving can be understood as the 'thesis' (positive), the 'antithesis' (negative) and 'synthesis' (negating the negative). The predominant feature of dialectics is the replacement of the logical 'thesis' space with the logical 'synthesis' space as the 'thesis' 'antithesis' 'synthesis' process advances. However, the logic talked about here is not the logic of formulas but the logic of meaning, so it's probably better to call these logical spaces 'meaning spaces' instead, because syllogisms that involve formal logic cannot give birth to new propositions or meanings. Hegel named the creation of new logical spaces 'sublation' (aufheben), which serves to negate and simultaneously preserve. Put more directly, no matter whether a proposition can be found to be true or false, any 'true' proposition will have an 'opposite' counterpart that negates it. The solution to this opposing positive and negative situation is not to make

---

10   Hegel's dialectics are used in similar methods of inquiry into pragmatism, e.g. Peirce's i) abduction, ii) deduction, iii) induction, or Dewey's i) problematic situation, ii) defining of the problem, iii) hypothetical investigation, iv) deduction, v) testing, vi) conclusions (guaranteed assertions), although these methods are more rooted in the scientific method. In general, dialectics is the process of 'thesis', 'antithesis' and 'synthesis', where 'synthesis' will also give rise to 'antithesis' that subsequently seeks a new 'synthesis' ... etc., which can turn into a perpetual process. Nevertheless, the qualitative aspect of dialectics changes with the emergence of 'conversions of quantity and quality', 'interpenetrations of conflict' and 'negating the negative' – all of which serve to bring forth new knowledge and meaning that moves beyond ordinary dichotomies.

an either/or selection and eliminate one of the choices, but to 'sublate' with a both/and selection and retain the advantages of each option, which leads to propositions of a higher dimension (new meaning spaces).

In dialectical thinking truth is dynamic, and the processes of 'thesis', 'antithesis' and 'synthesis' help to develop creative dialogue. Productive dialectical thinking starts with 'conflict and coexistence', 'reconciliation and unification', and 'negating the negative'. However, in practicing this process of 'thesis' 'antithesis' and 'synthesis' in real-life business situations, rather than engage in the western Hegel school of 'hard dialectics' that aims to eliminate contradiction, it's better to embrace inconsistencies as natural and dynamic phenomena, allow ambiguity, and practice the 'soft dialectic'[11] of the eastern approach to achieve balance. In this kind of 'soft dialectic' approach, instead of interpreting things as elemental and abstract 'absolute truths', they should be understood in terms of the whole context and their relationship to it, to dynamically create a 'mean point' beyond compromise. Accordingly, team members must investigate new meanings and processes that pose the question 'how can this be produced?' rather than engage in the formal logic of syllogisms that ask whether something exists as a truth or not. To practice this kind of 'contradictory productivity', business people need an open way of thinking that accepts contradiction as they get into the details (meanings) of the matters at hand. Business people need both self-assertiveness and humility to personally develop to a higher dimension and become a conduit for contradictions and confrontation with others, and need to develop an awareness that they themselves are not infallible (Osono, Kodama, Yachi and Nonaka 2005).

The concept of 'the mean point' of 'soft dialectics' is clearly reflected in the characteristics of BTs. These characteristics can be defined as i) 'the mean of knowledge'; ii) 'the mean of relationships'; iii) ' the mean of boundaries'; and iv) 'the mean of thought-worlds'. We can describe these BT features through the case of Apple's product development of the iPod.

i) The Mean of Knowledge

As managers in the world's leading corporations drive project management through the formation of BTs, they simultaneously practice collaboration and coordination among existing organizations and engage in the business of linking up any number of different projects. Projects in leading companies start out as either formally or informally formed projects with participation from personnel in a range of existing functional organizations, and typically promote the sharing and mutual transfer of knowledge and know-how of these organizations. In companies with notably low levels of personnel turnover, there are many cases of project teams consisting of colleagues who have worked together in the past, bosses and subordinates, and staff members who are old friends. Accordingly, the level of knowledge and information sharing among project teams in the first-class companies is higher than project organizations in which members meet up for the first time in companies with a high staff turnover.

---

11   Nisbett (2003) describes dialectical thinking by contrasting the analytical skills of Western thinking with the broad-view understanding of Eastern thinking as analogous to eastern thinking looking across the whole forest, whereas western thinking stares at a single large tree.

The base knowledge in BTs does not only depend on the individual skills and know-how of certain people or the individual specialized knowledge as in a Col.oP; rather, the collective and organizational knowledge with proven track records achieved through real-world practice is also merged, as is the case in a Com.oP organization. This can be referred to as the 'harmonized knowledge' of a BT. New product development projects in high-tech companies are staffed from personnel within the company (and sometimes outside the company), and these project members smoothly share the knowledge and know-how accumulated between their Com.oPs, whether they are given additional postings to their regular departments, or dispatched by their bosses to participate in a project.

In the Apple iPod development project case, CEO Steve Jobs appointed Mr. Jonathan Rubinstein as system designer to steer the project (Rubinstein worked on Apple's original Mac, through to the water cooled workstation, and took charge of iPod development until 2006, when he resigned to become CEO of Palm). Rubinstein made use of the technological know-how he had accumulated, intentionally sought out technologies outside the company, and scouted for people who had experience with this type of music player. The key person recruited was Anthony Fadell, who greatly contributed to the development of the iPod (previously he had worked for General Magic and Philips before starting his own company. After joining Apple, he later took over iPod operations from Rubinstein). Accompanied by Stan Ng, Apple's marketing director, Fadell engaged in portable music player market research, and began detailed technological investigation and product development under the supervision of Rubinstein.[12]

Apple already had know-how with FireWire (wireless LAN data transfer technology that had the potential to transfer tunes to the music player at high speed) and PC peripheral development, and had purchased the rights to SoundJamMP that became the base for the company's iTunes product. The iPod development involved a range of departments within Apple as well as associations with external corporations (first-class part makers and EMS companies etc.). Within the structure at Apple, iTunes developer Jeff Robin was put in charge of developing the iPod internal software, software to link up with iTunes, operability and the user interface. The iPod design was entrusted to well-known industrial designer Jonathan Ive, while the iPod hardware development was driven along mainly by Rubinstein, Fadell and Ng.

In the iPod development project, many of the ideas about the device came through creative dialogue between the different departments at Apple. The iPod developers gained a lot of stimulating ideas from a wide range of Apple's internal organizations such as the FireWire development group,[13] PowerMac supervisors, software developers and the company's documentation section. Apple staff are fully aware of the confidentiality surrounding new product development, and have a deep understanding of each other's situations (new product developers), and do not spare any efforts to assist each other, even when the iPod development team made seemingly impossible requests.

---

12   Based on market research results reported in April of 2001, Apple's top management (Steve Jobs, Phil Schiller) gave the go-ahead for the new product development. However, to be ready for the Christmas shopping rush, they ordered that this high-quality product be completed within six months. The development team members were quickly assembled, and to facilitate easy dialogue with the iTunes division, the iPod division was set up next door. Then, on the 23rd of October in the same year, Steve Jobs announced the first iPod at Apple's headquarters in California, with the catch copy 'Say hello to iPod. 1000 songs in your pocket.'

13   Not only did the company incorporate software such as iTunes to make iPod easy-to-use. The ability to link up the device with a personal computer also played a big role (for instance, the use of the IEEE1394 interface that Apple called 'FireWire'). To develop this function, Apple's FireWire team capabilities were also called upon.

Rubinstein had the following to say:

The iPod was not developed from scratch. We already had hardware engineering groups that we could rely on – if you need a power supply, there is a power supply group, if you need a display, there is a display group. The architecture group also helped us. The product is a collection of the technologies that Apple already had.

And Mr. Ngcommented commented:

We got help from a lot of different departments at Apple. CAD supervisors, designers, software developers … We opened all the drawers in the Apple cupboard and pulled out whatever personnel we needed. The iPod development was a bit like starting up a venture business, but if it had been a real venture we would never have been able to get the thing ready in such a short time. We were only able to because we had the support of the whole company. Everybody was happy to help out – even if it had little or nothing to do with their own business area.

Greg Jozwiak, Apple's Vice President of Hardware Product Marketing said that it wasn't possible to grasp exactly how many people were involved in the iPod development:

There were engineers who were hired full-time for the iPod project, but there were also a lot of other people in the company who worked on it as well. Probably, there were several tens of people at the core of the development, but probably hundreds of people who had some hand in it. Apple employs at least 1000 hardware engineers, and more than 1000 software engineers, but only a handful of those are dedicated to specific products. The rest are involved in projects as the need arises.

This characteristic of Apple's approach to product development projects is typical of a BT, and the 'harmonized knowledge' mentioned earlier is embedded in the company's BTs as part of Apple's product development culture. These BTs are drivers that bring about the 'creative collaboration', 'boundary penetration' and 'shared thought worlds' discussed next. Illustrated in Figure 8.4 and discussed in more detail later, projects like the iPod development formed as BTs that merge knowledge in and out of the company raise potentials and realize hybrid innovation.

ii) The Mean of Relationships

In one way, the pragmatic boundaries that characterize BTs are often breeding grounds for various problems and issues that arise in the relationships among members and business processes due to the high degree of novelty and uncertainty in their business contexts. It's natural for conflict and friction to occur between project members, and project members find themselves faced with a range of compromises and trade-offs in many cases due to time and cost constraints. These patterns are a notable feature of Col.oPs. However, they are not the only solutions that project organizations should choose. Rather than aim for compromise, project teams that aim to genuinely combine and synthesize contradictions by amassing creative abrasion and productive friction through creative dialogue among project members have been observed in many of the world's leading corporations. Apple is one of these top-level global corporations that conducts itself in this way. Because

Apple aspires to bringing the best possible products to its customers (like the iPod), the company never compromises on any of its developmental elements.

The Japanese corporation Canon Marketing Inc. has also described similar characteristics of their projects in which there is 'a productive battle devoid of compromises'. Honda also talk of creative dialogue in their meetings, and Sharp, described in Chapter 7, outline their policy of ' helping each other's projects and lending a hand' through collaboration and support across different project teams and organizations. Apple's iPod development also exemplifies this same kind of corporate culture. Because this means that the organizational behaviors of project members in BTs simultaneously pursue the merging of conflicting knowledge of individuals in Col.oPs with the familiar knowledge in Com.oP groups and organizations, this behavior can be called 'creative collaboration' in BTs. As illustrated in Figure 8.1, members in BTs characteristically combine Col.oPs as pragmatic boundaries with the semantic boundaries of Com.oPs to find a middle path and bring about creative collaboration.

iii) The Mean of Boundaries

Innovation in BTs lies in the nature of unique knowledge boundaries. Obviously, knowledge is the source of a corporation's competitiveness, and the knowledge possessed by human beings is the origin of strategic formation and execution. The tacit knowledge of skills, know-how and core competencies is embedded in the thinking and behavior patterns of individual people. Importantly, in the knowledge integration process necessary for BTs aiming for innovation, Col.oPs that transcend knowledge boundaries of diverse human knowledge inside and outside companies must be put together, while at the same time, knowledge at the tacit level in Com.oP groups and organizations must be shared and merged. The thinking and actions of BTs that create new knowledge across these knowledge boundaries can be called 'boundary penetration'. Apple's iPod product development is a case realized through the occurrence of boundary penetration between the knowledge boundaries of many different areas of expertise (design, human interface, hardware, software etc.).

iv) The Mean of Thought Worlds

BT members must also have the flexibility to view things from the points of view of diverse business functions and specialist areas. For example, managers who have technological backgrounds in leading corporations demonstrate the potential to propose new technologies from the point of view of marketability, while on the other hand, managers with experience in marketing and sales express their desire to learn about technology, though they may have little experience in the area. In this way, everybody involved focuses on making efforts to find the relevance between technology and the market. As illustrated by the Apple development case based on its culture of embedded mutual learning between different specialist areas, this is the 'thought world' that exists in BTs – the crossover career paths of managers, crossing over the Col.oP values rooted in business and specialist knowledge of individual people with the Com.oP values rooted in group and organizational knowledge. These can be called the 'shared thought worlds' of BTs.[14]

Boundary teams encourage the dialectical elements of these four middle-path Col.oP and Com.oP characteristics – harmonized knowledge, creative collaboration, boundary penetration and shared thought worlds. As quoted from Panasonic Director Ohtsubo in section 8.2.2:

There is always some degree of overlap formed between different business functions, which greatly empowers the whole company. Most Japanese corporations have this culture of collecting and combining wisdom across their design, manufacture and resource sectors.

Ohtsubo's comment reflects the harmonized knowledge and shared thought worlds of BTs.

Similarly, as former NEC president Yano says:

Adjacent organizations that are continually aware that they are working together can open up any number of new possibilities. Actually, we have advanced our cooperative relationships across organizational barriers quite substantially. ... So, I think now as much as ever, to break through the 'growth barrier', it's important to continue to team up and cooperate with each other.

This comment reflects the creative collaboration and boundary penetration in BTs. And as previously stated, this feature of BTs is not limited to Japanese corporations, but is a project culture common throughout the leading high-tech companies of the world such as Apple.

Figure 8.3 illustrates the concepts and positioning of BT, Com.oP and Col.oP[15] organizational systems. The BT is an organizational system that lies midway between the

---

14   In one of Japan's major telecommunications carriers (in which the author has worked), staff involved in technology are assigned to business sections and research departments once they join the company. Engineers assigned to business sections are rotated through various functional departments on a two to three-year basis. For example, after joining the company an engineer's career path might start in the technology department (as a communications equipment or communications service development supervisor), then move to a business section (as a section chief or assistant manager of a facilities division), then move back to a technology department (as a development manager), then back to the business division (as a sales and facilities manager), then become the manager of the technology department, then become a departmental chief in the business division, and then become a director in the marketing and sales division. Different individuals follow different career paths – there are also cases of staff that have moved from the business section to become R&D managers. Engineering staff assigned to the research department initially begin working on separate R&D proposals, but can then become occupied as R&D managers through promotions, while there are also scientists and engineers who follow career paths exclusively in their respective fields. There is no small number of cases of researchers who have moved into the technology divisions within business departments or marketing and sales – there is always a vibrant dialogue going on between the research and business ends of the company, and after gaining experience in business divisions often people return to their original research departments. This is a consistent personnel education system oriented towards coupling business with research and development – in other words a mechanism to avoid the so-called 'Valley of Death'.

15   The axes in Figure 8.3 illustrate the characteristics of knowledge, the level of knowledge boundaries between actors and their thought worlds, and the degree of conflict and friction in the relationships between business people in these Com.oPs and Col.oPs. In a Com.oP, business people with knowledge about the same job functions and areas of specialization (where the knowledge boundaries between actors are small) embed new knowledge in their group or organization by mutually engaging in deep dialogue and collaboration (there is little friction between business people) based on the knowledge they have retained through similar experience. By contrast, business people in a Col.oP with knowledge in different areas of specialization and who possess different thought worlds, engage in collaboration and coordination based on minimal common knowledge, and it is through the merging of these individual professional

Com.oP and Col.oP (the midpoint) and includes some of the features of both.[16] IBCs are these three organizational systems dynamically adjusted to respond to changing business circumstances.

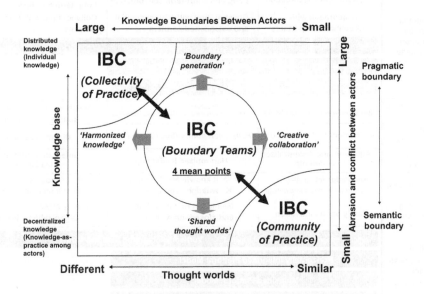

Figure 8.3   Three features of dynamically changing IBCs
Note: this figure was generated based on Kodama (2007c)

8.2.4 ELEMENTS OF IBC MANAGEMENT

Next, let's sort out the features of IBC management that pertain to these three organizational systems (see Figure 8.4).

Com.oP Features

In a Com.oP, long-term collaboration is encouraged among members in specific areas of specialization and workplaces under common values, while outside the company, this and organizational learning are also important for smooth knowledge transfer to share technological know-how emerging from prolonged dealings with established partners. In terms of the collaboration networks discussed in Chapter 3, collaboration among members takes a closed form with certain leaders and managers selected from particular areas of specialization who operate under a hierarchical governance structure in the Com. oP (an elite circle).

---

capabilities in the Col.oP that products with new goals are born. There are also concepts that involve interplay of these Com.oP and Col.oP characteristics.

16   The author has proposed the concept of 'strategic communities' (SCs) through his fieldwork to date. An SC can mean the two types of BT and Col.oP systems. See Kodama (2007c).

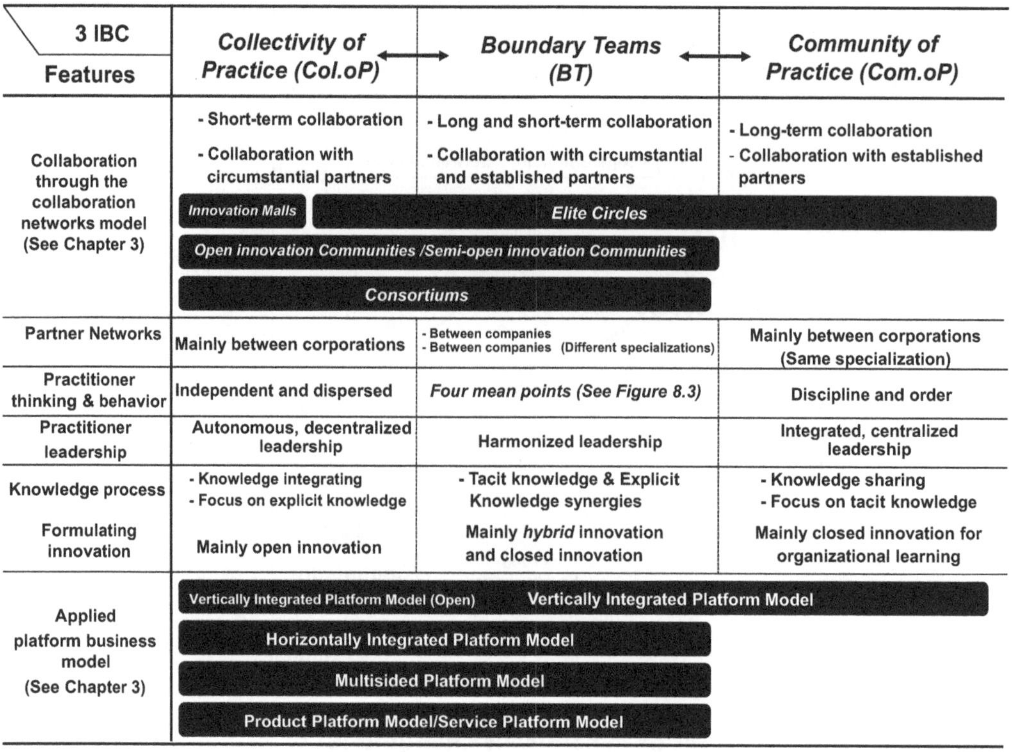

3 IBC Features	Collectivity of Practice (Col.oP)	Boundary Teams (BT)	Community of Practice (Com.oP)
Collaboration through the collaboration networks model (See Chapter 3)	- Short-term collaboration - Collaboration with circumstantial partners	- Long and short-term collaboration - Collaboration with circumstantial and established partners	- Long-term collaboration - Collaboration with established partners
	Innovation Malls	*Elite Circles*	
	Open innovation Communities /Semi-open innovation Communities		
	Consortiums		
Partner Networks	Mainly between corporations	- Between companies - Between companies (Different specializations)	Mainly between corporations (Same specialization)
Practitioner thinking & behavior	Independent and dispersed	*Four mean points (See Figure 8.3)*	Discipline and order
Practitioner leadership	Autonomous, decentralized leadership	Harmonized leadership	Integrated, centralized leadership
Knowledge process	- Knowledge integrating - Focus on explicit knowledge	- Tacit knowledge & Explicit Knowledge synergies	- Knowledge sharing - Focus on tacit knowledge
Formulating innovation	Mainly open innovation	Mainly *hybrid* innovation and closed innovation	Mainly closed innovation for organizational learning
Applied platform business model (See Chapter 3)	Vertically Integrated Platform Model (Open)	Vertically Integrated Platform Model	
	Horizontally Integrated Platform Model		
	Multisided Platform Model		
	Product Platform Model/Service Platform Model		

Figure 8.4   Elements of IBC management

The Com.oP is also an organizational platform for organizational learning focusing on tacit knowledge for closed innovation. As elements of the thinking, behavior and leadership of practitioners in the Com.oP, practitioners require integrated and centralized leadership based on discipline and order (called 'integrated leadership'). Also, in terms of the platform business model discussed in Chapter 3, the Com.oP is formed through the deep collaboration and commitment of practitioners and is a fundamental element of the organizational platform needed to structure a vertically integrated platform model.

Col.oP Features

Conversely, in the Col.oPs mentioned earlier, partners are selected from inside and outside the company depending on strategic objectives, and short-term or temporary collaboration is encouraged among members to share and merge the specialist knowledge possessed by individual participants. As a collaboration network, the Col.oP is especially advantageous as an organizational platform for collaboration with external partners. For instance, this kind of Col.oP organizational platform is effective under either flat or hierarchical governance structures, for collaboration (consortiums and elite circles), for joint business and development among certain closed corporate leaders, or for collaboration among unspecified numbers of external partners in a flat and open environment (an open innovation community), or collaboration among unspecified numbers of external partners working under an authoritative governance structure with decision-making powers (an innovation mall).

Col.oPs especially focus on the explicit specialist knowledge of external partners, and so require clarified mutual interfaces between the technologies and business processes of the companies involved. On the other hand, to encourage collaboration through open innovation with global partners with leading capabilities, it is important for companies to form Col.oPs that are able to dynamically and constantly change to integrate a diverse range of knowledge. As elements of Col.oP practitioner thinking, behavior and leadership, practitioners need autonomous and decentralized leadership (called 'distributed leadership'). Collaboration in Col.oPs formed under open and flat governance structures can be carried out through organizational platforms that take the form of a range of different business models (the multisided platform model, horizontal integrated platform model, product platform model/service platform model etc.). This is because depending on the business environment and context, the open and flat collaboration system enables partners to be flexibly included in the Col.oP and thus realizes optimized collaboration with partners when needed, which brings about new knowledge created through the resulting synergies (the three synergies – see Chapter 3).

BT Features

As stated earlier, the four mean points form the basis for practitioners' thinking and behavior in BTs. As a hybrid featuring characteristics of both Col.oPs and Com. oPs, practitioners in BTs display 'harmonized leadership' through the hybridization of distributed and integrated leadership elements. BTs focus on 'established and circumstantial' collaborative activity to make best use of the company's knowledge and flexibly absorb knowledge from other companies at the same time – characteristic of the hybrid innovation process that seeks to integrate the company's knowledge. In terms of collaboration networks, BTs are an effective organizational platform for engaging in the knowledge integration process through collaboration between organizations within the company and with external partners.

Similarly to the Col.oP, BTs are useful for joint development and business among certain corporate leaders in closed systems under flat or hierarchical governance structures (consortiums and elite circles), but are also effective in sustaining collaborative relationships with partners as required, regardless of whether they are inside or outside the company. While BTs can maintain strong relationships with some best partners under flat and hierarchical governance structures, on the other hand they are organizational platforms that encourage collaboration without establishing any particular fixed partnerships through a 'semi-open innovation community' in which partnerships are optimized to respond to changing circumstances.

Practitioners in BTs advance the tacit knowledge established within their own company as in a Com.oP, as well as absorbing and learning the explicit knowledge of external partners and convert this external knowledge into their company's own tacit knowledge while encouraging the sharing of their tacit knowledge. Then, practitioners convert this integrated tacit knowledge into explicit knowledge of the company to achieve hybrid innovation for new products and services, in other words, BTs encourage synergies (Nonaka and Takeuchi 2005) between tacit and explicit knowledge. While the knowledge integration process through the synergies between tacit and explicit knowledge encourages hybrid innovation, it also simultaneously reinforces the company's closed innovation processes. As well as that, this kind of BT formation is a suitable organizational system for all platform business model structures. As collaboration networks, the heart of the matter is really how to form these IBC and boundary networks in the business workplace. This can be illustrated by breaking them down into different models.

8.3 IBC and Boundary Networks Patterns

8.3.1 IBCS IN AND BETWEEN COMPANIES – HORIZONTAL IBCS

IBC and boundary networks are formed in time and space around different organizational and knowledge boundaries. Generally, the following six patterns illustrate these different types of formations (see Figures 8.5, 8.6 and 8.7).

The first pattern is formed from informal IBCs and boundary networks (vertical value chain network) across a company's functional organizations (research, product planning, development, manufacture, sales etc.). Organizational platforms that form creative and efficient value chains through the encouragement of coordination and collaboration among business processes are examples of this pattern. Equivalent to BTs, IBCs that reflect this pattern can be seen in the case examples of the vertical value chain models of NTT DOCOMO (Chapter 3), Chunghwa Telecom (Chapter 5), HTC (Chapter 6) and others.

The second pattern (networks between corporations) illustrates IBC and boundary networks formed across related or different businesses and industries, and are organizational systems for realizing the creation of new business models. IBCs and boundary networks in this pattern have the potential to give corporations a foothold into new business through the induction and creation of new business models via 'business model matching' and 'pursuit of the three synergies' discussed in Chapter 3. This is especially noticeable in the co-evolution model born through network effects in ICT industries (e.g. mobile telephone, game, content delivery businesses and so forth), and has a great potential to give birth to business ecosystems for sustained growth of new industries. The characteristics of IBCs in this pattern correspond to BTs or Col.oPs. Actual cases of this can be seen with NTT DOCOMO/Apple/Google (Chapter 3), Qualcomm/TSMC/eSilicon/Fujitsu (Chapter 4), Chunghwa Telecom (Chapter 5), HTC (Chapter 6), and the examples of convergence discussed in Chapter 1.

The third pattern describes IBCs formed as temporary projects or the cross functional teams (CFTs) that transcend the barriers between different organizations within a company. This type of IBC is either a formal and authorized, or an informal organization within a company. Numerous corporations regularly form many of these types of organizations, and they are wide-ranging, depending on the scale of the CFT or project (resource distribution such as personnel materials and capital), and can be formed at the management level. These IBCs also have the characteristics of BTs, and actual examples can be seen with Chunghwa Telecom (Chapter 5), Sharp (Chapter 7) and others.

The fourth pattern (a knowledge network) is a boundary network for knowledge sharing as an IBC formed as departmental organizations in the product planning, technology and sales departments etc. within a company (a Com.oP), or an IBC formed across departments (a BT). This type of IBC encourages knowledge activities to share and accumulate the company's best practices and know-how based on knowledge sharing and organizational learning within certain areas of specialization in the same department. By contrast, IBCs formed across different departments are organizational entities that function to formulate product concepts and specifications through conflict between the marketing and technological sides involved in new product development. These are knowledge boundaries between different areas of expertise along which intense collisions occur, and are formed through knowledge sharing and collaboration among members across different departments. IBCs that reflect this pattern can be found in NTT DOCOMO/Apple (Chapter 3), Chunghwa Telecom (Chapter 5), HTC (Chapter 6) and others.

The fifth type of pattern (project) is an organizational system observed in companies involved in development. These are IBCs for projects that span across a range of different sectors (Col.oPs and BTs) and boundary networks formed among IBCs within the same sector (Com.oPs). These are also IBCs formed as project networks between official project organizations (Col.oPs or BTs). Organizational learning through knowledge, technology and know-how sharing and transfer between organizations through the boundary networks formed among Com.oPs in the same department and initially in projects serves to raise the level of problem solving capability for a project. Apple's iPod product development case is an example of this. Also, the second type of project networks does not only raise mutual synergies among project organizations and execute project strategies, but also enables new project strategy generation.

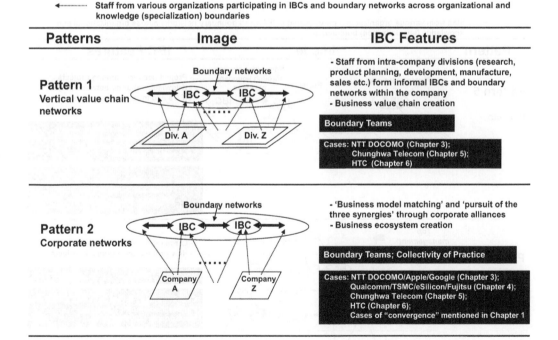

Figure 8.5   IBC and boundary network patterns (pattern one and two)

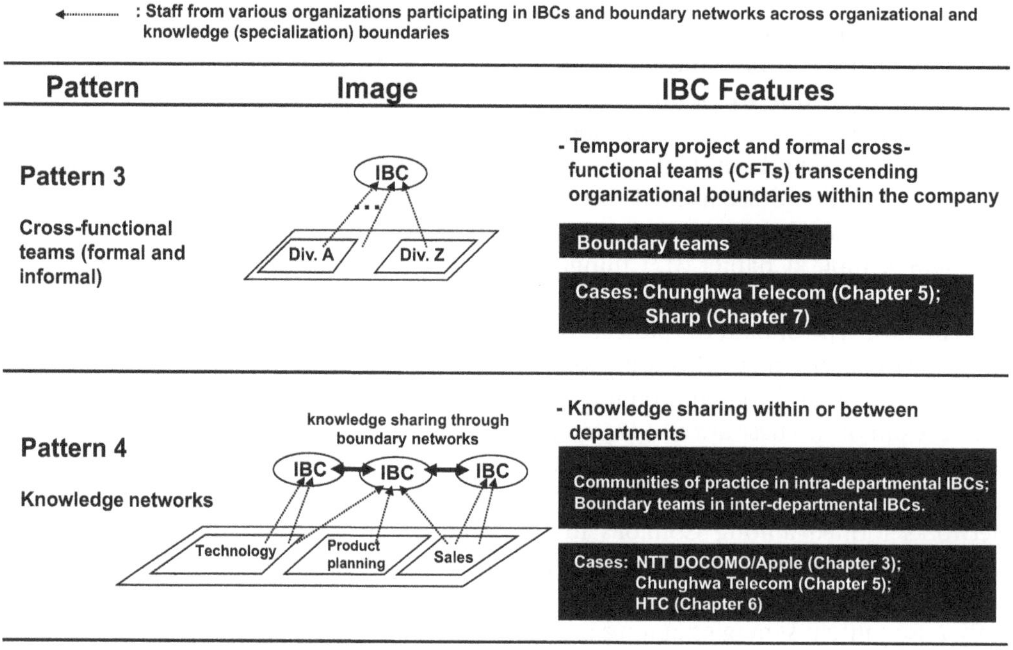

◄············· : Staff from various organizations participating in IBCs and boundary networks across organizational and knowledge (specialization) boundaries

Pattern	Image	IBC Features
Pattern 3 Cross-functional teams (formal and informal)		- Temporary project and formal cross-functional teams (CFTs) transcending organizational boundaries within the company **Boundary teams** **Cases:** Chunghwa Telecom (Chapter 5); Sharp (Chapter 7)
Pattern 4 Knowledge networks		- Knowledge sharing within or between departments Communities of practice in intra-departmental IBCs; Boundary teams in inter-departmental IBCs. **Cases:** NTT DOCOMO/Apple (Chapter 3); Chunghwa Telecom (Chapter 5); HTC (Chapter 6)

Figure 8.6   IBC and boundary network patterns (pattern three and four)

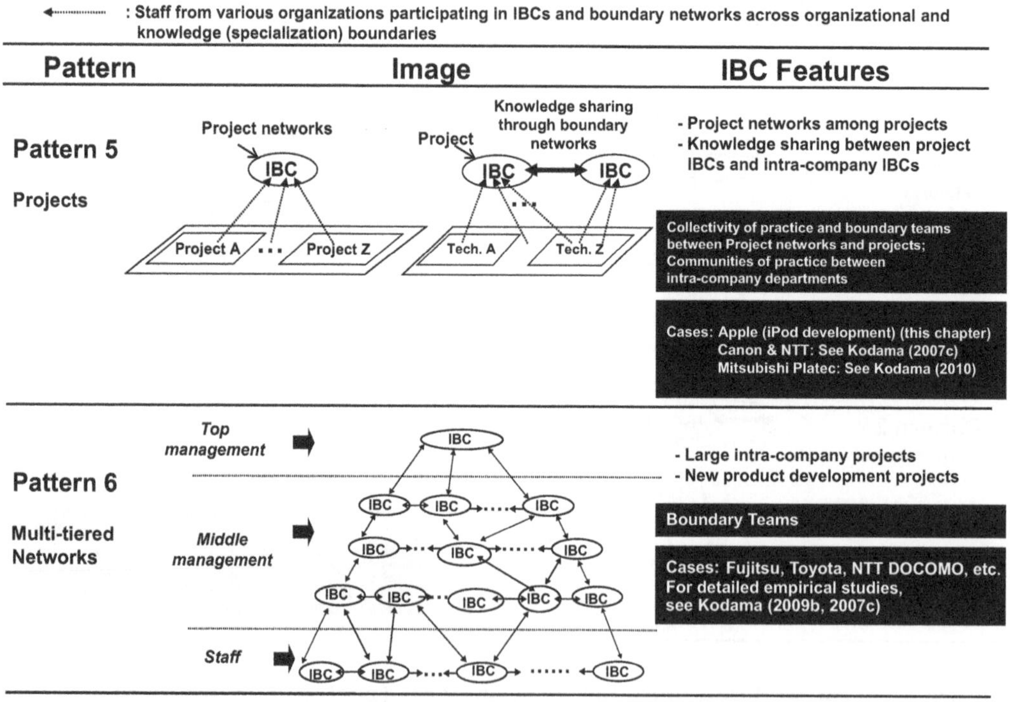

◄············· : Staff from various organizations participating in IBCs and boundary networks across organizational and knowledge (specialization) boundaries

Pattern	Image	IBC Features
Pattern 5 Projects		- Project networks among projects - Knowledge sharing between project IBCs and intra-company IBCs Collectivity of practice and boundary teams between Project networks and projects; Communities of practice between intra-company departments Cases: Apple (iPod development) (this chapter) Canon & NTT: See Kodama (2007c) Mitsubishi Platec: See Kodama (2010)
Pattern 6 Multi-tiered Networks		- Large intra-company projects - New product development projects **Boundary Teams** Cases: Fujitsu, Toyota, NTT DOCOMO, etc. For detailed empirical studies, see Kodama (2009b, 2007c)

Figure 8.7   IBC and boundary network patterns (pattern five and six)

8.3.2 MANAGEMENT HIERARCHY IBCS – VERTICAL IBCS

The IBC patterns described in the previous section are networked horizontal IBCs formed within and between companies. As well as those, in reality, the intra-company IBCs illustrated in Figure 8.7 (pattern 6) exist as strata across the formal organizations and layers of management within a company, and are networked together. These multitiered networks are the sixth pattern. The larger a corporation is, the more complicated the layers of IBC and boundary network formations. However, there are not many corporations that have these multilayered collaboration networks statically formed within themselves; rather, the tendency to apply this pattern is observed in the world's leading high-tech corporations as a mechanism for their intra-company strategic problem solving, or as a structure for large-scale projects that involve the whole company.

One example of this is Toyota, who form multitiered horizontal and vertical IBCs as cross functional tasks teams in all levels of management within the company (including groups, sections, departments, divisions and at the executive level). Task teams at the group and sectional levels regularly take measures to solve ongoing and technological problems, while task management teams formed from section leaders and departmental heads look beyond individual problems to engage in activities to generate solutions that can be applied universally. The total task management teams at the executive level engage in activities connected with measures for new global production systems and the creation of high-level technology through the strengthening of alliances between departments. Also through their IBC activities, they form joint total task management teams that include suppliers both nationally and internationally to ensure a high level product reliability.[17]

Toyota's IBCs do not only include departments involved in technology. To continue to provide customers with even better vehicles, the company has complete linkages from its sales departments through to development, design and manufacturing businesses (thirteen departments in all), as well as administrative departments (technological, manufacturing, procurement, sales, information technology and quality assurance departments), clerical and indirect departments (general management, TQM promotion, advertising and publicity, safety, hygiene, environmental, external affairs, finance and accounting, international business, personnel and general affairs), each linked and layered through seamless organizational connections to invigorate resources and capabilities and optimize both the individual sections and the company as a whole. Toyota has multitiered horizontal and vertical IBCs at various levels of management to unify the characteristics of its bureaucracies and networks. Important proposals are decided across the IBCs formed among the company's managers and leaders (managers appointed at all levels of management), and prompt action is taken for strategic objectives and important issues by its business divisions and group companies. These IBCs have the features of BTs.

The above illustrates the diverse range of vertical and horizontal IBC and boundary network patterns that span within and between companies, and are compound collaboration networks consisting of the three IBC organizational systems. To manage the structure of these complicated collaboration networks, practitioners must practice

---

17   Amasaka (2004) referred to Toyota's multitiered task teams as 'strategic stratified task teams'. This valuable suggestion was provided by Professor Kakuro Amasaka of Aoyama Gakuinn University (a former director of Toyota's TQM Promotion Division).

leadership (distributed leadership, harmonized leadership, integrated leadership) of individual IBCs to suit the characteristics of the collaboration networks. The following section describes the multifaceted leadership frameworks needed for companies to achieve innovation through the integration of diverse knowledge.

8.4 Innovation through Leadership Integrative Capability

The previous section describes the different types of IBC and boundary network patterns, but in actual fact, networks in business workplaces are usually more complicated, and as illustrated in Figures 8.1 and 8.3, the three characteristic IBCs – Com.oPs, Col.oPs and BTs – shift dynamically with changing business environments and the daily dealings of practitioners, and there are mixtures of patterns one to six described in Figures 8.5, 8.6 and 8.7 both inside and outside companies, and on top of that, the three characteristic IBCs themselves also dynamically transform. This means that to execute corporate strategic objectives, IBC and boundary networks must be optimally created and managed on-the-spot. Furthermore, the larger a Corporation is, the more dispersed business organizations exist within it, and the more diverse the range of strategic objectives, which means top management must be skilled in formulating and managing a variety of IBCs and boundary networks.

The important issue is to structure the most optimal IBC organizational platform for creating these patterns, and create IBC and boundary networks most appropriate for dealing with multimodal business models, including the platform businesses discussed in Chapter 3. As illustrated in Figure 8.4, the three characteristic IBCs take the form of diverse collaboration network systems among practitioners (elite circles/open innovation communities/semi-open innovation communities/consortiums/innovation malls). In other words, for companies to advance their strategies, it is important to be able to combine any number of the three characteristic IBCs (Com.oPs, Col.oPs or BTs) to assemble IBC and boundary networks as effectual complex collaboration networks. The business strategies of Apple, Google and NTT DOCOMO described in Chapter 3 are cases of simultaneous and distinct use of combinations of collaboration networks formed from IBC and boundary networks aptly applied to individual target platform business models.

The simultaneous existence of collaboration networks based on the three characteristic IBC organizational platforms (Com.oPs, Col.oPs, BTs illustrated in Figure 8.4) inside and outside companies means practitioners must also apply the right kind of leadership to the individual organizational systems (distributed leadership, harmonized leadership, integrated leadership, described in Figure 8.4). Especially, managers working at the routine business level have to form IBCs, and practice individual leadership styles (distributed leadership, harmonized leadership, and integrated leadership) to deal with different businesses. However, to form, maintain and develop multiple IBCs or boundary networks across companies and between companies, top leaders such as executives and managers (boundary architects) involved in serious decision-making such as resource distribution also need to simultaneously incorporate these three leadership styles.

Boundary architects must use the corporate capabilities and business design capabilities fundamental to boundary vision (the seven boundary vision capabilities – see Chapter 2) and practice leadership that gives birth to new business innovation through the integration of superior knowledge inside and outside their companies, and they must be able to merge the three leadership styles above, and have the leadership integrative capability (See Chapter 2 and Chapter 3) fundamental to dialectical thinking and action to synthesize wide-ranging IBC and boundary networks across the company and between companies. 'Leadership integrative capability' is the driver that dialectically synthesizes these three leadership styles which are necessary to formulate and manage diverse IBCs and boundary networks.

The leadership integrative capability of boundary architects dynamically formulates internal and external integration networks as boundary networks to merge the knowledge inside and outside companies, and depending on circumstances, is a necessary skill to generate open or closed innovation and create valuable hybrid innovation (see Figure 8.8).

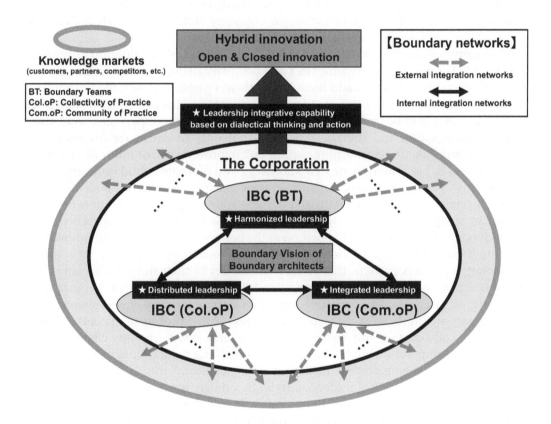

Figure 8.8   Innovation through leadership integrative capability

8.5 Leadership as Process

From the discussion above, IBC and boundary networks formulated, maintained and developed as diverse collaboration networks will be increasingly important as business elements of leading innovation companies to execute their strategies into the future. The three IBC organizational platforms (Com.oPs, BTs and Col.oPs) that form the basis of collaboration networks can change characteristics in response to changing circumstances, and at the same time bring about the diverse collaboration network patterns (the six patterns described in Figures 8.5, 8.6 and 8.7) though the formation of boundary networks between these IBCs. In these IBC and boundary networks, the new knowledge needed for new business models, products and services is steadily created through the sharing and inspiration of tacit knowledge of individual boundary architects through the creative dialog and dialectical thinking and action of team members.

Boundary architects use boundary vision in different areas of specialization to integrate new knowledge, and create dynamic IBCs and boundary networks to meet strategic and personal objectives, while IBC and boundary networks promote close collaboration and encourage dynamic human networks to merge and integrate diverse specialist knowledge for critical and urgent business contexts. Members, including boundary architects, share their common values and strategic objectives, not only to encourage organizational learning to bring about new meaning, reform and improvements, or innovation in their main businesses, but also to create new knowledge and promote hybrid innovation.

For this reason, boundary architects must practice diverse collaboration and leadership styles, to create, maintain and develop wide-ranging collaboration networks as sources of this type of innovation. In this regard, a number of research documents have advocated open and flat collaboration as the best method for successful innovation, but this is not a universal solution. Boundary architects have to construct a range of collaboration network patterns that respond effectively to their strategic objectives and business situations. Furthermore, boundary architects also need to recognize that these patterns must be constantly adjusted to cope with shifting business environments.

Boundary architects must develop an awareness of the 'process of dynamic change' for forms of collaboration and leadership styles in these ever-fluctuating circumstances. In short, leadership should not be thought of as something rigid: it should be interpreted as a constantly changing process. In these evolving environments, boundary architects need to engage in a variety of leadership styles in a timely manner. Boundary architects are aware of these dynamic leadership processes from a microscopic point of view, and practice strategy through the proper application and combination of diverse collaboration networks through the formation of IBC and boundary networks.

'Leadership as process' means particular leadership styles are always changing to respond to actual events and episodes as they occur (Kodama 2009a). Practitioners of 'leadership as process' constantly renew their own knowledge and skills through experience of actual events and episodes in the past, present and future. This dynamic and ongoing accumulation of experience and knowledge gives a person greater capacity for open-mindedness, and thus enriches their boundary vision.

As a practical proposition for practicing a variety of leadership capabilities, it will be even more important in the future for practitioners to develop capabilities to acquire new knowledge and insight from diverse and complicated boundaries through boundary vision. In addition to acquiring the boundary vision elements of 'context architect capability' for designing new contexts in response to diverse business contexts, 'boundary consolidation capability' for encouraging and inspiring new knowledge, and 'knowledge integrative capability' for integrating diverse and unfamiliar knowledge, 'leadership integrative capability' is a crucial business element needed to understand leadership as process, and create and synthesize a range of leadership models.

Boundary vision also makes new proposals: 'boundary architecture' – the conceptual capability of realizing new business models through the merging of different boundaries, and 'boundary innovation' – innovation across the boundaries between different businesses and industries. Boundary architects use boundary vision to draw up grand designs for new boundary architecture, to achieve knowledge integration across a wide range of boundaries, and to create new business models as hybrid innovation. In the twenty-first century, the new knowledge of leadership integrative capability that understands the dynamic nature of leadership and knowledge integration processes realized through the boundary vision of boundary architects will be increasingly important as the frameworks and concepts for new innovation in the businesses of the future.

Chapter 8 Conclusions

1. As organizational platforms that respond to changing business environments, IBCs characteristically exist as three types – 'communities of practice', 'boundary teams', and 'collectivities of practice'. The four dialectical elements of 'harmonized knowledge', 'creative collaboration', 'boundary penetration' and 'shared thought worlds' are important in encouraging creative dialog in boundary teams.
2. There are also diverse collaboration network characteristics and management leadership styles created with these three IBC systems.
3. There are six basic patterns that illustrate IBC and boundary networks, and collaboration networks formed from these dynamically change to respond to corporate strategic objectives.
4. Through the formation of IBC and boundary networks, boundary architects integrate and apply the best type of collaboration networks to produce optimal collaboration patterns to deal with their strategic objectives.
5. Through the integration of new knowledge, boundary vision is a perspective that brings about a variety of innovations including hybrid innovation, open innovation and closed innovation. Based on their boundary vision, boundary architects must practice 'leadership integrative capability' to manage leadership styles and diverse collaborations in IBCs and boundary networks.
6. As instigators of corporate innovation, it is important for boundary architects to recognize and understand that leadership is a continually changing process. The concept of 'leadership as process' is an important business element for flexible, creative, and strategic thinking and action that is not well understood by many leaders in rigid hierarchical systems.

9 *Conclusions – Creating Knowledge Integration Firms*

9.1 Knowledge Integration through Dynamic Practical Processes

This book has discussed the strategies, organizations, technologies, business models and leadership styles for a variety of mechanisms to achieve innovations such as hybrid innovation, through the formation of interactive business communities (IBCs). The book focused on the processes behind the formation of IBCs through in-depth case studies of high-tech corporations in Japan, Taiwan and the United States, and described the management and leadership styles observed in those corporations.

The essence of strategic management in corporations begins with the dynamic practical activities of practitioners based on the knowledge integration process. Strategy formation and execution by business people through trial and error, and based on high-quality practical knowledge, is also essential for innovation. Furthermore, the process of acquiring knowledge is a dynamic one, and knowledge is gained by individuals or organizations through the strategic thinking and action of business people and spiralling applied processes of introspection that deeply embed it as tacit knowledge in the experience of individuals.

While the recent phenomenon of fusing together different technologies with ICT – known as 'convergence' – has spurred the development of new technologies and products, it has also brought with it business models based on new rules that span different industries, and even more complexity than the traditional competitive business model. The source of this accelerating convergence, and of new industries and markets, is the dynamic knowledge integration processes of individuals and organizations in companies, between companies, and between companies and customers.

The collaboration among business people in and between companies, and with customers, involves the formation of IBC and boundary networks across these wide-ranging boundaries, and in turn, these collaboration networks become breeding grounds for extensive innovation processes such as knowledge integration and hybrid innovation. Looking through a lens at the processes of generating the invisible resources of 'knowledge' and pushing them through to business activities in IBC and boundary networks provides valuable insights into how companies can develop their organizational capabilities and establish themselves at their target market positions through the strategic creation of new knowledge.

This is why the 'boundary architects' in corporate organizations have to develop excellent 'boundary vision' as part of their strategic thinking to merge and manage multiple diverse boundaries, and dynamically design their corporate boundaries, at the same time as engaging in strategy transformation to respond to (or create) new business environments. Dynamic IBC and boundary network formation by boundary architects is the core engine to bring about business model innovation through new convergence.

9.2 Convergence Accelerates Hybrid Innovation!

In the current era of convergence, many conventional business structures in all kinds of industries are being greatly affected by novel innovation especially in the ICT and environmental technology areas. In the twenty-first century paradigm of mass production and mass retailing, corporations focused their resources on their own core competencies and pursued economies of scale and domain to provide consistent products and services. Based on closed hierarchical organizational systems, companies established and executed strategies within a predictable range of possibilities, since markets were not particularly volatile most of the time. This meant that companies had full control of their innovation processes under the conditions of these closed and autonomous systems and hierarchical organizations. However, in the age of convergence with its ever-changing and diversifying business environments, the old-style closed innovation system for achieving new innovative success is reaching the end of its usable life.

Conversely, in the wildly changing high-tech fields of the twenty-first century, corporate collaboration with various partners is becoming increasingly important for businesses whose competitiveness is intrinsically linked with their R&D and productive capability to respond to (or create) market situations and win out. As well as that, wide-ranging technological innovations, especially in ICT field, are having a huge impact on the business environment. The current era is one in which ICT is used in many different businesses to provide customers with new value beyond conventional product and service frameworks, which has forced companies in all kinds of industries to incorporate ICT into their core strategies and engage in networked business. This also means that every business will have to develop new business models using ICT to meet the demand for mass customization, a whole host of business solutions, individual customer needs and levels of personalization that can respond to new expectations. In other words, all industries will become information industries. These information industries will demand economies of customer value and speed, and companies will have to engage in urgent measures to bring about valuable innovations ahead of competitors.

These are the reasons companies must be ready to swiftly deal with the high-quality and diverse knowledge that is born through the convergence and consolidation of knowledge existing in different technological fields and industries. Because business environments are changing though the convergence phenomenon, companies can no longer rely solely on their own resources (core knowledge such as technology, know-how etc.), and must make efforts to form strategies to make the best use of the resources available through partnerships including certain customers, prominent corporations and even universities.

In these innovation systems, the process of integrating internal and external knowledge via company-wide and inter-company IBC and boundary network formation (internal and external integration networks) for collaborative strategies in corporations and between partners is essential. Hybrid innovation in these innovation systems can combine the elements of closed and open innovation and become semi-open innovation.

Convergence that cuts across multiple industries and technologies is bringing with it new market opportunities (new products, services and business models), and is accelerating the formation of IBC and boundary networks as collaboration networks between organizations and companies. Global high-tech corporations can raise their potential to achieve new and unique hybrid innovations for their companies through the formation of these wide-ranging collaboration networks. The success of these hybrid innovations can also induce the potential to pioneer new markets and technologies for new convergence. More new proposals will be presented to companies as the phenomenon of convergence accelerates hybrid innovation progressively into the future (see Figure 9.1).

The age of convergence means that companies can no longer rely on the conventional closed innovation systems, and must recognize the importance of the dispersed skills and creativities of external partners all over the world, and the essential nature of the knowledge integration process that transcends the borders between companies and industries. Management of this type of dispersed-knowledge innovation requires new approaches to governance. It is becoming increasingly important for management to openly integrate the top-class knowledge dispersed inside and outside companies and among customers to maintain their competitiveness in the knowledge economy. The author has significant theoretical and practical propositions regarding the structure of business systems for knowledge integration models with hybrid innovation. It also goes without saying that companies must maintain and develop their hard-to-imitate core competencies while they work towards achieving hybrid innovation.

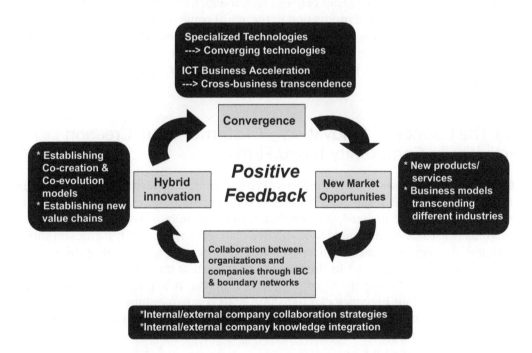

Figure 9.1   Convergence accelerates hybrid innovation!

Companies can incorporate certain aspects of open innovation to respond to business environments, but if there is too large a tendency towards open innovation, companies run a higher risk of problems in structuring core competencies that are difficult for other companies to mimic. Basically, open innovation provides companies with the capability of accessing knowledge from anywhere in the world and making the best use of it to bring about new products and services. However, because competitors can also operate under open innovation conditions, it is possible to gain a temporary or short-term competitive lead through open innovation, but it cannot guarantee competitiveness in the long-term. This is because licensing and technological transfers to other companies based on explicit knowledge make it easier for competitors to copy product and service developments.

To create and develop valuable and hard-to-imitate knowledge, and develop products and services using this knowledge, time is needed to accumulate tacit knowledge and advance existing human capabilities that are the foundations of technological and organizational capabilities, not just accumulate technological and organizational capabilities themselves. To create high-quality tacit knowledge, and transfer it as unique explicit knowledge, closed innovation elements through the formation of basic IBC 'communities of practice' (Com.oPs), and 'boundary teams' (BTs) are indispensable. There is an urgent need for companies to establish their own unique knowledge integration processes through hybrid innovation, as new innovation systems that enable companies to flexibly incorporate elements of both open and closed innovation.

To reiterate, new knowledge that is born through the IBC and boundary networks created by merging the boundaries between technologies, organizations, companies and industries is the wellspring of innovation in the age of convergence. The practical actions applied across collaboration networks formed from diverse IBC and boundary networks existing inside and outside companies, and with partners and customers, induce a dynamic view of strategy in practitioners and give rise to new organizational capabilities to generate innovation.

9.3 The Essence of Innovation – Customer Value Creation Activities in Community-based Firms

It is important for bosses to place the focus of corporate management on 'customer value creation businesses' as a top priority. This is fundamentally different from the value-oriented management inclined to shareholders that streamlines business with easy and individualistic values. This kind of short-sighted management, that only focuses on short-term gain through overzealous efficiency and production, lies at the root of the wave of problems seen in recent times in the United States, such as the sub-prime problem and the Lehman shock. In the age of convergence, however, it is important for corporate leaders to think about how they can transform their companies into 'community-based firms' that are centered on customers and staff, and move away from management that prioritizes short-term profits for shareholders.

The late Peter Drucker said:

Excellent managers pierce through the bad habit of not considering whether things will be beneficial for customers, although it is also common knowledge that thinking about business in the long-term also means big profits for shareholders in the end.

These are not just leading American 'excellent companies' (Peters and Waterman 1982) or 'visionary companies' (Collins and Porras 1994) that succeed in generating continuous profits; top management in Western family businesses (Miller and Breton-Miller 2005) (companies like Wal-Mart, Cargill, Estée Lauder, Levi Strauss in the US; Porsche, BMW, Fiat, Hermès, Ferragamo, Michelin, and Sparr etc. in Europe), and traditional leading companies in Japan don't focus on profit pursuit as the main priority to please shareholders: they consider investments in R&D, employee education and motivation to be their most important business elements. In short, companies with good business results think (O'Reilly and Pfeffer 2000) that the most valuable asset they have is their personnel. Companies can thoroughly rationalize costs and efficiencies to generate short-term profits, but the more they do this, the more they are prone to cheapen customer value. Although it's certainly possible to achieve short-term profits by restructuring and cost reductions, too much emphasis on pursuit of short-term profit by restricting investment in R&D, production technology and personnel training lowers the 'intrinsic motivation' (Osterlof and Frey 2000) of staff, and presents a risk of collapsing the IBC and boundary network organizational platforms formed for coordination between people, between communities, between teams and between projects. This can stifle new innovation for future business development through R&D activities (Vogel 2006, Handy 2002). Therefore, companies can achieve competitiveness through the creation of customer value and sustained innovation by doggedly continuing to invest in management that focuses on long-term customer satisfaction, rather than immediate profit in the short-term.

In the future, companies will not only have to continue to invest in long-term R&D and personnel training strategies for customer value creation businesses, but also have to share their values with customers, staff and partner companies through the sharing of visions and missions via deep dialogue to achieve their business objectives. Promoting profound creative dialogue encourages the sharing and resonance of values among staff members, between companies and their partners, and between companies and their customers, and serves to build trust. This raises the level of motivation and commitment among staff members, and has great potential to bring corporations closer to the 'community-based firm' concept. Moreover, community-based firms encourage the formation of IBC and boundary networks internally and externally and include their customers to fortify collaborations among participants.

In the pursuit of customer value generation, the knowledge integration firms considered in this book are also examples of templates of corporate models rooted in a community spirit forged among all stakeholders. Knowledge integration firms which flexibly form and reconfigure IBCs and boundary networks respond efficiently to environmental changes (or create new business environments themselves) and give birth to new knowledge that structures value chains and business ecosystems in line with their customers. Twenty-first century top management needs to understand the seamless nature of these knowledge integration firms that are rooted in communities formed among managers, staff, partners, shareholders and customers, and steer their businesses based on the values and trust fostered in these communities that bring about new knowledge through the formation of IBC and boundary networks.

9.4 Creating Knowledge Integration Firms

With the expansion of integration, diversification and refinement of knowledge in the age of convergence and networked economies, another issue is the necessity for integration and consolidation of knowledge between different industries. To achieve the hybrid innovation of the future, the processes of knowledge integration of high-quality knowledge dispersed across corporations and industries in IBC and boundary networks that conquer and transcend the boundaries within and between companies, will be the most critical elements. This is why collaboration and coordination capabilities with external partners and customers are going to be more and more important.

The strategic activities of those knowledge integration firms that create win-win relationships for their stockholders, customers and staff, and with their partners, will become indispensable as elements of corporate governance. In other words, corporations that aim for 'customer value creation businesses' as 'community-based firms' must place emphasis on the strategic importance of creating win-win situations among all stakeholders. And, as well as providing customers with new value, corporations must develop capabilities to bring about competitive business models and 'optimized profit structure generation' as they mutually work towards 'business model matching' and 'pursuit of the three synergies' with their partner corporations (See Chapter 3). Because this kind of corporate thinking and action serves to bring profits to shareholders at the same time as achieving long-term profit through the critical issue of innovation, it is a driver that gives rise to sustained corporate competitiveness.

And central to these win-win business models for corporations that encourage hybrid innovation are the diverse collaboration networks formed among best partners around the world through which corporations coordinate and collaborate with each other. Especially, IBC and boundary networks formed across different industries can raise the potential to generate the types of business ecosystem described in this book. For knowledge integration firms, IBC and boundary networks formed as knowledge networks are also important core frameworks for the new governance models needed for the formation, maintenance and development of these business ecosystems.

Furthermore, for knowledge integration firms to practice the leadership that achieves boundary innovation, conquering and overcoming a range of diverse boundaries, business people must have the capability to use the 'boundary vision' described in this book to gain new insight into these diverse and complex boundaries. Boundary vision is a management capability that enables the merging of unfamiliar knowledge, the creation of new business models through the merging of different boundaries, and furthermore, boundary vision is an imaginative and creative 'business design capability' that presents new points of view for creating new business models across the borders between corporations and industries (see Chapter 2).

Boundary vision is a perspective that gives birth to 'hybrid innovation' – new innovation born through the merging of knowledge. Business people who function as boundary architects use their boundary vision to draw up grand designs as new 'boundary architecture' to achieve hybrid innovation; but to achieve hybrid innovation, boundary architects must bring leadership that synthesizes the multiple viewpoints and diverse knowledge in IBC and boundary networks that are constantly changing.

Boundary architects must recognize that in managing the IBC and boundary networks that comprise wide ranging collaboration networks, leadership is a constantly changing process, and they must practice 'leadership integrative capability' to lead and manage the diverse collaborations across these various networks. The concept of 'leadership as process' is an important business element for flexible, creative, and strategic thinking and action that is not well understood by many leaders in rigid hierarchical systems, but these types of practical processes enacted by boundary architects will become the foundation stones of the leadership that integrates the knowledge needed to create the new business models of the twenty-first century.

References

Abernathy, J. (1978) *The Productivity Dilemma: Roadblock to Innovation in the Automobile Industry*. Maryland, US: Johns Hopkins University Press.

Allen, T.J. (1977) *Managing the Flow of Technology*. Cambridge, MA: MIT Press.

Amasaka, K. (2004) Development of science TQM, a new principle of quality management: effectiveness of strategic stratified task team at Toyota. *International Journal of Production Research*, 42(17), 3691–706.

Baatz, E. (1999) Rapid growth changes rules for purchasing. *Purchasing*, 126(10), 33–36.

Belous, R. (1989) *The Contingent Economy: The Growth of the Temporary, Part-time and Subcontracted Workforce*. National Planning Association.

Boudreau, K. and Lakhani, K. (2009) How to manage outside innovation. *MIT Sloan Management Review*, 50(4), 69–76.

Bourgeois, J. (1981) On the measurement of organizational slack. *Academy of Management Review*, 6(1), 29–39.

Brown, J.S. and Duguid, P. (1991) Organizational learning and communities-of-practice. *Organization Science*, 2(3), 40–57.

Brown, J.S. and Duguid, P. (2001) Knowledge and organization: a social-practice perspective. *Organization Science*, 12(6), 198–213.

Brown, S.L. and Eisenhardt, K.M. (1995) Product development: past research, present findings, and future directions. *Academy of Management Review*, 20(2), 343–78.

Brown, S.L. and Eisenhardt, K.M. (1998) *Competing on the Edge*. Boston, MA: Harvard Business School.

Buckman, R. (2003) *Building a Knowledge-driven Organization*. New York: McGraw Hill.

Carlile, P. (2002) A pragmatic view of knowledge and boundaries: boundary objects in new product development. *Organization Science*, 13(4), 442–55.

Carlile, P. (2004) Transferring, translating, and transforming: an integrative framework for managing knowledge across boundaries. *Organization Science*, 15(5), 555–68.

Checkland, P. (1981) *Systems Thinking, Systems Practice: Includes a 30-year Retrospective*. New York: Wiley.

Chesbrough, H. (2003) *Open Innovation*. Boston, MA: Harvard Business School Press.

Chesbrough, H. (2006) *Open Business Models: How to Thrive in the New Innovation Landscape*. Boston, MA: Harvard Business School Press.

Christensen, C.M. (1997) *The Innovator's Dilemma: When New Technologies Cause Great Firms to Fail*. Boston, MA: Harvard Business School Press.

Christensen, C.M. and Raynor, M. (2003) *The Innovator's Solution*. Boston, MA: Harvard Business School Press.

Collins, J. and Porras, J. (1994) *Built to Last: Successful Habits of Visionary Companies*. NY, US: HarperCollins.

Davis-Blake, A. and Uzzi, B. (1993) Determinants of employment externalization: a study of temporary workers and independent contractors. *Administrative Science Quarterly*, 38, 195–223.

Day, G. and Schoemaker, P.J. (2005) Scanning the periphery. *Harvard Business Review*, 83(11), 135–48.

DiMaggio, P. and Powell, W. (1983) The iron cage revisited: institutional isomorphism and collective rationality in institutional fields. *American Sociological Review*, 48, 147–60.

Dougherty, D. (1992) Interpretive barriers to successful product innovation in large firms. *Organization Science*, 3(2), 179–202.

Eisenhardt, K.M. and Martine, J. (2000) Dynamic capabilities: what are they? *Strategic Management Journal*, 21(10–11), 1105–21.

Eisenhardt, K.M. and Sull, D.N. (2001) Strategy as simple rules. *Harvard Business Review*, 79(1), 106–16.

Eisenmann, T., Parker, A. and Alstyne, M.W.V. (2006) Strategies for two-sided markets. *Harvard Business Review,* 84(10), 92–101.

Eppinger, S. (1991) Model-based approaches to managing concurrent engineering. *Journal of Engineering Design*, 2(4), 283–289.

Galbraith, J.R. (1973) *Designing Complex Organizations*. Reading, MA: Addison-Wesley.

Gawer, A. and Cusmano, M.A. (2004) *Platform Leadership*. Boston, MA: Harvard Business School Publishing.

Global Views Monthly, Moving Forward: Hong Qi, The Smiling Curve, February 2004 (Chinese language).

Govindarajan, V. and Trimble, C. (2005) *Ten Rules for Strategic Innovations*. Boston, MA: Harvard Business School Publishing.

Granovetter, M. (1973) The strength of weak ties. *American Journal of Sociology*, 78(6), 1360–80.

Grinyer, P. and McKiernan, P. (1994) Triggering major and sustained changes. In: stagnating companies, in Daems, H. and Thomas, H. (eds), *Strategic Groups, Strategic Moves and Performance*, New York: Pergamon, 173–95.

Hamel, G., Doz, Y. and Prahalad C.K. (1989) Collaborate with your competitors and win. *Harvard Business Review*, 67(1), 133–9.

Hamel, G. and Prahalad, C.K. (1994) *Competing for the Future*. Boston, MA: Harvard Business School Press.

Hamel, G. and Prahalad, K. (1993) Strategy as stretch and leverage. *Harvard Business Review*, 71(2), 75–84.

Handy, C. (2002) What's a business for? *Harvard Business Review*, 80(12), 49–55.

Hargadon, A. and Sutton, R. (1997) Technology brokering and innovation in a product development firm. *Administration Science Quarterly*, 42, 716–49.

Henderson, R. and Clark, K. (1990) Architectural innovation: the reconfiguration of existing product technologies and the failure of established firms. *Administrative Science Quarterly*, March, 9–30.

Hobday, M. (1995) East Asian latecomer firms: learning the technology of electronics. *World Development*, 23(7), 1171–1193.

Holmes, J. (1986) The organization and locational structure of production subcontracting. In: M. Storper and A.J. Scott (eds), *Production, Work, Territory: The Geographical Anatomy of Industrial Capitalism*, 80–106, Boston, MA: Allen & Unwin.

Jantsch, E. (1980) *The Self-organizing Universe*. Oxford, UK: Pergamon Press.

Kim, W.C. and Mauborgne, R. (2005) *Blue Ocean Strategy*. Boston, MA: Harvard Business School Publishing.

Kitada, H. (2010) *Brand Strategy in SHARP AQUOS* (in Japanese), Tokyo, Toyo Keizai.

Kodama, M. (2001) Creating new business through strategic community management. *International Journal of Human Resource Management*, 11(6), 1062–84.

Kodama, M. (2005a) Knowledge creation through networked strategic communities: case studies in new product development. *Long Range Planning*, 38(1), 27–49.

Kodama, M. (2007a) *The Strategic Community-based Firm*. UK: Palgrave Macmillan.

Kodama, M. (2007b) *Knowledge Innovation – Strategic Management as Practice*. UK: Edward Elgar Publishing.

Kodama, M.(2007c) *Project-based Organization in the Knowledge-based Society*. London, UK: Imperial College Press.

Kodama, M. (2008) *New Knowledge Creation Through ICT Dynamic Capability: Creating Knowledge Communities Using Broadband*. US: Information Age Publishing.

Kodama, M. (2009a) *Innovation Networks in Knowledge-based Firm – Developing ICT-Based Integrative Competences*. UK: Edward Elgar Publishing.

Kodama, M. (2009b) Boundaries innovation and knowledge integration in the Japanese firm. *Long Range Planning*, 42(4), 463–494.

Kodama, M. (2008) *Knowledge Integration Dynamics – Developing Strategic Innovation Capability*. SI: World Scientific Publishing.

Kodama, M. (2010) *Knowledge Integration Dynamics – Developing Strategic Innovation Capability*. SI: World Scientific Publishing.

Kogut, B. and Zander, U. (1992) Knowledge of the firm, combinative capabilities and the replication of technology. *Organization Science*, 5(2), 383–97.

Lave, J. and Wenger, E. (1991) *Situated Learning. Legitimate Peripheral Participation*. Cambridge, UK: Cambridge University Press.

Lawrence, P. and Lorsch, J. (1967) *Organization and Environments: Managing Differentiation and Integration*. Boston, MA: Harvard Business School Press.

Lei, D., Hitt, M. and Goldhar, J. (1996) Advanced manufacturing technology: organizational design and strategic flexibility. *Organization Studies*, 17(3), 501–523.

Leonard-Barton, D. (1992) Core capabilities and core rigidities: a paradox in managing new product development. *Strategic Management Journal*, 13(S1), 111–25.

Leonard-Barton, D. (1995) *Wellsprings of Knowledge: Building and Sustaining the Sources of Innovation*. Boston, MA: Harvard Business School Press.

Lepak, DP. and Snell, SA. (1999) The human resource architecture: toward a theory of human capital allocation and development. *Academy of Management Review*, 24(1), 31–48.

Levitt, B. and March, J.B. (1988) Organization learning. In: Scott, W.R. and Blake, J. (eds), *Annual Review of Sociology*, 14, Palo Alto, CA: Annual Reviews, 319–40.

Lindkvist, L. (2005) Knowledge communities and knowledge collectivities: a typology of knowledge work in groups. *Journal of Management Studies*, 42(6), 1189–1210.

Malone, T. and Crowston, K. (1994) The interdisciplinary study of coordination. *ACM Computer Surveys*, 26(1), 87–119.

Markides, C. (1998) Strategic innovation in established companies. *Sloan Management Review*, 39(3), 31–42.

Martines, L. and Kambil, A. (1999) Looking back and thinking ahead: effects of prior success on managers' interpretations of new information technologies. *Academy of Management Journal*, 42(6), 652–61.

Miller, D. and Breton-Miller, I. (2005) *Managing for the Long Run: Lessons in Competitive Advantage from Great Family Businesses*. Boston, MA: Harvard Business School Press.

Mintzberg, H. (1978) Patterns in strategy formation. *Management Science*, 24(9), 934–48.

Mintzberg, H. and Walters, J. (1985) Of strategies deliberate and emergent. *Strategic Management Journal*, 6(2), 257–72.

Nikkei Biztech (2004) *Don't Just Praise the Craftsmanship!* (in Japanese), Nikkei Business Publications.

Nisbett, R. (2003) *The Geography of Thought*. New York: The Free Press.

Nonaka, I. (1988) Toward middle-up-down management: accelerating information creation. *Sloan Management Review*, 29(3), 9–18.

Nonaka, I. and Takeuchi, H. (1995) *The Knowledge-creating Company*. New York: Oxford University Press.

Noria, N. and Gulati, R. (1996) Is slack good or bad for innovation? *Academy of Management Journal*, 39(5), 1245–1264.

Ohshima, M. (2010) *Enabling Method of New Idea Generation* (in Japanese), Tokyo, Japan: Aki Publishing.

Ohtsubo (2006) Interview (In Japanese), *Voice*, 11, 153–158.

Orr, J. (1996) *Talking About Machines: An Ethnography of a Modern Job*. Itheca, NY: ILP Press.

Orton, D. and Weick, K. (1990) Loosely coupled systems: a reconceptualization. *Academy of Management Review*, 15(2), 203–223.

Osono, E., Kodama, M., Yachi, T and Nonaka, I. (2006) *Practice Theory for Innovation* (in Japanese), Tokyo, Japan: Hakuto Shobo.

Osterlof, M. and Frey, B. (2000) Motivation, knowledge transfer, and organizational forms. *Organization Science*, 11(3), 538–50.

O'Reilly III, C. and Pfeffer, J. (2000) *Hidden Value: How Great Companies Achieve Extraordinary Results with Ordinary People*. Boston, MA: Harvard Business School.

O'Reilly III, C. and Tushman, M. (2004) The ambidextrous organization. *Harvard Business Review*, 82(4), 74–82.

Peters, T. and Waterman, R. (1982) *In Search of Excellence*. New York: Harper & Row.

Pfeffer, J. and Salancik, G. (1978) *The External Control of Organizations: A Resource Dependence Perspective*. New York: Harper & Row Publishers.

Pisano, G. and Verganti, R. (2008) Which kind of collaboration is right for you? *Harvard Business Review*, 86(12), 78–86.

Pisano, G. (1994) The governance of innovation: vertical integration and collaborative arrangements in the biotechnology industry. *Research Policy*, 20(3), 237–249.

Powell, W. and Brantley, P. (1992) Competitive cooperation in biotechnology: learning through networks? In: N. Noria and R.G. Eccles (eds), *Network and Organizations: Structure, Form and Action*, 366–394, Boston, MA: Harvard Business School Press.

Powell, W., Koput, K. and Smith-Doerr, L. (1996) Inter-organizational collaboration and the locus of innovation: networks of learning in biotechnology. *Administrative Science Quarterly*, 41, 116–146.

Roberts, J. (2006) Limits to communities of practice. *Journal of Management Studies*, 43(3), 623–639.

Rose, E. and Ito, K. (2005) Widening the family circle: spin-offs in the Japanese service sector. *Long Range Planning*, 38(1), 9–26.

Rosenberg, N. (1982) *Inside the Black Box: Technology and Economics*. UK: Cambridge University Press.

Rosenkopf, L. and Tushman, M. (1998) The coevolution of community networks and technology: lessons from the flight simulation industry. *Industrial and Corporate Change*, 7(1), 311–346.

Sanchez, R. and Mahoney, T. (1996) Modularity, flexibility, and knowledge management in product and organizational design. *Strategic Management Journal*, 17 (winter special issue), 63–76.

Sawhney, M. and Prandelli, E. (2000) Communities of creation: managing distributed innovation in turbulent markets. *California Management Review*, 42(4), 24–54.

Schilling, M. and Steensma, H. (2001) The use of modular organizational forms: an industry-level analysis. *Academy of Management Journal*, 44(6), 1149–1168.

Shannon, C. and Weaver, W. (1949) *The Mathematical Theory of Communications*. Urbana, US: University of Illinois Press.

Shibata, T. and Kodama, M. (2007) Knowledge integration through networked strategic communities – cases of Japan. *Business Strategy Series*, 8(5), 394–400.

Shibata, T. and Kodama, M. (2008) Managing technological transition from old to new technology: case of Fanuc's successful transition. *Business Strategy Series*, 9(4), 157–162.

Shibata, T. and Kodama, M. (2009) Japanese mythology and leadership. In: *Japan, Cultural Mythology and Global Leadership*, E. Kessler and D. Wong (eds), UK: Edward Elgar Publishing.

Siggelkow, N. (2001) Change in the presence of fit: the rise, the fall and the renaissance of Liz Claiborne. *Academy of Management Journal*, 44(4), 838–57.

Simon, H. (1996) *The Sciences of the Artificial*, 3rd Edition. US: MIT Press.

Simon, H. (1997) *Administrative Behavior*, 4th Edition. US: Free Press.

Spender, J.C. (1990) *Industry Recipes: An Enquiry into the Nature and Sources of Managerial Judgement*. Oxford: Basil Blackwell.

Teece, D.J. (1982) Towards an economic theory of the multiproduct firm. *Journal of Economic Behavior and Organization*, 3(1), 39–63.

Teece, D.J., Pisano, G. and Shuen, A. (1997) Dynamic capabilities and strategic management. *Strategic Management Journal*, 18(3), 509–33.

Thompson, J.D. (1967) *Organizations in Action*. New York: McGraw Hill.

Tushman, M. and Nadler, D. (1978) Information processing as an integrating concept in organizational design. *Academy of Management Review*, 3(3), 613–24.

Tushman, M.L. (1977) Special boundary roles in the innovation process. *Administrative Science Quarterly*, 22, 587–605.

Utterback (1994) *Mastering the Dynamics of Innovation: How Companies can Seize Opportunities in the Face of Technological Change*. Boston, MA: Harvard Business School Press.

Vogel, S. (2006) *Japan Remodeled: How Government and Industry are Reforming Japanese Capitalism*. US: Cornell University Press.

Wenger, E.C. (1998) *Community of Practice: Learning, Meaning and Identity*. Cambridge: Cambridge University Press.

Weerd-Nederhpf, Wouters, Teuns and Hissel (2007) The architecture improvement method. *R&D Management*, 37(5), 425–435.

Winter, S. (2003) Understanding dynamic capabilities. *Strategic Management Journal*, 24(10), 991–995.

Wu, Z-X. (2007) *HTC Fight to Defend the Top Stock Position – Cher Wang's Discernmenr and Ambition* (in Chinese), Taipei, Wunan Tushu.

Yano (2006) Interview (in Japanese), *Voice*, 11, 159–164.

Zollo, M. and Winter, G. (2002) Deliberate learning and the evolution of dynamic capabilities. *Organization Science*, 13(3), 339–351.

Index

Abernathy, J. 142
Acer 133, 134
a-huei phone 118, 119, 120, 128
Aisin 8
Allen, T.J. 172n.
alliance strategies 135, 139, 144, 145
Altera 102
Amazon 11, 69, 70, 71, 78
ambidextrous organization 42, 43
Amkor Technologies 97
Android Market 66, 81–2
Android PDAs 135, 139, 144
A123Systems 21
Apache 79
Apple 9, 10, 11, 32, 38, 40, 41, 42, 43,59,
    66, 67, 70, 73, 75, 86, 90, 123,
    144,186ff.
  and boundary teams 170, 179–80, 182
  and external partners 73, 80–81, 85, 176
  and iPod development 179, 180
application innovators 65, 67, 68–9, 70, 71,
    72, 73, 74, 76, 78–9, 80, 81, 83, 88,
    89, 90
AppStore 10, 11, 66, 70, 73, 78, 82
AQUOS 15, 150, 153–5, 157, 159, 160, 163
architectural innovation 56, 125, 147, 163
architecture thinking 53–7, 60, 61, 125,
    130, 132, 147, 163
ARM 91n., 93, 96, 97
Artisan Components 97
ASEAN countries 134
Asia 125, 135, 140
ASIC 93, 96
ASP 69, 71, 78, 79
Asus 133, 134
AT&T 139
au 135, 139
Austria 110
automobile makers 18, 20

automotive industry 7, 8–9, 15–18

'ba' xii, 119, 123
Baatz, E. 105
back-end design 91, 97, 101, 108
Barnes & Noble 11
battery makers 20
Belous, R. 105
black box 32, 58, 161, 164
'blue ocean strategy' 141
BMW 20, 137, 139, 199
books 10, 11, 70
Bosch 20
bottom-up approach 38, 48, 50, 51–2, 53,
    57, 126, 130, 131, 147, 156, 160, 162
Boudreau, K. and Lakhani, K. 68
boundary architects 27, 169, 170, 175, 176,
    190–91
  and boundary vision 192–3, 195–6, 200
boundary architecture 27, 33, 34, 61, 66,
    68, 74, 75, 86, 88, 169, 193, 200
  see also boundary architects
boundary characteristics 170–72, 175
boundary innovation 27, 169, 193, 200
boundary networks 25, 32, 36, 39, 40, 44,
    45, 46, 60, 66, 67, 80ff., 86ff., 90
  and knowledge integration 84–5
  patterns 186–90
  in Taiwan 119–21, 125–9
  and vertical value chains 128
boundary penetration 180, 181, 182, 193
boundary teams (BTs) 170, 172, 174, 175,
    182, 183, 184, 187, 188, 191, 193,
    198
  and dialectics 177–8
  features 185–6
boundary vision 68, 109, 126, 149, 150,
    159–62, 164, 165, 191, 192, 193,
    195, 200

capabilities 34–61, 66, 129–32, 159ff., 190
definition 169
and external knowledge integration networks 67
and hybrid innovation 27–32, 146–8
types of 170–71
Bourgeois, J. 43
branded products 133–4, 140, 141, 142, 144
break-through innovation 39
Broadband 67, 69, 70, 97, 103, 108, 113
Brown, J.S. and Duguid, P. 22, 28, 169, 170n., 171n., 172n.
Brown, S.L. and Eisenhardt, K.M. 172n.
Buckman, R. 174
Buckman Laboratories 174
business design capabilities 34, 53, 57, 61, 130, 147, 149, 162–4, 190
business ecosystems 60, 61, 65, 70, 145, 146, 186, 199, 200
business model matching 67, 78, 75–6, 86, 87, 88, 89, 90, 186, 187, 200
business model typology 77
BYD 20, 21

Cadence 96, 97
camera phones 151, 153, 159, 160
Canon 32, 143
Canon Marketing 181
Carlile, P. 28, 169, 171, 172
Chang, Morris 98
Cher Wang 134, 138, 146
Chesbrough, H. 23, 25
China 13, 20, 95, 110, 127n., 134, 140
chipsets 94, 95
Chou, Peter 134, 138–9
Christensen, C.M. 3, 22, 173n.
Christensen, C.M. and Raynor, M. 40
Chrysler 18, 21
Chun Shui Tang 117
Chunghwa Telecom 32, 113–32, 138, 139, 175, 186, 187, 188
and boundary vision capabilities 129–31
business design 130–31
and IBCs 117–28
and boundary networks119–21, 125–9

marketing and sales 117–18ff.
network collaboration business 116
organizational capability 114–15
organizational reforms 115
product strategies 119–20
R&D 114, 122–3, 128
technological philosophy 130
Cingular 135
closed innovation 5, 23, 24, 30, 73, 74, 85, 92, 110, 111, 124, 184, 186, 191, 193, 198
inadequacies of 196, 197
in semiconductor industry 106, 107, 109
closed systems 67, 185
CMOS sensor 151
co-creation 4, 7, 59, 65, 66ff., 75, 76, 86, 87, 89, 90, 100, 138, 145, 197
co-evolution 4, 7, 59, 65, 66ff., 75, 76, 87, 89, 90, 94, 100, 138, 145, 197
collaboration networks 77–85, 90, 175, 183, 184, 189–90, 193, 195, 197, 198
and BTs 185
changes in 80–81
combining 80
integration 81–4
and leadership 192, 200
types of 79–80
collaborative strategies xi, xii, 5, 8, 9, 13, 15, 17, 18, 21, 22, 26, 32, 42ff., 61, 91, 100, 102, 103, 104, 106, 110, 114, 115, 130, 139, 147, 148, 196
and hybrid innovation 67, 121
and IBCs 5–7, 74, 95, 124, 125, 129
and knowledge integration model 23–5
and open service 97
and organizational capability innovation 22–3
collectivities of practice (Col.oPs) 172, 173, 181, 184–5, 187, 190, 193
Collins, J. and Porras, J. 199
community leaders 45, 46, 147
communities of practice (Com.oP) 44, 170n., 172, 173n., 181, 183–4, 187, 190, 191
community-based firms 198–9, 200
competency traps 22, 173n.

competition 21, 28, 41, 115, 120, 122, 124,
    140, 142, 156, 163
competitiveness 21, 23, 27, 28, 30, 59, 89,
    113, 142, 173, 176
conflicts 22, 39, 46, 115, 116, 172, 173
consortiums 69, 77, 79, 81, 83, 184, 185,
    190
consumer electronics makers 93–4
content innovators 68, 70, 71, 74, 75, 76,
    82, 83, 86, 87, 89, 90
content providers 7, 9, 32, 66, 119, 124
convergence 3, 4, 5, 7ff., 22, 23, 24, 25,
    149, 159, 161, 187, 195
  and automotive industry 8–9
  and hybrid innovation 196–8
  and new value chains 12
  and PDAs 7, 8, 9
  smart grid 15
  and semiconductors 17n., 110
core competencies 22, 25, 28, 30, 44, 85,
    92, 96, 109, 130, 149, 181, 196, 197,
    198
core rigidities 22, 173n.
core technology 36, 67, 72, 78, 93, 145
corporate capability 34, 37, 61, 130, 131,
    160, 165
corporate social responsibility 114
corporate vision 17, 98, 116, 161
costs 14, 17, 20, 21, 23, 42, 69, 71, 84, 94,
    95, 100, 142, 163, 199
creative collaboration 175, 180, 181, 182,
    193
creative dialogue 150, 155, 160, 175, 177,
    178, 179, 180, 181, 199
'creative reactions' 159–60
creativity 6, 8, 24, 25, 28, 33, 39, 45, 46, 76,
    80, 116, 129, 143, 149, 161, 169
cross-functional teams (CFTs) 6, 46, 165,
    186, 188, 189
cross organizational IBCs 6, 123, 130
cross organizational teams 123, 127, 128,
    156
'crowdsourcing' 73–4, 77
'customer convenience' 120
customer services 97, 99, 116, 119, 120,
    128, 129
customer value creation 198–9, 200

customer-designed services 98
customers 93, 96, 97, 100
customs 171
CyberShuttle 98
cycloid design 154, 155

Daimler 18, 21
data communications 113, 122, 127, 129,
    144
data processing 139, 141
Davis-Blake, A. and Uzzi, B. 10
Day, G. and Schoemaker, P.J. 29
Death Valley 41
deep involvement 87, 88, 89, 90
Denso 8, 18
design and development companies 92
Design Centre Alliance (DCA) 98, 108
design service alliances (DSAs) 98
developed countries 140
development 3, 4, 6, 7, 9, 17, 18, 19, 21,
    22, 23, 31, 36, 39, 48, 50, 55, 73,
    109, 110, 122–3, 125 see also product
    development
'development vision' 126
dialectical thinking and action 87–90, 177,
    178, 191, 192
dialogue 7, 23, 39, 44, 46, 86, 87, 90, 97,
    130, 138, 155, 159, 160, 174, 177ff.,
    181, 199
digital cameras 32, 56, 58, 149, 150ff., 159
digital content 163, 164
DiMaggio, P. and Powell, W. 87, 89
distributed leadership 185, 190, 191
distribution 11, 12, 13, 35, 39, 54, 69, 114,
    134, 144, 186
distributors 12, 32, 120
DoD 12
dominant design 142
Dopod CHT9000 123, 127–8
Dopod International 127n., 128, 137
Drucker, Peter 137, 198
DuPont 8
DVD players 32, 40, 58, 93, 143
dynamic capability 30n.
dynamic change process 192
dynamic practical processes 195
dynamic strategy view 23, 25, 27, 40, 198

e-books 10, 163
ECU 17
EDA 94, 98, 101, 109
Eisenhardt, K.M. and Martine, J. 30n.
Eisenhardt, K.M. and Sull, D.N. 30n.
Eisenmann, T., Parker, A. and Alstyne,
    M.W.V. 69, 74
electric power trains 18
embeddedness, high 87, 88, 89, 90
emergent strategies 37–40, 45, 130, 160
EMOBILE 135, 139
'emome' mobile portal 124
EMS businesses 133–5, 140, 141, 142, 146,
    179
EnerDel 20, 21
engineers 36, 50, 55, 73, 81, 96, 97, 107,
    108, 122, 143, 149, 151, 155ff., 159,
    161, 180
environmental technology 13, 189, 196
environmental vehicles 7, 8, 9, 19–22, 48,
    74
EPC Global 12
Eppinger, S. 57n.
Eriksson 124
Esaki, R. 38, 39
eSilicon 91, 96–7, 105, 106, 108, 109, 111,
    176, 186, 187
Europe 18, 20, 50, 137, 144, 199
Evonic Industries 20
'excellent companies' 137, 199
explicit knowledge 39, 51, 108, 184, 185,
    198
external integration networks 24, 31, 32,
    33, 68, 100, 107, 109, 119, 170, 191
external knowledge integrative capability
    34, 35–7, 41, 44, 46, 60, 61, 99, 129,
    130ff., 146, 147, 160, 164
external partners 5, 6, 7, 24, 28, 44, 61, 70,
    71, 72ff., 78, 80, 82, 83, 87, 97, 109,
    124, 126, 127, 130, 184, 185, 200

'fabless' companies 32, 42, 73, 84, 91, 92,
    93, 94, 96, 98ff., 105, 106, 109, 110
'Fab-lite strategies' 104, 107, 109, 110, 111
Fadell, Anthony 179
Fanuc 41, 42, 43
FDA 12

feedback 10, 33, 34, 59, 79, 87, 108,, 109,
    119, 120, 121, 197
FeliCa 69
FireWire 179
Fisker Automotive 21
flat systems 77, 78, 79, 80, 81, 99, 147, 184,
    185, 192
Fleming, Alexander 38, 39
Ford 18, 20, 21, 22, 142
formal organizations 100, 150, 170, 171n.,
    176, 189
foundries 91, 92, 93, 94, 95, 98, 99, 103,
    104, 105
FPGA 103
front-end design 91, 95
Freescale Semiconductors 8, 18, 110
friction 7, 22, 39, 42, 43, 150, 161, 173,
    175, 180, 182n.
Fujitsu 8, 42, 43, 83, 91, 92, 103–4, 106,
    109–11, 163, 186ff.

Galbraith, J.R. 171n.
Gawer, A. and Cusmano, M.A. 72n.
GE 8, 21
Germany 21, 110
Gigabyte 134
globalization 5, 18, 28, 48, 55, 113, 115,
    141
GM 18, 21, 22
Google 3, 9, 10, 11, 59, 65, 66, 67, 69, 70,
    71, 80, 86, 90, 123, 139, 144, 145,
    186, 187, 190
    collaboration patterns 85
    platform model 81–3
    and technology synergy 75–6
    see also Android Market
Govindarajan, V. and Trimble, C. 43n.
GPS 52
Grand design 27, 48, 49, 50, 51, 52, 162
Granovetter, M. 87
Grinyer, P. and McKiernan, P. 171n.
GS Yuasa Corporation 20

half-open innovation 24, 26
Hamel, G. and Prahalad, C.K. 25, 74
Handy, C. 138, 199
Harding, Jack 96

hardware 18, 51n., 58, 59, 66, 67, 68, 71, 73, 76, 78, 80, 82, 86, 89, 91, 139, 147, 151, 156, 179, 180
Hargadon, A. and Sutton, R. 22, 30n.
harmonized knowledge 35, 179, 180, 182
harmonized leadership 184, 185, 190, 191
Hayakawa, Tokuji 156
Hegel 177
Henderson, R. and Clark, K. 30n., 56
hierarchical collaboration 79
hierarchical innovation 85 *see also* closed innovation
hierarchical networks 77, 79, 80
hierarchical structures 23, 79, 170, 171, 183, 184, 185, 193, 196, 201 *see also* closed systems
high performance products 18, 21, 42, 56, 91, 101, 104, 105, 110, 111, 147, 156, 157
Hiroshima 150ff., 155
Hitachi 8, 20, 22, 92
Hobday, M. 133n.
Hochen Tan 115, 125
Holmes, J. 105
Honda 9, 10, 18, 21, 181
horizontal boundaries 29, 30, 31, 32, 33, 34, 66, 67, 74, 75, 160, 169
horizontal business model 103, 108
horizontal integration platform model 74–5, 77ff., 81, 82, 87
horizontal specialization 25, 91, 92, 93
household appliances 93, 110, 161
HTC 86, 123, 127, 128, 134–48
    alliance strategies 139–46
    and boundary vision 146–7
    branded products 134, 140, 141, 142, 144
    business design capabilities 147
    and IBCs 135, 138, 142, 145, 148
    management 137–9
    R&D 136, 138, 139, 140, 141ff., 146, 148
    smartphones 134–5, 136ff., 139, 142
    vision 136
HTC Touch 136
Hu, Chenming 100
human capability 35, 40

human resources 96
hybrid cars 8, 149
hybrid information 121, 125, 129
hybrid innovation xii, 4, 5, 24, 25, 26, 34, 36, 39, 61, 67, 68, 76, 85, 90, 104, 111, 146, 196–7
    and boundary vision 27–32, 60, 146–8
    and Chughwa Telecom 113–32
    and HTC 135, 145
    in semiconductor industry 91–111
    and TSMC 100
hybrid innovation-based firms 107, 108
Hyundai 18, 20

IBCs (interactive business comunities) 5–7, 9, 21, 22, 23ff., 28, 31, 32, 33, 40, 44, 45, 61, 67, 74, 76, 84, 87, 88, 90, 95, 111, 143, 175
    and Chunghwa Telecom 116–31
        marketing 117–18
        networks 119–21
        sales 118–19
    concepts 170–86
    definition of 5
    dynamically changing 183
    external 124–5, 129
    horizontal 186–9
    and HTC 135, 138, 142, 144, 148
    internal 122–4, 129
    management 183–6
    multi-tiered 35, 36, 39, 82, 83, 127, 145, 160
    and Panasonic 58
    and Qualcomm 95
    and Sharp 150, 151, 152, 155, 160
    and TSMC 99–100ff.
    vertical 189–90
ICT 3–4, 5, 7, 12, 13, 14, 22, 25, 99, 113, 114, 114ff., 149, 156, 186, 195, 196, 197
    and modular companies 43
    and platform innovation 65ff.
    and semiconductor firms 91ff.
IDM Model 17n., 91, 92, 93, 94, 96, 98, 101, 103–5, 106, 107, 109–10, 111
    see also virtual IDM
image processing chips 109

imaging 151, 159
i-mode 3, 4, 9, 10, 38, 42, 59, 65, 69, 70,
    78, 82, 83, 86, 124, 150
incidental emergent strategies 37, 38, 39
individuals 22, 36, 39, 71, 171, 181
industrial equipment 149
information 9, 10, 11, 19n., 35n., 56, 65,
    66, 76, 82, 87, 89, 97, 99, 106, 108,
    118–19ff., 125, 127, 129, 141, 154,
    161, 171ff.
    distribution 70, 72
information communications network 70
information sharing 106, 108, 120, 121,
    178
information-processing boundaries 171
innovative leadership 45, 46, 87
innovative practitioners 35–6, 39, 40
InSilicon 97
Institute for Information Industry 110
integrated fabless manufacturing (IFM) 94,
    101
integrative capabilities 34–61, 98ff.,
    129–30ff., 162, 164, 193
integrity 88, 98, 143
Intel 82, 97, 104, 106
intellectual property 92, 93, 96, 97, 98
intended strategies 37, 130, 146, 160
intentional emergent strategies 37, 38, 39,
    40
interactive information sharing 120
internal integration networks 24, 30, 31,
    100, 108, 170, 176, 191
internal knowledge 5, 23, 24, 26, 30–31, 67,
    97, 99, 100, 104, 121, 129, 130, 147
internationalization 114
Internet 82, 89, 99, 114, 121
Internet businesses 4, 8, 9, 10, 38, 65, 66,
    71, 73, 74, 76
    shopping malls 69, 78
intrinsic motivation 40, 199
Intumit data management system 120, 121
in-vehicle graphics technology 110
involvement see deep involvement
IP providers 92, 93, 97, 100, 101, 102, 109
iPad 3, 4, 9, 10, 11, 12, 23, 40, 56, 59, 65,
    69, 73, 86, 163
    and e-books 66

iPAQ 135
iPhone 3, 4, 9, 10, 11, 12, 23, 40, 56, 59,
    65, 69, 73, 86
iPod 3, 4, 56, 65, 73, 86, 91, 96, 178,
    179–80, 181, 187, 188
'issue-driven community' 174
ITS 18
ivory soap 38, 39

Jantsch, E. 171, 172
Japan 8, 9, 10, 12–13, 14, 17n., 18, 20, 29,
    32, 42, 54, 57, 69, 74, 91, 92, 107,
    118, 121, 139, 140, 144, 150, 153,
    170, 176, 199
Japanese corporations 8, 18, 19, 21, 42, 43,
    48, 50, 51, 56, 57, 109, 177, 182
Japanes semiconductor companies 8, 106–7
Jobs, Steve 179
joint development 5, 9, 10, 31, 83, 106,
    108ff., 123, 124–5, 126, 127, 128,
    139, 151, 185
joint ventures 5, 42, 55, 111, 153, 163
J-Phone 150, 151, 152, 153
Jozwiak, Greg 180
JR 10, 69

KDDI 7, 9, 10, 54, 151
Kim, W.C. and Mauborgne, R. 141n.
Kindle 10, 11, 163
Kitada, H. 157
KJ method 50
knowledge boundaries 7, 8, 28, 97, 143,
    150, 158, 169, 171ff., 181, 182n.,
    183, 186, 187
knowledge innovators 65, 66, 67, 68,
    69–70, 90
    and boundary networks 86, 87
    collaboration networks 77, 85ff.
    dialectical thinking and action 87–90
    synergies between 75ff., 85–6
'knowledge integration firms' 31, 61, 110
knowledge integration model 23–5, 28, 92,
    99, 107, 108, 110, 111
knowledge integration path 33, 34, 66
knowledge integration process 7, 9, 31, 40,
    51–2, 66, 126, 181, 185, 195, 197
knowledge integrative capability 27, 34, 193

see also external knowledge integrative
    capability
knowledge sharing 151, 186–7
Kodama, M. 3, 4, 5, 6, 8, 31, 35, 40, 41, 42,
    43, 44, 46, 48, 59, 159, 174, 183,
    188, 192
Kogut, B. and Sander, U. 28, 169
Koike, Susumu 55
Korea 18, 20, 32, 87n., 92, 95, 106, 134,
    140

landline telephone services 113
Lave, J. and Wenger, E. 170n.
Lawrence, P. and Lorsch, J. 171n.
layout design 97
LCD screens 153–4, 156, 157, 158, 160
leader teams (LTs) 40, 44, 45
leaders 28, 34, 35, 44
    see also community leaders
'leadership as process' 192–3, 201
leadership integrative capability 34, 44–6,
    61, 87–9, 90, 129, 130, 131, 132,
    147, 149, 159ff., 164, 170, 190–91,
    193, 201
Lei, D., Hitt, M. and Goldhar, J. 105
Lenovo 133
Leonard-Barton, D. 22, 23, 28, 30n., 169,
    172n., 173n.
Lepak, D.P. and Snell, S.A. 105
Levitt, B. and March, J.B. 22, 30n., 173n.
LG Chemical 20
LG Electronics 32, 163
liberalization 113, 124
libraries 98, 100, 101, 102, 109
licensing 92, 94
Lindkvist, L. 173n.
linking 5, 7, 8, 9, 10, 30, 32, 39, 40, 44, 46,
    47, 54, 60, 78, 85, 96, 108, 120, 127,
    142, 147, 175
Linux 79, 83, 163
liquid crystal display 155, 163
Liu, Mark 102
logic 177
logistics 12, 54, 120, 134
loosely coupled organization 105, 106, 107,
    173
low-cost products 3, 21, 104, 114, 141n.

LSI design 8, 17n., 40, 48, 49, 51, 58–9, 92,
    93, 97, 98, 102n., 103, 107ff., 157,
    163

Machida, Katsuhiko 150, 157, 158, 159,
    160, 161
macro level 29, 32n., 37, 50, 51, 52, 130,
    147
M&A 5, 31, 32, 74, 75, 107, 109, 110, 111
Malone, T. and Crowston, K. 171n.
management 4, 24, 27, 28, 35, 37, 40, 42,
    44, 46, 87, 89, 115ff., 124, 137,
    154ff., 160ff., 183–6 *see also* middle
    management
manufacturing 16, 17n., 2, 32, 36, 40, 48,
    96, 97, 98, 99, 101ff., 143, 144, 145,
    146, 153, 156, 170, 176, 189
    contracts 105, 133, 134, 140, 142
    IBC 128
    methods 51, 56, 142, 171, 172
    rules 107, 108, 110
    see also IDM Model
market analysis 126
marketing 5, 6, 10, 12, 32, 36, 99, 117
marketing IBCs 117–18
marketing strategies 3, 5, 65, 116, 119
markets 142, 160, 175, 191, 195
Markides, C. 43
Martines, L. and Kambil, A. 22, 30n., 173n.
mass production 21, 23, 41, 85, 93, 94, 95,
    106, 108, 136, 140, 171, 196
mean of boundaries 178, 181
mean of knowledge 178–80
mean of relationships 178, 180–81
mean of thought worlds 181–3
'mean point' 178, 179ff., 183
Mebius PC 157
MegaChips 91, 93
Meidensha 22
mental models 22, 28, 29, 35, 169, 171,
    173, 175
micro design 48, 49, 50, 52, 162
micro processes 28, 29, 32n., 37, 169
Microsoft 38, 59, 75, 86, 127, 128, 134,
    135, 138, 139, 144, 145
    and automakers 9
    game business 3

middle management 37, 40, 42, 44, 45, 130, 131, 147, 156, 159, 160, 162
Miller, D. and Breton-Miller, I. 137, 199
miniaturization 100, 104, 107, 108, 109, 147
Mintzberg, H. 37
Mintzberg, H. and Walters, J. 37
Mitarai, Fujio 143
Mitsubishi 8, 10, 13, 14, 18, 22, 188
MMS 124, 125–6
mobile phone businesses 3, 8, 20, 29, 32, 38, 40, 43, 54, 65, 74, 93, 94, 117ff., 124, 134ff., 156
mobile phone carriers 7, 9, 54, 83, 86, 124, 144
mobile phone modules 52, 53
mobile phone platforms 53, 83, 163
mobile phone/cameras 151, 153, 159
mobile terminals 94
modular innovation 56, 125, 130, 147
modular organization 41, 42, 43, 47, 51, 52, 57, 59, 92, 100, 105–6, 107ff., 111
Moore's Law 100
Motorola 8, 118, 123, 139, 161, 163
Mozilla Firefox 79
MPU 104
multimedia services 8, 9, 65, 84, 125, 126, 136, 163
multi-sided platform model 69–71, 78, 79ff., 83, 84, 87
  open 82
  semi-open 81, 82, 83
mutual learning 86, 88, 172
mutual understanding 45, 87, 126, 130

Nakamura, Kunio 143
NATC 17, 18n., 19
NATO 12
NC 149
NEC 8, 19–20, 73, 83, 163, 177, 182
NEC Electronics 17n., 92
'needs-oriented' ideas 36
network collaboration business 116
networked modular organizations 42, 43, 106, 108, 109, 111
networks 7, 9, 10, 12, 19, 22, 23, 24, 25, 26, 29, 30–31, 32 see also boundary networks; IBCs

'New IDM' company 91, 92, 107, 109, 110, 111
new integrated model 102–3, 106, 108, 111
new knowledge 5, 8, 9, 23, 27, 28, 29, 31, 35, 36, 39, 44, 75, 114, 159, 169, 175, 185, 192, 198, 199
  boundaries 171–2
  integration difficulties 127
new meanings 172
Nexus One smartphone 139
Ng, Stan 179
Nippon Oil Corporation 13, 14
Nippon Television 10
Nisbett, R. 178n.
Nissan 9, 17–19, 21
  Revival Plan 17
Nokia 118, 119, 123, 125, 139, 144, 161, 163
Nonaka, I. xii, 143n., 160
Nonaka, I. and Takeuchi, H. 28, 42n., 169, 185
Noria, N. and Gulati, R. 43
NTT DOCOMO ix, 7, 9, 32, 41, 42, 54, 59, 65, 66, 86, 135, 138, 141n., 151
  business model 90
  collaboration patterns 83–4, 85, 139, 163, 187, 190
  and IBCs 74, 84, 176, 186, 188
  integrated structure 43
  platform model 70, 73ff., 83–4
NTT group 13, 14, 42
NVIDIA 91, 93

objectives 33, 43, 47, 51, 85, 116, 119, 121, 123, 147, 184, 189, 190, 192, 193
OBM 133, 134, 144
ODM 133, 134, 136, 137, 139, 140, 144
OEM 133, 134, 135, 139, 140, 141, 144
Ohshima, M. 149
Ohtsubo, Fumio 176–7, 182
one-of-a-kind products 154, 155, 156ff., 164
open innovation 4, 5, 24, 25, 73, 74, 78, 79, 98, 106, 108, 109, 110, 111, 184, 185, 190, 193, 196, 198
open service system 97
optimized profit structure 67, 68, 75–6, 200
Orange 134, 135, 139
O'Reilly III, C. and Pfeffer, J. 137, 199

O'Reilly III, C. and Tushman, M. 43
organizational architecture xiii, 25, 27, 54
organizational boundaries 150, 158, 170, 171
organizational integrative capability 34, 41–4, 46, 60, 129, 130, 131, 132, 147, 160, 164
organizational platform 5, 26, 84, 88, 184, 185, 190
organizational systems 40, 42, 85, 105, 124, 143, 165, 175, 182–3, 186, 189, 190, 196
    in semiconductor industry 106ff.
Orr, J. 170n.
Orton, D. and Weick, K. 105
OS systems 163
Osaifu-Keitai systems 59
Osono, E., Kodama, M., Yachi, T. and Nonaka, I. 178
Osterlof, M. and Frey, B. 137–8, 199
O2 134, 135
outsourcing 5, 6, 30, 31, 32, 104, 105, 107

packaging 23, 95, 96, 99, 100, 103, 104, 109, 110
P&G's Ivory soap 38, 39
Palm PDA 134, 135
PalmChip 97
Panasonic 8, 19, 32, 40, 54, 55, 73, 83, 92, 106, 143, 163
    UniPhier system 58
Panasonic EV Energy 19
paper manufacturing technologies 174
parts makers 8, 18, 21, 22, 139, 152
Pasteur, Louis 38, 39
path dependencies 22, 28, 30n., 33, 34, 169, 173
PCB technology 151–2
PCs 9, 29, 38, 40, 66, 72, 93, 104, 133, 134, 136, 142, 149, 157, 179
PDA devices 9, 22, 40, 66, 134–5, 136, 139, 140–41, 143, 146, 151, 152, 157
PDA terminals 143
personnel training 137, 138, 199
Peters, T. and Waterman, R. 137, 199
Pfeffer, J. and Salancik, G. 171
Pfizer 38

photovoltaic business 4, 13, 14
Pisano, G. 30n.
Pisano, G. and Verganti, R. 77
platform business innovation 65, 68, 69ff., 78, 83ff., 88, 184, 186, 190
platform leader corporation 59
platform strategies 57, 59, 60, 82, 88, 163, 164
platform thinking 34, 57–9, 61, 125, 130, 131, 132, 147, 149, 162, 163, 164, 165
Playstation 4, 42, 65, 78, 86
Powell, W., Koput, K. and Smith-Doerr, L. 32n.
Powell, W. and Brantley, P. 32n.
pragmatic boundaries 172–3, 180, 181
prices 8, 108, 117, 119, 120
Prius 19, 51n.
privatization 113, 114, 116
product development 3, 17, 19, 35, 36, 38, 39, 42, 47, 51, 54ff., 59, 77, 81, 109–10, 122–3, 128, 129, 141, 144, 146, 150ff.
product planning 117, 140–43, 151, 156, 162ff.
product platform model 69, 72, 78, 79, 81, 82, 83, 87, 184, 185
product strategies 119–20
product/service development 122–4
    see also product development
production yield management 99
productivity dilemma 142–3, 178
profits 20, 42, 71, 82, 101, 113, 137, 138, 142, 198, 199
    see also optimized profit structure
project partnership system 19
project teams 158, 187
project-based organizations 6, 174
'proven technology' 32
publishers 11
purikura 150

QC activities 50
Qualcomm 10, 32, 42, 43, 52–3, 59, 72, 84, 86, 91, 93, 105, 106, 107ff., 111, 134, 135, 138, 139, 144, 145, 176, 186, 187

business model 94–5

radical innovation 32, 39, 56, 125, 147, 163
Rakuten 10
Rambus 93
R&D 17, 20, 23, 32, 35, 36, 41, 58, 73, 80,
    94, 99, 122, 123, 128, 129, 137, 199
    and Chunghwa Telecom 114, 122–3, 128
    and HTC 133, 136ff., 140, 141ff., 146,
        148
    and Sharp 156, 158
reflective practitioners 35
Renault 17, 18, 20
Renesas 17n., 18, 83, 92, 106, 163
resonance of values 46, 75, 86, 87, 88, 89,
        90, 100, 161, 172, 199
retailers 12, 118, 120, 121
RF license technology 110
RFID 4, 7, 12–13, 22, 23, 48, 74
rich content 76, 118, 124, 156
RIM 144
Roberts, J. 173n.
Robin, Jeff 179
Rose, E. and Ito, K. 43
Rosenberg, N. 22
Rosenkopf, L. and Tushman, M. 32n.
RTL 48
Rubinstein, Jonathan 179, 180

SaaS 67, 69, 71, 78, 89
sales 80, 81, 82, 94, 99, 109, 114, 117,
        118–19, 120
Samsung 18, 32, 92, 106, 163
Sanchez, R. and Mahoney, T. 105
Sawhney, M. and Prandelli, E. 23
SCE 42, 43
Schilling, M. and Steensma, H. 105
SCM 12
'seed-oriented' ideas 36
segmentation 96, 105, 169
segregation 91, 93, 102, 103
selection and consolidation 32, 36
selection and convergence 25, 30
semantic boundaries 171–2, 173, 175, 181
semiconductor industry 18, 91–111, 159
    changing value chains 91–4
    and integrative capability 96ff.

networked modular organizations in
        105–6
semiconductor sector business model 92,
        106ff.
semi-open innovation 78, 79, 81ff., 185,
        190, 196
Sen, Anjan 96
servant leadership 45, 46
service platform model 71–2, 78–9, 81, 82,
        83, 87, 184, 185
Seven Boundary Vision Capabilities 34–61,
        129–31, 190
7-Eleven 29, 69, 74, 75
Shanghai Automotive 20
Shannon, C. and Weaver, W. 171, 172
shared thought worlds 35, 180, 182, 183,
        193
shared values 43, 76, 87, 89, 175
Sharp 8, 15, 32, 54, 73, 83, 150–65, 175,
        181, 188
    business design 162–4
    R&D 158
Shi Chen-Jung, Stan 133n, 134
Shibata, T. and Kodama, M. 41, 42, 47, 55,
        58, 149
Siggelkow, N. 30n.
'sign-off' concept 93
Simon, Bernard 35
Simon, H. 35n.
sincerity 161
Singapore 95
small-world structures 44
smart grid 4, 7, 13–14, 15, 16, 19, 22, 23, 48
smartphones 11, 17n., 81, 84, 96, 134–5,
        136ff., 144–6, 147, 149
'smiling curve' 144
SoC design 17, 57, 58, 92, 93, 104, 108, 109
social networking 70, 124
soft dialectics 178
Soft System methodology 50
SoftBank 7, 9, 10, 54, 66, 75, 135, 138, 139,
        150, 155
software development 11, 50–51, 76, 81,
        94, 110
solar cells 7, 14–15, 23
Sony 3, 10, 32, 41, 42, 43, 44, 65, 66, 67,
        70, 86, 90

e-book store 11
    and lithium-ion batteries 20
    see also SCE; Sony Bank
Sony Bank 66
specialization 91, 96, 99, 106, 108, 160,
    169, 171
Spender, J.C. 28, 169, 171n.
SPICE model 102
Sprint 135
staff 35, 90, 96, 115, 116, 120, 136, 138,
    138, 154, 156, 159, 161, 174, 176,
    178, 182n., 188, 199
standardization 10, 12, 13, 54, 93, 95, 105,
    142
strategic alliances 5, 6, 8, 9, 17, 22, 31, 32,
    69, 74, 77, 92, 97, 107, 109, 120,
    124ff., 137, 140ff.
strategic integrative capability 36–41, 44,
    46, 60, 61, 129, 130, 131, 132, 146,
    160, 161
'strategy establishment' 126
'strategy execution' 126
strategy transformation 29, 33, 34, 38, 40,
    67, 102, 124, 133–47, 196
structural reform 114
Suica Card 69
Sumitomo 152, 153
supply 95
supply chain models 12, 72
support 96, 97, 108
Symbian OS 72, 73, 163
synergies 12, 25, 33, 36, 40, 53, 60, 67, 69,
    83, 84, 127, 143, 187
    of leadership 130, 147
    see also 'Three Synergies'
syntactic boundaries 171, 172, 173, 174
system parts 47, 48, 50, 51, 53, 54, 56, 57
systems thinking 34, 46–53, 55, 57, 58, 59,
    60, 61, 126, 130, 131, 132, 147, 162,
    164, 165

tacit knowledge 22, 39, 107, 143, 159, 181,
    185, 192, 195, 198
Taiwan 42, 84, 91, 92, 110, 113ff., 139ff.,
    142, 143, 170, 195
    EMS businesses 133–5, 140
    see also Chunghwa Telecom; HTC

'Tatami Project' 158
Techforum 174
technology convergence 149–50ff.
technology elements 125, 130
technology integration 155ff., 163
Teece, D.J. *xiin.*, 30n.
Teece, D.J., Pisano, G. and Shuen, A. 30n.
Telematics 8–9, 10, 53
testing companies 94, 96, 101
Texas Instruments 92, 98, 106
Think Global 21
Thompson, J.D. 171
'thought world' 181
'Three Synergies' 75–6 , 86, 87, 88, 89, 90,
    185, 186, 187, 200
3G mobile phones 94, 144
3M's post-it 39
T-Mobile 135, 138, 139
Tokyo Electric Power Company 10, 13, 14
Tokyo Gas 13
Tokyo Institute of Technoloy 13, 14
top-down approach 42, 46, 48, 49, 50,
    51–2, 53, 55, 57, 126, 130, 131, 147,
    156, 159, 162, 171
Toshiba 8, 20, 21, 32, 92, 106
Total Quality Management (TQM) 172, 189
Toyota 10, 18, 19, 21, 51n., 188, 189
training 107, 122, 123, 129, 137, 138, 158,
    159, 199
transport systems 18
Tsai, Dr Rick 99, 103
TSMC 41, 42, 43, 59, 84, 92, 97, 105, 106,
    108, 109, 110, 111, 176, 186, 187
    hybrid innovation 100
    integrative capacity 98–105
    platform solutions 98, 100
    strategy 93–4
turnkey system 95, 97, 98
Tushman, M. and Nadler, D. 172n.
Tushman, M.L. 172n.
TV 10, 32, 40, 76, 93, 150, 154, 155, 157,
    158, 160, 163
two-sided platform model *see* multisided
    platform model

uncertainty 172, 173, 174, 175, 180
unified product planning 140–43, 146

UniPhier 58
United Microelectronics (UMC) 91, 108
United States 12, 20, 21, 51, 52, 87n., 92,
    93, 96, 104, 107, 110, 138, 139, 163,
    195, 198, 199
upstream processes 101, 134
'urgent project' 155–9
Utterback, J.M. 142

value 4, 9, 10, 35, 36, 44, 46, 53, 91, 101,
    140, 142, 181
value chains 7, 8, 9, 14, 15, 29, 32, 33, 45,
    66ff., 141, 146, 186, 199
    integrated 23, 30, 99, 100, 101, 111, 128
    vertical 128, 129
Verizon 135, 138, 163
vertical boundaries 29, 30, 31, 32, 33, 66,
    170
    and TSMC 101, 108
vertical business model 103, 108
vertical integration platform model 69, 71,
    72–4, 77, 80, 81, 82, 83, 84
vertical value chains 128–9
Viagra 38
video 8, 9, 10, 12, 70, 82, 150, 154, 155,
    156, 159, 163
video cameras 151
Viewcam 157
virtual corporations 5, 100
virtual IDM 85, 94–5, 101, 102, 103, 105–6,
    107FF., 111
    and eSilicon 96–7
virtual integration 42, 91, 99–100
    vertical 91, 99, 101, 111
    see also virtual IDM
Virtual Silicon 97

virtual space 155
vision 17, 98, 116, 126, 130, 138, 161
    see also boundary vision; corporate
    vision
visionary companies 137, 199
Vodafone 10, 135, 138, 139, 150, 163
Vogel, S. 199
Volkswagen 18, 21

wafer processing 96
Wal-Mart 12, 71, 137, 199
WAP 124, 125
wearable mobile devices (WMDs) 52, 53
Web services 99
Wenger, E.C. 44, 173n.
Western companies 54, 57, 137
West Chip Star 110
Wii/DS 4, 38, 56, 65, 69, 78, 86
Wikipedia 79
WiMax 110
win/win situation 59, 68, 75, 78, 85ff., 90,
    94, 100, 101, 110, 130, 145, 200
Windows 136, 142
Windows mobile 134, 135, 138, 139, 144
wireless services 9, 11, 12, 94, 95, 103,
    124ff., 134, 136, 179

Xilinx 93, 97

Yachi and Nonaka 178
Yahoo 3, 9, 10, 65, 69
Yano, K. 177, 182
Yun-Hua Telecom 121, 123

Zaurus PDA 151, 152, 157
Zollo, M. and Winter, G. 30n.

CPI Product Safety Systems and Information Please contact our EU-representative GPSR@taylorandfrancis.com, Easton & Fitzroy Verlag GmbH, Kandelstrasse 28, 80931 Ludwigburg, Germany

For Product Safety Concerns and Information please contact our
EU representative GPSR@taylorandfrancis.com Taylor & Francis
Verlag GmbH, Kaufingerstraße 24, 80331 München, Germany